Lands and Peoples
THE WORLD IN COLOR

VOLUME 2

SCANDINAVIA

CENTRAL EUROPE

ITALY

THE GROLIER SOCIETY • NEW YORK • TORONTO

Copyright © 1959, 1957, 1956, 1955, 1954, 1953, 1952, 1951, 1949, 1948, 1946, 1943, 1941, 1940, 1938

by THE GROLIER SOCIETY INC.

B*

Copyright 1932, 1930, 1929 by THE GROLIER SOCIETY

Copyright © 1959, 1957, 1956, 1955, 1954, 1953, 1952, 1951

by THE GROLIER SOCIETY OF CANADA LIMITED

The Library of Congress has cataloged this publication as follows:

Lands and peoples; the world in color. New York, Grolier Society [1959]

    7 v. illus. (part col.) ports., maps. 25 cm.

1. Geography—Pictorial works.

G138.L35   1959   910   59–5161

Library of Congress

Volume 2

TABLE OF CONTENTS

	PAGE
THE LAND OF FIORDS—*Norway and Its People* 10 Pictures in Full Color	4
SWEDEN—*Modern Democracy on Ancient Foundations* 15 Pictures in Full Color	24
THE LAND OF A THOUSAND LAKES—*Finland and Its Progressive People* 3 Pictures in Full Color	48
ISLANDS OF FIRE AND ICE—*Iceland's Norsemen and the Eskimos of Greenland* 5 Pictures in Full Color	67
EUROPE'S OLDEST KINGDOM—*Denmark and Its People* 9 Pictures in Full Color	88
THE HEARTLAND OF EUROPE—*Germany and Its People* 18 Pictures in Full Color	109
BERLIN IN ECLIPSE—*Where the Iron Curtain Is Visible*	144
A STATE WITH A GLORIOUS PAST—*How Poland Rose and Fell*	153
IN THREE BALTIC COUNTRIES—*People of Esthonia, Latvia and Lithuania* 3 Pictures in Full Color	173
CZECHOSLOVAKIA—*Land between Yesterday and Tomorrow* 5 Pictures in Full Color	191
AUSTRIA—*"A Land So Fair . . ."* 18 Pictures in Full Color	217
A LINK BETWEEN EAST AND WEST—*The Magyars and Gipsies of Hungary* 2 Pictures in Full Color	236
SWITZERLAND AND THE SWISS—*Beautiful Countryside of the Alpine Republic* 6 Pictures in Full Color	253
THE TOY STATES OF EUROPE—*Tiny Countries and Their Self-reliant People* 3 Pictures in Full Color	277
THE LURE OF ITALY—*Its Vital People and Their Land* 22 Pictures in Full Color	295
THE CITY THAT RULED THE WORLD—*Rome and Its Splendid Ruins* 7 Pictures in Full Color	335
BEAUTIFUL VENICE—*Born of the Marriage of Land and Sea* 10 Pictures in Full Color	354
THE JEWEL OF THE MEDITERRANEAN—*Sicily's People and Historic Places* 6 Pictures in Full Color	371

Norwegian Information Service
THE FLYDALSJUVET, A GORGE IN GEIRANGER FIORD
Geiranger Fiord is an inland arm of the Stor Fiord, in the northern Fiord Country, and cuts deep into the mountains. In this gorge the rocky walls rise almost vertically for thousands of feet, above a farmstead on the shelf of land at the fiord's edge. The large ocean-going vessel seems almost like a toy boat in the midst of the majestic spectacle.

The Land of Fiords

Norway and Its People

The Scandinavian Peninsula reaches down for more than a thousand miles like a giant's mitten, with a very big thumb, about to grasp Denmark. The "mitten" shuts off the Baltic from the North Sea, and a ridge of mountains running north and south divides Sweden from Norway. Did giants create Norway, here thrusting up a high peak, and there digging a deep fiord? One can believe that Thor once hurled his thunderbolts in these wild mountains. In the spray of the many waterfalls, rainbows glimmer—and long ago the old Norse gods rode daily to and fro across the Bifrost Bridge, which is the rainbow.

"THE sea unites us; the land divides us," has long been a saying of the Norwegians. It helps to explain both the character of the people and the rugged beauty of their country. Through countless ages, wind, ice and water have chiseled what might be called a single huge stone into a complex pattern of mountains, plateaus (*vidda*) and deep U-shaped valleys. Sending long probing fingers inland, the sea formed fiords; and off the coast a chain of more than 150,000 rocky islands and islets—skerries—arose. Thus an inner ocean passage was made, sheltered from gales. From early times this sea route has been known as Norvegr, or "the Northern Way."

If we sail around the coast, beginning in the southeast, our ship passes, first, through the Skagerrak (the strait that separates Norway and Denmark). Then, where the waters of the Skagerrak and the North Sea mingle, we pass the most southern tip of Norway, the headland called The Naze, or Lindesnes. Rounding into the North Sea, at about Stavanger we pass into the North Atlantic Ocean. Beyond Floroe, our course changes to the northeast. A further voyage of about 450 miles brings us to the Arctic Circle, and from here on, around North Cape, we are in the Arctic Ocean.

The highest range of mountains in the whole Scandinavian Peninsula rises along the west side and from early times has been called Kjoelen, or The Keel. The name of Kjoelen Mountains is also given to that part of the range which marks the natural boundary between Norway and Sweden. Though the peaks of the Kjoelen Mountains soar higher in northern Sweden, the Scandinavian spine south of Trondheim Fiord lies within Norwegian territory. Between the Kjoelen Mountains and the Gudbrandsdal (*dal* means "valley"), the highland of plateaus and rounded summits is called Dovre. South of Dovre and running all the way to the southern coast, the mountain mass is called Langfieldene, the Long Mountains. Included in the Langfieldene are the Hardangervidda and the magnificent Jotunheim Mountains.

Though Norway is narrow—the width varies from about 4 to 275 miles—it has a length of about 1,100 miles. However, the coast is so deeply indented that the actual shoreline is about 12,000 miles long. Norway also has territory far within the Arctic Circle—the Svalbard archipelago, which includes Spitsbergen. These islands are in the same latitude as northern Greenland. Though one-third of Norway proper is within the Arctic Circle, the climate is surprisingly mild. This is because of the Gulf Stream, the ocean current that forms in the tropical Caribbean Sea, and swerves across the Atlantic in a great arc. To western Norway, the Gulf Stream brings abundant rainfall, mild winters and cool summers. However, on the eastern side of the mountains in southern Norway, the climate is drier, with hotter summers and colder winters.

The visitor to Norway by ship or plane generally lands at Oslo. It is a crisp, spacious city, with many green vistas and no slums. From the inner harbor, where

THE LAND OF FIORDS

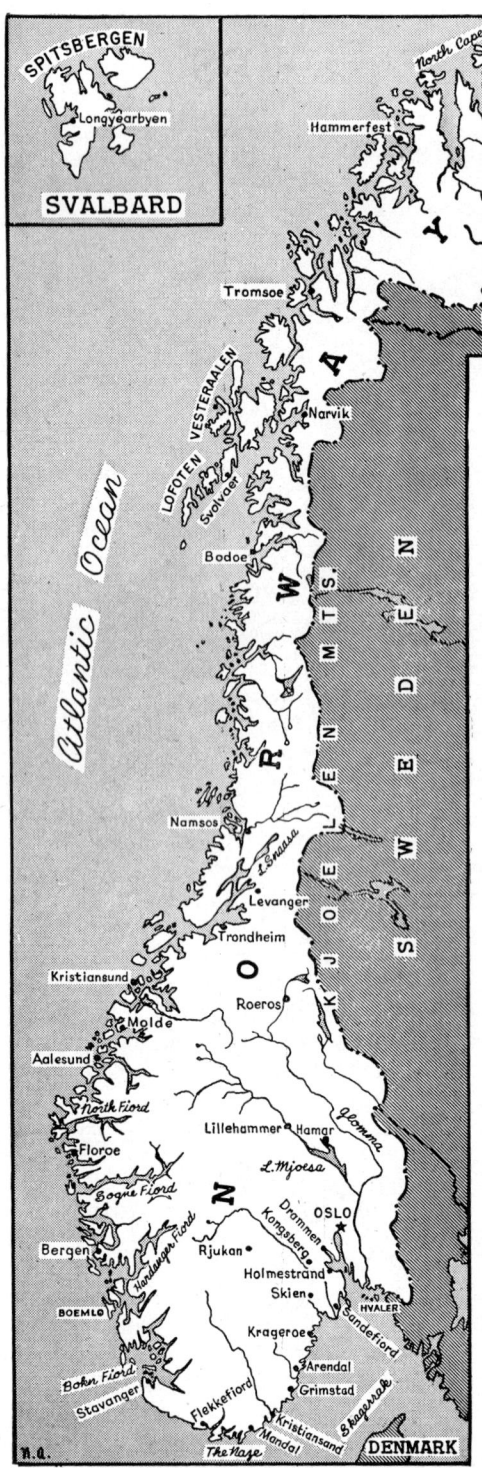

HOMELAND OF THE NORWEGIANS

passenger ships and freighters from all over the world ride at anchor, the city rises toward rounded hills clothed in pine and spruce. Conspicuous at the edge of the water front is the City Hall, a square-looking structure with two towering wings. The very modern appearance of this big building is in sharp contrast to the gleaming white Royal Palace, classic in design, that surmounts a near-by hill.

A town named Oslo was founded around 1050 at the eastern side of the harbor. However, in 1624, Christian IV, king of Denmark and Norway, established a town on the western shore, after the old town burned down. There he laid out a city with broad avenues and rectangular blocks and named it for himself, Christiania. In 1924 the Storting, the Norwegian Parliament, voted to restore the old Norse name of Oslo.

A rocky peninsula, on which Akershus Castle stands—it was a fort and a royal residence long ago—divides the port in two: Bjoervika, the old town, to the east; and Pipervika, to the west. An inviting park stretches from north of the castle to the Storting (Parliament House), and within the park is the National Theater, which Norway's foremost playwright, Henrik Ibsen (1828-1906), helped to make world-famous.

On the outskirts of Oslo, in the park at Frogner, is the lifework of the sculptor Gustav Vigeland, who died in 1943. Starting as a design for a fountain, which is in bronze, the group was added to year by year, the later works being carved in granite. The central piece alone—a column fifty feet high—has 121 intertwined human figures.

On the Bygdoe Peninsula, to the west of Oslo, is the fascinating open-air Norwegian Folk Museum, where the visitor steps into the Norway of medieval times. Among the old wooden buildings is a

THE LAND OF FIORDS

stave church. Carved in the portals are intertwined dragons, a favorite Viking design, which was often used in ship carving. The steep gables of the stave churches give them an oddly Oriental look. Why such a style developed under Gothic skies and in Norway is a mystery. In a building near the Folk Museum are several ships that tell stories covering centuries of adventure on the high seas: high-prowed Viking ships—the Oseberg, the Gokstad and the Tune; the celebrated Fram, on which Fridtjof Nansen and Roald Amundsen explored the Arctic and the Antarctic; and the fragile Kon-Tiki raft, on which Thor Heyerdahl and five companions made a 4,000-mile voyage across the South Pacific in the interests of twentieth-century science.

Oslo Fiord is wider and has more gently sloping ledges than the western fiords. The eastern shore—Oestfold County—is a fertile and thickly populated region of green meadows and large tracts of forest. Timber has always been one of Norway's most valuable raw products, and since the Middle Ages one of its chief exports. Norway's largest river, the Glomma, flows through Oestfold on its way to the Skagerrak. Just south of the mouth of the Glomma is one of the larger skerries off this coast—Hvaler—where fishermen and coast pilots like to gather and spin their salty yarns. In summertime, farther up the east shore, white sails fly before the wind in the regattas held at Hankoe.

On the western side of Oslo Fiord—Vestfold County—cliffs and sandy beaches mark the shoreline. Vestfold is a bustling center of industry and shipping. The largest whaling ships in the world come from the small ports here; and the town of Sandefiord is the main base of the whaling fleet. Holmestrand, called the

Norwegian Information Service

OSLO'S HANDSOME MODERN TOWN HALL

As one comes into Oslo by water, the massive building at the edge of the inner harbor draws the eyes at once. The twin towers give this part of Oslo a twentieth-century skyline; and the Town Hall is a meeting place of modern Norwegian art. Sculptures relieve the severe lines of the exterior; and inside there is a series of large murals of Norwegian life.

Norwegian Information Service

A BIT OF OLD NORWAY IN THE TELEMARK COUNTRYSIDE

On many farms one may still see a *stabbur*, a storehouse raised above the ground to protect a family's provisions from dampness and wild beasts. Usually such storehouses were two-story buildings, with an outer staircase leading up to a gallery around the upper floor. Some of those still standing have been in continuous use for more than six hundred years.

"aluminum town," is a center for one of Norway's most important industries.

Aluminum is produced from a clay called bauxite, and to extract the aluminum requires tremendous amounts of electric power. In Norway, electric power means hydroelectric (water) power. As the rivers cascade down to the sea from the mountains, the rapids and falls have given Norway a greater amount of hydroelectric power in proportion to population than any other country in the world. Thus far only about a fifth of this power has been developed. Norway does not have bauxite. Nevertheless, the falling-water resources and their nearness to ice-free harbors make it profitable to send the clay from other countries to be processed. In turn Norway exports aluminum metal and articles made from it.

Fanning out north of Oslo and cutting deeply into the mountain plateau are the Eastern Valleys, U-shaped, sprinkled with sparkling lakes, and divided from each other by rolling highland moors. The valley farthest to the northeast, Oesterdal, is sometimes called "Norway's hidden valley." It once seemed far more remote than it does today, and few travelers glimpsed its brooding conifer forests carpeted with leafy mosses, its deep mirrorlike tarns and foaming rivers, including the upper course of the Glomma. Elk still slip through the woods, and occasionally roe deer. Among the many game birds is the capercailzie, which figures so often in Norwegian folk tales.

The largest and most important valley is the broad, fertile Gudbrandsdal, which spreads between the Dovre and the northern end of Lake Mjoesa, the largest lake in Norway. Though narrow, it is almost sixty miles long. The gateway to the Gudbrandsdal is the town of Lillehammer, on the lake. Sigrid Undset, who won a Nobel Prize in literature, lived just outside Lillehammer. Her greatest book, KRISTIN LAVRANDSDATTER, is considered the most important Norwegian literary work of the twentieth century. The scene of the trilogy is thirteenth-century Norway, but the characters are seen through modern eyes. Kristin is one of the most alive and memorable women in all fiction.

The Gudbrandsdal, Norway's "valley of valleys," and the region between it and Oslo contain the most fertile and level stretches of land and make up the chief farming district of Norway. Mountains and forests leave only about 4 per cent of

THE MONOLITH, 50 feet high with 121 intertwined human figures, is the center piece of Vigeland's park of sculptures, just outside Oslo.

the total area of the country suitable for raising crops. Nevertheless about one-third of the Norwegian people earn their living by farming in combination with forestry. (Along the coast a farmer may also be a fisherman.) Agriculture and lumbering have this close relationship because many of the farmers themselves own the forests. Besides, the farms are quite small: more than 90 per cent are less than 25 acres in extent; and only about 40 farms in the whole country are 250 acres or more. Though thrift and skill and the widespread use of fertilizers make the crop yields exceptionally high, not enough foodstuffs can be raised to meet the needs of the population. Only in the production of potatoes is Norway self-sufficient. Taking just two items, the country must buy from other nations about 40 per cent of its cereals (grains) and 15 per cent of its fodder (for livestock).

Saeters and Modern Creameries

The raising of livestock is an important part of the farmer's work. To this must be added the raising of fur-bearing animals, particularly silver foxes. Norway has developed its own breeds of cattle and horses, among them the Doele cattle that are raised in both the Gudbrandsdal and the Oesterdal. In addition to forests, many farmers own mountain pastures in common, where their cattle and sheep are put to graze in summer. In times past, milk was churned into butter and cheese was made in mountain dairies—the lonely saeters that, in Norwegian folklore, are often haunted by trolls. Today, however, the raw milk is sent to creameries in towns and villages. Norway, with other Scandinavian countries, was a pioneer in the co-operative movement. Most simply, this means that those who produce a certain article—milk or cheese, for instance—band together in an association that markets and sells the article without benefit of a middleman, or distributor. In Norway, the marketing of agricultural products is handled almost entirely by co-operatives.

There are several valleys, west of the Gudbrandsdal, in the enchanting lake district of Valdres. One of them extends to the slopes of the Jotunheim range—the name means "Home of the Giants"—where the mountains of Norway soar highest. Here Galdhoepiggen lifts its rocky summit 8,098 feet above sea level. It is the highest mountain in Europe north of the Carpathians. However, a near-by peak, Glittertind, appears even higher because of its thick cloak of eternal snow.

South of the Valdres district is the Hallingdal, through which the railway between Bergen and Oslo passes. The route provides a thrilling moutain ride, and from the train one sees a cross section of the magnificent Norwegian landscape. To the east of the Hallingdal lies a roadless forest called Vassfaret, where an occasional bear still lurks.

The farthest south of the Eastern Valleys is the Numedal. Its chief town is Kongsberg, which was an important silver-mining center as early as 1800. Metal for Norwegian coins still comes from these mines. Of more interest in the Numedal today are the number of stave churches still standing in their original settings. The one at Uvdal has a gorgeous "rose painting," and is an outstanding piece of Norwegian folk art.

The Norwegian Riviera

From Stavanger to Krageroe the coast of southern Norway is called Soerlandet, or the "Norwegian Riviera." Indented by many bays and tiny fiords and protected from the open ocean by thousands of skerries, the Soerlandet lures all those who love salt water and sun. From centuries-old ports along this coast—Arendal, Grimstad, Kristiansand, Tvedestrand—generations of mariners have braved the perils of the sea.

Telemark, Home of Skiing

Telemark, in the central part of South Norway, is a district of winding valleys. On many of the farms one may still see examples of the folk architecture that developed during the Middle Ages. Among these wooden buildings, adorned with carving, is the *stabbur,* a storehouse that rests on pillars.

Norwegian Information Service
RJUKAN—FOREST-CLAD RAVINE AND CHEMICAL PLANT
The little cable car carries workers from the plant to the high surrounding plateau. Extracting nitrogen from the air, this factory produces fertilizers, of great importance to agriculture. The process of nitrogen extraction was developed by Norwegian scientists. It uses enormous amounts of electric power, made possible by the country's vast water-power resources.

SEVEN SISTERS WATERFALL, in Geiranger Fiord, is a dazzling sight in spring. Then melting snows add to the headlong rush of foam.

A **MODERN HIGHWAY** winds through the Romsdal valley, following an ancient route between west and central Norway. In the background looms Romsdalshorn.

STAVANGER is a bustling port, where the old and new blend happily. Though the city has a number of industries, it is best known as a fish-canning center.

THE LAND OF FIORDS

The glittering white cap of Mount Gausta dominates Telemark. Near this peak is the town of Rjukan, which is a center of Norway's important electrochemical industry. This is another industry that has grown along with the development of water power. Vast quantities of cheap electricity have opened the way for the production of chemicals, of "heavy water" (used in atomic-energy plants), and for the extraction of nitrogen from the air, a process worked out by Norwegian scientists. The factories at Rjukan are among the largest in Norway and—a unique combination of beauty and utility —they nestle at the bottom of a deep, forest-clad ravine.

Telemark is also the home of skiing, the national sport, and has given its name to a kind of skiing technique. Skis have been in use all over Norway for at least a thousand years, though skiing was not considered a sport until the middle of the nineteenth century. During the four "white" months, Norwegian boys and girls learn to glide over the crust almost as soon as they can walk. Easter is a special skiing holiday, when the worker in office or factory takes his family to the mountains for the sport. It is not surprising that Norwegian skiers usually take the lead in the Winter Olympics.

To the west of the mountains lies the breathtakingly beautiful Fiord Country. At the same time that the glaciers of the ice age were scouring out the deep Eastern Valleys, similar valleys were formed on the west coast separated by rounded mountain ranges extending toward the ocean like huge fingers. After the ice age the coastline began to sink, and the sea flooded the valleys to form the fiords. After the period of sinking, a slight rising occurred so that a shelf of lowland pushed above the water in the south as well as in the west. Today the greater part of Norway's population lives on this shelf. When it was formed, the chain of skerries also appeared that forms a natural breakwater along the coast.

The fiords are extremely deep. In places in Sogne Fiord, the water has a depth of more than 4,000 feet. At their mouths, the fiords are broad and smiling, with farmlands on either side; but gradually they narrow and the walls rise sheer and ever higher above the water. In many places the sides are so nearly vertical that large ocean-going vessels may ply within a few yards of the fiord's edge. On the steeper slopes there is little soil, but elsewhere there are groves

Scandinavian Airlines
COLORFUL GARB FOR FUN ON ICE AND SNOW
Many of the intricate designs are traditional, developed by generations of Norwegian women, busily clicking their needles through the long winter dusk. The star pattern (at left on the rack) comes from the Selbu area near Trondheim.

of pine and birch, where graceful red deer may be seen now and then. The islands that stand sentinel in the open sea look barren from a distance, but in sheltered coves and in crannies in the rocks there are thickets of oak and birch, aspen and rowantree.

Some of Norway's most important cities are at the mouths of the western fiords. Stavanger is a quaint old seaport, bustling with shipping and trade. It is the center of the fish-canning industry. During the summer a constant stream of smacks bring silvery cargoes of brisling to the quays. Brisling are small fish, and those canned are sold as "sardines." From Stavanger one may sail inland, weaving in and out among the teeming isles of Ryfylke and beyond into narrow fiords. One of the most enthralling of these is Lyse Fiord, where farms perch, at the edge of steep walls, hundreds of feet above the water. On such farms, the sturdy, sure-footed "fiord horse" does yeoman service.

One of the loveliest fiords of all is Hardanger, between Stavanger and Bergen. In the springtime the orchards along the shore are a drift of white blossoms. Farther inland, upland pastures show green and lush. Rising above the head of Hardanger Fiord is a lake-studded plateau rimmed with snow-covered peaks —Hardangervidda. On the edge of it, the power of both Laatefoss and Voeringfoss (*foss* means "falls") has been harnessed in superb engineering feats.

Although the colorful costumes of old time are rarely worn any more and the folk costumes are disappearing from everyday life, the visitor to the Hardanger

Burton Holmes from Ewing Galloway, N. Y.

THE HANSEATIC WHARF ON BERGEN'S WATER FRONT

In these gabled buildings the German merchants of the Hanseatic League once bargained for fish in exchange for grain. Bergen has been an important port ever since that medieval period. Today modern docks line the busy harbor, a haven for ships of all flags.

region may be lucky enough to witness an old-fashioned wedding. The women in the bridal party wear white blouses, and over them stiffly beaded or embroidered bodices; and knee-length skirts of black or dark-blue homespun. The men may be decked out in bibbed trousers with elaborately embroidered vests, and broad-brimmed hats, or sometimes tight-fitting knee breeches, scarlet vests with silver buttons and silver-buckled shoes. If the people live inland, the bridal procession winds down a country road led by a fiddler playing the curious eight-stringed "Hardanger fiddle." (Four of the strings are set below the others, and they give out rich overtones when the fiddle is played.) Bride and groom follow, riding in state, the bride wearing a crown, a tradition that has come down from medieval times. The crown, wrought of silver, is probably a family heirloom. If the fiord is near by, the procession will be made up of a number of small boats.

Bergen was already an important city in the Middle Ages, when merchants settled there from the free towns of the

LODGE along the Trollsteg mountain road between Valldal and Aandalsnes, western Norway.

FLOWER MARKET in Oslo. From June to September there is a profusion of blossoms.

STAVE CHURCH at Borgund, built some time in the 1200's. Upper ridge ends have the shape of dragons—viking symbol.

THE LAND OF FIORDS

Hanseatic League in northern Germany. Side by side with gabled buildings, including the Hanseatic Wharf, that date from this period, and even earlier reminders of the Vikings, are modern hotels and restaurants and shops.

Though industry is taking a more important part in the life of Bergen today, it is still one of Norway's chief shipping centers. The country's prosperity has long been dependent on world trade; and before World War II, Norway had the fourth largest fleet of merchant ships of any country in the world. During the heroic but doomed struggle against the Germans in April 1940, seven-eighths of this fleet managed to escape to Allied ports. Thereafter it carried men and supplies to every theater of the war; and numbers of the ships and the Norwegian seamen who manned them were lost. One of Norway's chief problems after the war, therefore, was to rebuild its merchant marine. Norwegians could take pride in the fact that by 1951 their shipping was greater than it had been in 1939. Norway now ranks third in world shipping.

The largest and deepest of the fiords, and perhaps the most wildly magnificent, is Sogne Fiord. It winds inland for 110 miles, where it meets the cold fingers of the Jostedal Glacier, the largest ice field in northern Europe. The really high mountains of Norway—the Lom, the

Burton Holmes from Ewing Galloway, N. Y.

OLAF TRYGVESSEN STILL STANDS GUARD OVER TRONDHEIM

The market place is in the center of Trondheim, at the base of a statue of King Olaf Trygvessen, who founded the city in 997. A daring Viking chief, his romantic story weaves through Norwegian legend and poetry. Olaf's vessel, the Long Snake, was the mightiest in the north. During a fierce battle in 1000, Olaf fought on until he was about to be overwhelmed and then leaped into the sea.

Jotunheim, the Hemsedal and the Voss—lie in a semicircle around the innermost arms of Sogne Fiord.

The most northerly part of the Fiord Country consists of the districts of Moere, Romsdal and Trondelag. Kristiansund is the most important town of Moere, and most of its citizens are sea fishermen. Aalesund is the chief fishing center and one of the most important in the world. Inland, the streams, their headlong rush to the sea broken by numerous falls, teem with trout and salmon. Hare and ptarmigan may be flushed on the upland moors; and elk roam in the forests around Lake Snaasa. The forests of this region are second in value only to those of South Norway. All supply the country's tremendous pulp and paper industry.

Trondheim, Once Called Nidaros

The city of Trondheim, in Troendelag, is almost exactly in the center of Norway from north to south. It was founded by King Olaf Trygvessen in 997 as the capital of Norway and was then called Nidaros. The spires of Nidaros Cathedral dominate the modern city's skyline; and Norwegian kings are still crowned in the beautiful medieval building.

Beyond Troendelag lies North Norway, the Land of the Midnight Sun. The greater part of it is within the Arctic Circle. At North Cape, the farthest tip of Norway, the sun never sets from about May 14 to July 30. In the winter the shimmering curtain of the aurora borealis, or northern lights, brightens the long nights with unearthly splendor.

To North Cape by an Ancient Route

One of the most exciting experiences in Norway is to take a trip in summer on one of the comfortable coastal steamers that ply the Northern Way between Bergen and North Cape. A wall of rocky cliffs, rising sheer from the icy Arctic waters, the headland stands out in lonely grandeur. The round trip on the ship takes about twelve days. However, you can vary the tour by returning overland. There are excellent roads and railways.

Not far south of North Cape, on the island of Kvaloey, is Hammerfest, the most northerly town in the world and the center for Finnmark, as the far northern region is called. Only about 70,000 people live in this district, on the weather-beaten coast or on lonely homesteads separated by vast stretches of moor. Here, in the brief summer months, under long hours of sunlight, plants grow so fast that one can almost *see* them sprout.

South from Hammerfest, the next important town is Tromsoe, the "Capital of the Arctic." It, too, is on an island. The Northern Lights Observatory is here and near by there is a Lapp camp. Narvik, further down the coast, is the chief port for shipping iron ore. Most of the country's considerable iron-ore resources are in North Norway.

Swinging out into the ocean, northwest of Vest Fiord, is the chain of the Lofoten Islands. They are the headquarters of the tremendous fishing industry of North Norway. Cod is the chief catch. Tons of it are exported, fresh or frozen, dried or salted. The herring fisheries are the next most important after cod, and a large part of this catch is canned. Since it was discovered some years ago that cod-liver oil is extremely rich in vitamins A and D, the oil has become an important item in Norway's international trade.

The Norwegian People of Today

Their mountainous and sea-girt country —almost an island—has molded the Norwegians in many ways. For all its beauty, the land requires hard labor of its inhabitants. Toil and hardship have made them sturdy and self-reliant; and the constant challenge of sea and mountain has made them proudly independent. From the dawn of their recorded history they have also had a great respect for law and order.

From about 800 to 1050, the people along the coasts of northwestern Europe trembled in fear of the bold Viking raids. Nevertheless, many Norsemen went to trade (dried cod was even then an item for barter) and in search of homes. Norse colonies were set up in Iceland, Scotland, the Faeroes and along the French coast (Normandy!) and in Ireland. Where-

WITH PRIDE a Norwegian girl displays a traditional costume and the mellowed-wood interior of an ancestral home.

PEER GYNT, scalawag of Norse folklore. The effigy perches on a hut at Dovre, in central Norway.

BERGEN HARBOR is cupped in mountains. One may climb the slopes or take an almost vertical funicular railway.

Norwegian Information Service

SVOLVAER, HOME OF THE LOFOTENS COD-FISHING FLEET

From January into April, the harbor swarms with thousands of vessels of fishermen who have gathered from all parts of the coast. It is then that the cod come to their spawning grounds at the base of the mountainous Lofotens. Nowhere else are such large quantities of cod found in so small an area, and the catch is enormous. More than half of it is salted.

ever they settled, they brought a respect for law. The feudal system, by which the great mass of European people were held in thrall during the Middle Ages, was never established in Norway. The peasants continued to live as free men. It is an interesting sidelight on the period of colonization that ancient Norse literature —the sagas, the eddaic and scaldic poems—found its richest expression in Iceland.

By 872 Norway was united under a single chief, Harald the Fair-haired. The kingdom was made even stronger by Olaf Haraldsson (Saint Olaf, 1016-29) who brought Christianity to Norway.

However, colonies were lost, and civil strife and the terrible Black Death swept away three-quarters of the Norwegian population during the thirteenth and fourteenth centuries. So in 1397 Norway was forced to submit to a union with Denmark and Sweden, from which Sweden gradually broke away. The Dano-Norwegian union nevertheless lasted until 1814. In that year Norway wrote a new constitution and agreed to join a union with Sweden. But throughout the nineteenth century the Norwegians strove by peaceful means for independence. Writers, composers and painters were inspired to produce works that would be thoroughly Norwegian in feeling, without the old Danish influence. Interest in the old folk arts took on new life. Asbjoernsen and Moe made their wonderful collection of folk and fairy tales, which until then had been handed down by word of mouth. Woven through the haunting music of Edvard Grieg (1843-1907), Norway's greatest composer, are threads of old folk melodies.

The union with Sweden ended in June 1905, when the Norwegian Parliament declared Norway's independence. For king, the Norwegian people elected Prince Charles of Denmark, crowned as Haakon VII.

The government of Norway is a constitutional monarchy. There are several political parties, of which Labor is the strongest. Norway was one of the first countries to develop a broad social-security program, which includes insurance against unemployment, illness and accident, and retirement pensions. The welfare services for children reach the most remote homes. Boys and girls have regular medical and dental examinations; and necessary treatment is usually free.

Other progressive nations have copied the "Oslo breakfast," served to the city's children at school before classes begin. It is a scientifically balanced meal, of whole milk, whole-grain bread, vitamin-rich spreads, and fresh fruit or vegetables in season—plus cod-liver oil!

Norway has a splendid public-education system. Boys and girls from the age of seven must go to elementary school for seven years. On remote farms and in little isolated schools, the radio helps to bring the children into closer contact with the outside world. In the last two grades of the elementary schools and in the secondary schools, English is usually taught as a second language. Oslo University is the mother institution of all the other Norwegian academic colleges.

The "big moment" in the lives of Norwegian children comes on Christmas Eve. It begins with a traditional dinner of boiled codfish and rice porridge. In the country a bowl of porridge is set out, in the barn, for the brownie who, according to legend, watches over every family. Boys and girls remember the birds, too, and for them a sheaf of oats is hung from the ridgepole. There is no lingering over dinner, for under a lighted tree gifts await the children—perhaps skis or ice skates, and mittens, sweaters or scarfs knitted in unique patterns that have come down through the centuries. As the joyous evening draws to a close, boys and girls join hands around the glowing tree and sing old Norwegian Christmas carols.

NORWAY: FACTS AND FIGURES

THE COUNTRY

Bounded on the north and northwest by the Arctic Ocean, on the west by the North Atlantic, on the south by the North Sea and the Skagerrak, and on the east by Sweden, Finland and Russia. The distance from north to south is about 1,100 miles; and the coastline, including the fiords and the shores of the islands, is about 12,000 miles. The total area is 126,099 square miles, and the population is about 3,250,000. The Arctic archipelago of Svalbard (which includes Spitsbergen), which is under Norwegian sovereignty, has an area of 24,101 square miles and a population of about 1,300.

GOVERNMENT

Hereditary and constitutional monarchy with legislative power in the hands of the Storting, or Parliament, for which women are eligible. The executive is represented by the king, who acts through a Cabinet. The constitution, which has been modified at various times, dates from 1814.

COMMERCE AND INDUSTRIES

Only 4% of the area is arable. Forests (mostly pine) cover 24% of the total area and are one of the chief natural resources. Cod, herring, mackerel, salmon, whale and seal fisheries are important. The mineral deposits include silver, copper, pyrites and iron, and coal is worked in Spitsbergen.

The principal exports are wood pulp and paper manufactures, edible animal products, base metals and articles made of them, oil seeds and fats. The principal imports are machinery, transport equipment, ships, base metals and articles made of them (different from those exported), fuel, oil, textiles and cereals. The krone (crown) is the monetary unit.

COMMUNICATIONS

In a recent year, the total registered merchant marine (ships above 100 gross tons only) was 2,393 vessels, 6,936,000 gross tons. Ships under construction at this time totaled 2,000,000 gross tons. Total railway mileage is 2,719 miles, mainly state-owned. Scandinavian Airlines operates most domestic routes. Radio broadcasting is state-controlled.

RELIGION AND EDUCATION

The Evangelical Lutheran Church is the national church and the only one endowed by the state. The clergy are nominated by the king. There is freedom of religion for all denominations.

Education is compulsory and primary schools are free. There are 2 kinds of secondary schools, and a number of vocational and technical institutions. There are 2 universities, Oslo and Bergen, and a technical university at Trondheim.

POPULATIONS OF CHIEF CITIES

Oslo, capital, population, 447,000; Bergen, 116,500; Trondheim, 60,000; Stavanger, 52,000; Drammen, 30,000; Kristiansand, 26,000.

EUROPEAN

J. BARNELL

ORPHEUS FOUNTAIN by Carl Milles, Sweden's most famous modern sculptor. The graceful figure of the musician in Greek myth stands, appropriately, in front of the Concert Hall in Stockholm.

EXQUISITE VASES, with the designs etched, that have come from the furnaces of the Orrefors glassworks. The company is a world leader in the production of wares prized for beauty and use.

SWEDEN

Modern Democracy on Ancient Foundations

Land of the midnight sun—the middle way—a modern democracy on ancient foundations—land of smörgåsbord—many phrases have been coined to describe the largest of the Scandinavian countries, this long and narrow land that lies within the same latitudes as Alaska and southern Greenland. Sweden stretches for almost a thousand miles from the southernmost tip of the province of Skåne to above the Arctic Circle. There Norway and Finland meet beyond Sweden's border. Of Sweden it has been said that the country is very like many of its male inhabitants: long and gangling, all bone and no fat.

IN spite of its position "in the shadow of the North Pole," Sweden has a surprisingly mild climate. The reason for this is the Gulf Stream, which brings warm, "livable" wind currents to the Scandinavian peninsula. However, there are marked differences in climate between the north and the south of the country. The south has an average of 60 days a year with temperatures below freezing, but the north has up to 220 days of below-freezing weather.

Consequently, the Swedish landscape offers considerable variety—from undulating fields in the south, through forests and lean country in the middle, to the rugged and wild mountain areas in the far north. The typical scene in Sweden is a charming mixture of farmland, green pastures, wooded hills and the shimmer of a lake or river. Though woodland areas abound in the south, the deep forests—the seven-league forests—are all north of the Stockholm area. The winds sigh through thick stands of spruce, pine and white birch.

Sweden ranks fourth in size among the European countries. Only Russia, France and Spain are larger.

As for the people themselves, like those everywhere else, the Swedes have been labeled with certain characteristics. Some of these are very much to the point; others are more the hasty judgments of visitors. The Swedes may truly be called ambitious, industrious and practical. They are also stolid, formal, shy, generous, opinionated, friendly and decent. They have a great weakness for anything foreign and their rivalry among themselves is something of a national trademark.

Sweden's three main divisions correspond to the nature of the land: Götaland (Land of the Goths), in the south; Svealand (Land of the Svears, which has become Swedes—*svenskar*) in the center; and Norrland (Northland).

Skåne is the southernmost province of Sweden. About 11 per cent of the country's total population lives in Skåne, on only 2.3 per cent of the total area. Skåne's chief city is the port of Malmö. The province is Sweden's leading agricultural area, a land of plenty whose fertile plains yield bumper crops vital to the economy of Sweden. It is a rolling countryside, strewn with wooded hills and rimmed with beaches of white sand. This prosperous farming province is rich in graceful manors and Renaissance castles.

The largest province in Götaland is Småland, north of Skåne. As land, Småland is rather lean and stony. However, the province is the home of some of Sweden's best-known glass works, among them Orrefors and Kosta. Their beautiful products are prized the world over. The city of Jönköping in Småland is the headquarters of the famous Swedish match industry.

Göteborg, the second largest city in the country, is on the west coast of Götaland. Göteborg is Sweden's main gate to the oceans and home port for a substantial part of the Swedish merchant marine.

MODERN HOME FOR THE AGED—the Stadshagsgårdens, in Stockholm. The tall structure was opened in 1956 and provides comfortable, cheerful quarters, which have specially designed, easy-to-use equipment. Sweden is a leader in the care of "senior citizens."

Among the city's leading industries are three of the four largest shipyards in the country. Göteborg is also the home of SKF, whose ball bearings help to keep wheels of all kinds turning smoothly.

The Göta Canal

Now let us move north from Göteborg toward the land of the Svears—Svealand. Our "highway" is the Göta Canal. It was built more than a century ago and connects the west and east coasts of Sweden. It winds through 347 miles of lovely countryside, including a chain of lakes. The trip through the canal takes three days on one of the small white steamers that are built especially for the narrow canal and its many locks.

We arrive in Stockholm, capital of the country and without doubt one of the most beautiful cities in the world. It is on the strait where Lake Mälaren—the third largest lake in Sweden—flows into the Baltic Sea. A "city on the water," it spreads out over thirteen islands and the surrounding shores. From the Old City, still the heart of the capital, Stockholm has grown into a show place of modern city planning. The Old City still has its narrow lanes while the ultramodern suburbs attract professional city planners from many other lands.

Even today the charming Old City reminds the visitor of the times when Sweden was a great international power. The quarter has an atmosphere all its own. Still standing are a number of the mansions the aristocrats of those days built for themselves. Today these structures are used as court houses or other government offices.

The Royal Palace, built in the eighteenth century, is reputedly the largest residence in the world. It faces the waterway entrance to the heart of Stockholm from the Baltic. On an island nearby is the celebrated City Hall, acclaimed by many architects for the beauty of its design. Its sleek tower, topped by the Swedish emblem—three golden crowns—reaches toward the sky.

"Venice of the North" and "Queen of Lake Mälaren"—such phrases well describe the Swedish capital. Numbers of well-kept parks give rest amid the bustle of a big city. There are flowers in profusion in summer, when Stockholm belies its geographical location. Most famous of the parks is Djurgården with its open-air museum, Skansen. There, ancient buildings from all over Sweden have been re-erected. In warm weather there is folk dancing and a constant round of other gay activities.

As one might expect, Stockholm is the center of Swedish cultural life. Here is the Royal Opera—home stage of Jussi Björling, Set Svanholm and other world-renowned singers—the National Museum of Art, and the Royal Dramatic Theater, an international leader in the theater arts. Several of the plays by Eugene O'Neill (American Nobel Prize winner) have had their first performance at the Dramaten, as the Swedes call the theater.

Industry is well represented in Stockholm. Among the best-known products are refrigerators and vacuum cleaners, telephones and automatic gas beacons.

Where Tradition Is King

The most picturesque province in Svealand is Dalarna, or Dalecarlia, affectionately known as the "heart of Sweden." Ancient customs and costumes are still very much in evidence there. The people of Dalecarlia are proud but friendly, well aware of the main role they have played in Swedish history. It was there, in the sixteenth century, that Gustavus Eriksson Vasa gathered his forces in his successful attempt to drive the ruling Danes from Swedish soil. In Dalecarlia, tradition is king. The people have deliberately preserved the way of life of their glorious past. You can still see them coming across enchanting Lake Siljan on Sunday mornings, rowing the large church boats. The people are dressed in old costumes, each with a distinct pattern and color. If you know the designs you can tell from what lake village the wearer has come. Fiddlers lead the way as the villagers walk from the lake shore to church.

One of the most grueling of all sports contests, the annual Vasa Ski Race, is

held in Dalecarlia. This fifty-four-mile cross-country race takes the path followed by Gustavus Eriksson Vasa on his flight from Sweden to Norway before he was called back to lead the farmers of Dalecarlia in the fight against the Danes.

Bergslagen, the oldest industrial region in the country, is dotted with mines, iron works and factories. Many of them are well known far from Sweden. Bofors, manufacturers of the famous antiaircraft guns of the second World War, is one.

Stora Kopparbergs Bergslags Aktiebolag, one of the oldest companies in the world still active, is another. The latter dates its history back to the 1280's. It still operates iron works and pulp factories in various sections of Bergslagen. Its once noted copper mine is nowadays just a tourist attraction, though at one time it financed the wars fought by Gustavus II Adolphus and Charles XII.

Dalecarlia's neighbor to the southwest is Värmland, the province of Selma

Lagerlöf, Swedish novelist who won a Nobel Prize. Her *The Wonderful Adventures of Nils* has delighted children in many lands. Värmland is an enchanting province of forest-clad hills, deep river valleys and white manor houses. Many *värmlänningar* have emigrated to North America. The ties between North America and the province of Värmland are very strong.

Perhaps to a visitor anything in Sweden would be very much "north," but to the Swedes only Norrland qualifies. It is the largest of the three main regions, stretching from a line well south of the geographical center of the country up to the northern mountain plains where the Lapps still roam the tundra with their reindeer herds.

Norrland is the part of Sweden where there are still enormous resources to be tapped—vast forests, unharnessed rivers, iron-ore deposits.

Far above the Arctic Circle lies the city of Kiruna. In sheer size, it is the largest city in the world. It is also prob-

DONJON OF VITTSKOVLE CASTLE. Long ago the tower was a grim reminder of feudal power. Today only the wind ever rustles these trees or ruffles the tranquil moat waters.

SWEDISH NATIONAL TRAVEL OFFICE

SWEDISH NATIONAL TRAVEL OFFICE

A MEDIEVAL AIR still lingers in Stockholm's Old City. It is on one of the capital's smaller islands. In this section are the Royal Palace and Stockholm's oldest church, now a cathedral. Its clock tower, with a belfry atop, rises above this narrow byway.

ably the only city on earth that can claim a near seven-thousand-foot mountain within its limits. Kiruna is a model community, founded about 1900. Then the mines of the vast Kirunavaara iron-ore mountain were opened. These are surface mines. Southeast of Kiruna lie Malmberget and Gällivare. There the net of electric railways through the galleries of the mines is said to be more extensive than London's whole subway system.

The mines yield some of the richest ore to be found anywhere. Yearly production is about seven million tons. Most is exported. An electric railroad transports the iron ore from the mines to the Norwegian port of Narvik, on the Atlantic, and to the Swedish port of Luleå, on the Baltic. Due to the Gulf Stream, Narvik harbor is open all year round in spite of its location above the Arctic Circle.

As we have indicated, Sweden is a land of forests. For every acre of arable land there are six of forest. Much timber is produced in the province of Svealand, but Norrland is by far the largest source. An intricate network of rivers, canals and other man-made waterways provides for floating the timber downstream to the sawmills and pulp factories.

As Sweden's greatest natural resource the forests are carefully controlled. The cutting and conservation of timber is governed by national laws and regulations. Forestry experts follow scientifically proved programs. About one half of the forests are owned by individuals, mostly farmers; one fourth, by industries; and the remaining fourth by the national Government or local municipalities.

Besides serving as highways for transporting timber, the rivers are also the source of electric power for Swedish homes and industries. By the mid-1950's Sweden had harnessed about one third of its potential water power. It is expected that all the power will be used by 1980. There are close to one thousand hydroelectric plants in Sweden. The two largest, Harsprånget (Hare's Leap) and Kilforsen, are built underground. This has the advantage of providing even tem-

GÖTEBORG, Sweden's second largest city, is the center of the country's shipping and shipbuilding. Fine avenues, parks and buildings reflect the enterprise of the Swedes.

MONKMEYER

peratures and smooth operation all year round. It also makes the plants safe against air attack. Operation could continue and power be delivered under the heaviest assault. In the late 1950's Harsprånget had generators second in size only to those at Grand Coulee Dam in the United States.

The development of hydroelectric power has been an absolute necessity for Sweden. It has no oil at all and only a limited supply of low-grade coal.

The availability of electric power has also put its stamp on the railway system. By the late 1950's all the main lines, together carrying 85 per cent of all the traffic in the country, were electrified.

Swedish Lapland

Lapland, the northernmost province of Norrland, is where you will see the midnight sun. For six weeks, in June and July, the sun never sets. It just dips close to the horizon, illuminating the sky with a riot of brilliant colors. The vast wilderness of majestic mountains, beautiful lakes and almost endless forests is the home of the Lapps. Reindeer-herding nomads, they still follow practically the same way of life as their forefathers did centuries ago.

Many of them, it is true, have been assimilated into the Swedish population and have settled in towns and cities. Nevertheless, there are still more than six thousand Lapps who remain nomads. These wear the old colorful garb and live in tents they make themselves.

These glimpses of Sweden from south to north have pointed constantly to the close relation of past and present in Sweden. Despite its reputation for being one of the most advanced nations in the world, Swedish civilization can be traced back to the oldest certain date in history. This is the emergence of the southern portion of Sweden from the glacial ice around 12,000 B.C.

About two thousand years later the first tribes of hunters ventured northward toward the receding ice.

Agriculture began in Sweden about 3000 B.C. and there remain huge stone tombs enabling us to trace the early farmers. Copper and bronze became known in Sweden about 1,500 years later. Swedish museums have large collections of the ornamented weapons preserved from that time. Neighbors to the south acquainted these early Swedes with iron, which they learned to extract from the bottom of lakes and rivers.

The first recorded mention of people living in the area of present-day Sweden is in *Germania,* written by the Roman historian Tacitus in A.D. 98.

Sweden was comparatively isolated until the vikings started to roam the seas. The viking age lasted from about A.D. 800 to 1050. Early in the spring every year the vikings from different parts of the Scandinanvian peninsula and from Denmark set out on long expeditions. They were tradesmen when they met friendly people in foreign lands, but became pirates and plunderers if they were not welcomed. They were no doubt a puzzling combination of contrasting qualities. Their good characteristics, however—courage, a sense of fair play, love of freedom—have left a more lasting imprint on history than their bad ones.

Vikings Who Turned East

Vikings from Denmark, which at that time included the south of modern Sweden, set out toward the south and west of Europe. The majority of the Swedish vikings, however, sailed across the Baltic Sea toward the east and Russia. (The name "Russia" is supposed to be of Swedish origin.) The vikings built strongly fortified stations along their trade routes and they extended their travel to regions where they traded with both Greeks and Arabs. Literally thousands of Greek and Arabic coins have been found in Swedish soil.

Here and there in the Swedish countryside, runestones (stones carved with runes, a strange early script) bear witness to the viking exploits. There are some 2,400 of these runestones, half of which are in the province of Uppland.

St. Ansgar came to Sweden in the ninth century, but the country was not definitely

PHOTOS, D. FORBERT

MATCH MANUFACTURE. From these bristling rollers the matches will fall into tidy arrangement in boxes. In 1855, a Swedish inventor, J. E. Lundstrom, produced the first safety matches.

BALL BEARINGS, in a variety of sizes, being inspected. Almost everywhere that machines run, Swedish-made balls of hardened steel are easing friction and increasing the machines' efficiency.

33

converted to Christianity, from the old gods Thor and Odin, until several hundred years later. Some churches built in the twelfth and thirteenth centuries still stand and are in use today. By then the Roman Catholic Church was firmly established in Sweden.

About this same time, procedures for electing the rulers were laid down; a council, forerunner to the modern cabinet, made up of members from the leading families in the land, ruled the country with the kings.

The first Swede to win international fame was a woman, St. Birgitta. She founded a monastic order and is the greatest figure in both religious and literary medieval Swedish history. She was canonized in 1391.

In the same period Sweden's trade developed extensively. The town of Visby on the island of Gotland in the Baltic Sea became one of the leading members of the Hanseatic League. Sweden thereby gained markets for such products as copper, iron, furs and fish. Visby in those days was encircled by a great wall, most of which is still standing. The town's sixteen medieval churches are today picturesque ruins.

In 1397 Queen Margareta, daughter of one king (a Dane) and widow of another (a Norwegian), tried to unite Sweden, Denmark and Norway under one crown. The idea was appealing then, as it was to be many times later. She was successful and thus created the largest kingdom in Europe at the time.

The Swedish Parliament, or Riksdag, was born in 1435. It was notable for the fact that the farmers were represented in it. The feudal system, then dominating the central European countries, had not been established in Sweden.

In 1523 Gustavus Eriksson Vasa was elected king. Two years before he had driven the Danes out and put an end to the union with Denmark. Now began one of the most significant periods in Swedish history. Vasa has been called the "builder of the country." His rule laid the foundations for modern Sweden. By the middle of the sixteenth century—Vasa ruled until his death in 1560—the throne had become hereditary.

Gustavus II Adolphus, who reigned 1611–32, is usually considered the greatest of Swedish kings. He was one of the leaders in the Thirty Years' War. His political genius, military talents and out-

A MECHANICAL BINDER at work. In the rolling fertile plain of the southernmost part of Sweden, modern farm machinery and methods are used to good advantage. The well-tended land yields bountiful harvests of oats, rye, wheat, barley, sugar beets, potatoes, hay.

AMERICAN SWEDISH NEWS EXCHANGE

AMERICAN SWEDISH NEWS EXCHANGE

GLEAMING ROLLS OF SILVERY METAL curl out of the press in an aluminum mill. Sweden has no bauxite, the source of aluminum, but plentiful electric power, which aluminum production requires. It is therefore economical to process the metal there.

standing administrative abilities made his campaigns extremely successful. Under him Sweden began a period of great influence in the politics of Europe.

Almost a century later came the last major war period in the history of Sweden. The Swedish empire at that time embraced an area twice as large as that of the twentieth-century nation. Charles XII lost the Battle of Poltava, in 1709, to Peter the Great of Russia. When the conflict ended later, Sweden was left with few of her former possessions and was about the same size as it is today.

We leap another century to the year 1810. The Swedish Riksdag elected a French marshal, who had served under Napoleon, as crown prince. The marshal was Jean Baptiste Jules Bernadotte. He succeeded to the throne in 1818, as Carl Johan, or Charles XIV. The Bernadotte family is still the reigning house of the country.

In 1814 Bernadotte united Norway and Sweden. This union lasted until 1905.

Sweden was neutral in both world wars of the twentieth century. Neutrality, however, has not kept Sweden from tak-

PHOTOS, THREE LIONS

A WATERFALL breaks the headlong rush of one of the many streams that thread through Värmland, in southwestern Sweden. It is an enchanting province, deeply forested and with many sparkling lakes as well as rivers.

SERVICES are still held in a church that was built during the turbulent thirteenth century. Only a few such churches remain. This one is at Mora, a town in the picturesque province of Dalecarlia (Dalarna).

36

IN DALECARLIA even the children still wear the old-time costumes. The people of the province—a serene island amid modern bustle—cling to traditional customs and dress. Here, in 1521, Vasa led the revolt against the Danes.

VISBY, on the island of Gotland in the Baltic, is a quiet, gracious town today. In the time of the Hanseatic League, however, it was the commercial center of northern Europe. Turreted walls and the ruins of churches recall that period.

D. FORBERT

J. BARNELL

PHOTOS, SWEDISH NATIONAL TRAVEL OFFICE

REINDEER ROUNDUP in Norrland (Northland). On such occasions the herds are handled just as cattle are. The animals are sorted, some for slaughter, and the fawns are branded.

LAPP CLOTHES for bitter weather. Usually the men wear tight pants and long blue tunics trimmed with strips of yellow, red or green leather. The bulky boots are stuffed with hay.

ing part in many kinds of international activity. For example, Sweden sent a hospital unit to South Korea during the Korean war and a detachment to the UN Emergency Force in Egypt in 1956–57.

Early in 1949 Sweden was close to quitting its traditional neutral course. The issue was whether or not to join a Scandinavian alliance. To do so would have been a drastic departure from long-established policy. Yet the country was willing to share unlimited mutual responsibilities for the defense of Scandinavia with Denmark and Norway. The negotiations failed, however. Norway and Denmark joined NATO. Sweden returned to its old neutrality and decided to stay out of the military great-power alliance.

As an old seafaring nation and with a long coastline to defend, Sweden maintains a comparatively strong navy. The air force was expanded rapidly in the 1950's and by 1957 was one of the strong-

SWEDEN

est in Europe. Its planes are jets and its bases are largely underground.

To many people, Sweden is the cradle of the modern idea of social welfare. The results achieved are studied with as much interest in a number of other countries as they are at home. The Swedish welfare system of today is sometimes called a "social smörgåsbord." There are perhaps too many courses for the "social stomach" of most other nations. But it cannot be denied that several dishes are tempting and that most people who come in contact with the Swedish welfare program are attracted to at least some part of it.

Social-welfare laws of some kind can be traced back several centuries in Sweden. Nevertheless, the real work did not begin until the opening of the 1900's. Since the early 1930's progress in this field has been rapid.

It has never been the aim of the Swedish social-welfare program to wipe out individual effort or self-reliance. Nor has this been the result. The program is based on the belief that the citizens of a country are entitled to certain protection, against the hazards of illness, age, unemployment. Most citizens could not afford the cost of such safeguards themselves. When the government takes on the responsibility, both the people and the nation gain. Thus health, according to this theory, is a matter of public concern.

FROM FOREST TO SAWMILL by way of swift rivers. During the spring and summer, logs cut in the forests are floated down the streams to the great sawmills along the coast.

SWEDISH NATIONAL TRAVEL OFFICE

VÄLLINGBY, a city within a city on the outskirts of Stockholm, is a planned community. It has space as well as skyscraper apartments, houses, recreation centers and a variety of shops.

A PLAYGROUND in Stockholm invites youngsters to clamber over amusing free-form structures. One looks a bit like a monster snail with its shell removed, to provide sand piles.

40

KETTLEDRUMS boom and trumpets blare as the king's guard goes on parade. Used to the sound, the handsome chestnuts stand quiet.

THE SLUSSEN ROUNDABOUT in the heart of Stockholm. A cloverleaf intersection, it was built, in 1935, to eliminate the city's worst traffic jam. The Slussen is a neck, connecting two of the main islands.

EUROPEAN

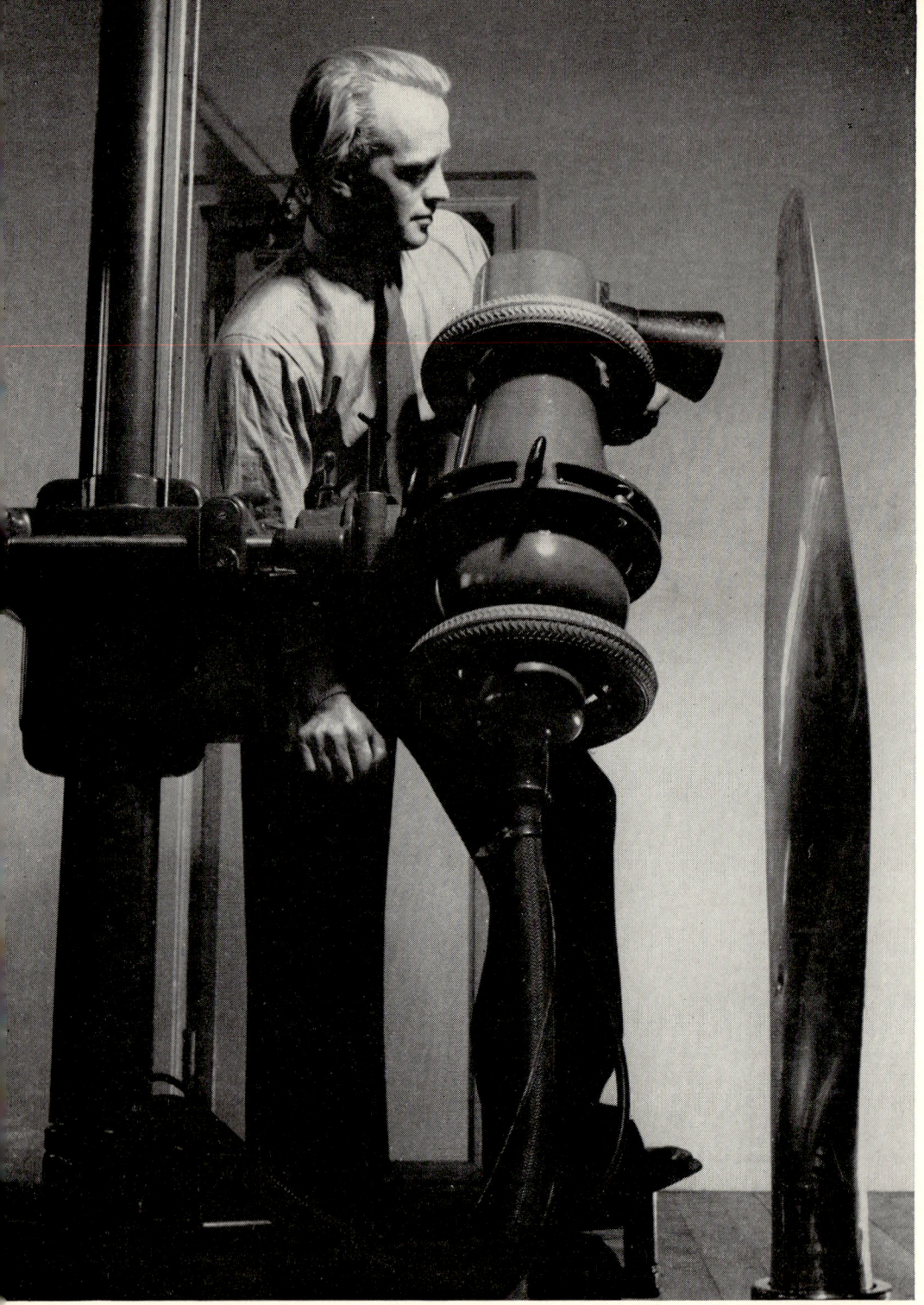

SCIENCE AND INDUSTRY work together. A blade of an aluminum airplane propeller is tested by X ray, which will reveal any flaws or cracks in the metal that would escape detection otherwise. Such advanced methods are typical of Swedish heavy industry. In efficiency and the quality of its products, it is a strong competitor for world trade.

SPACE AND LIGHT for work and play—an elementary school in Stockholm. Swedish children, regardless of family income, are assured of being able to get an excellent education. How far a boy or girl goes depends on his or her own talents and industriousness.

An important part of the welfare system is devoted to the care of families. Here care begins even before the cradle. Expectant mothers are given free examinations regularly. One result is that the Swedish infant death rate is the lowest of any country. Regular medical examinations are also given free to children.

Regarding care of the aged, the approach is summed up in the slogan, "Add life to the years, not just years to life." As the proportion of older people grows larger in all the advanced countries, this idea is gaining wide acceptance. For it means a longer period of working years and a later age when help may be needed.

The People's Home, as the Swedes call their social-welfare state, is a very expensive operation. More than 25 per cent of taxes, heavy, are applied to it.

Even so, Sweden today has a very high standard of living. It compares favorably with any country in Europe and in many respects even with Canada and the United States. In a recent year there were more automobiles per person in Sweden than in any other European country, and more telephones and more radios.

Sweden has an efficient educational system. Its foundations were laid by King Gustavus II Adolphus. Elementary education became compulsory in 1842. In the middle of the 1950's the Swedish schools started on a road that will lead to far-reaching changes by about 1975. Under this system, all children must take a nine-year general course. From the fifth grade on, study of English is obligatory. In the seventh grade a certain amount of choice of subjects begins. This is widened in the ninth grade. Some pupils then concentrate on vocational training while others prepare for the gymnasium (high school). Graduation from the gymnasiums qualifies students for attendance at the universities. Sweden has four. The most famous is the University of Uppsala, founded in 1477. The aim of the nine-year general course is chiefly to grade pupils more easily, according to individual aptitudes and interests. In other words, neither social rank nor family income influences how far a child goes in education.

The high level of literacy in Sweden is due in no small degree to the extensive educational activities outside the school

EUROPEAN

A BEDECKED MAYPOLE ready for the festival of midsummer eve, which comes on or near June 21. Though Maypoles are usually associated with May, they appear later in Sweden, as June is an even more joyous month there. Daylight lingers and the gloom of the short winter days is forgotten.

THREE LIONS

D. FORBERT

GRAZING on the frozen tundra of the far north. The Lapp and his wife, bulky in furs, wait while their reindeer burrow in the snow for lichens and moss, the only forage the tundra yields.

SUNDAY MORNING on a lake in Dalecarlia. Villagers don their most treasured costumes for church services, and row across the water in large boats, which are used only for church attendance.

THE OPERA HOUSE in Stockholm is a focus of the nation's lively interest in the arts. Behind the Opera House is St. Jacob's Church, which dates from the early seventeenth century.

CHANGING OF THE GUARD in the square of the Royal Palace in Stockholm. The palace, said to be the world's largest residence, was built on the site of a medieval castle.

PHOTOS, KOSTICH

system. Every organized group—labor, temperance, farmers and so on—provides its own form of adult education. The results are remarkable. Since a person joins of his own free will, he is usually likely to want to make the most of his time.

Sweden has a free and very vigorous press. Since 1812 a law guaranteeing freedom of the press has been part of the Swedish constitution. The country has about 230 daily newspapers with a combined circulation of over 3,500,000. As newspaper readers the Swedes are slightly ahead of North Americans but they are behind in reading magazines.

Swedes love the out-of-doors and sports. Soccer is the national sport in the summer, and skiing and skating, rather naturally, in the winter. Swedes are extremely active in international sports competitions. These athletes meet with scores of other Europeans every year in soccer, track and field, swimming, tennis, military pentathlon, skiing, ice hockey and the like. The whole population waxes enthusiastic over victories, and the newspapers and radio give wide coverage to the events. Through the years, Sweden has done very well in the Olympic games. Though it has only a small population, it has scored second in total number of points made.

The constitution of Sweden was written in 1809. It is thus the oldest written one in force in Europe. The country is a constitutional monarchy. Though the king is the nominal head of state and all state and governmental acts are performed in his name, he does not wield any political power. He is outside the political parties of the country and his role is as a symbol of national unity and continuity.

The chief executive of the Swedish Government is the prime minister. He is head of the cabinet. He is appointed by the king but depends on the support of the majority in the Riksdag for his power.

The Swedes are fond of their ruling family. In discussions of whether or not Sweden should change from a monarchy to a republic it has often been said that King Gustaf VI Adolf, who began his reign in 1950, would be certain to win the first presidential election if he chose to run. He could also have made a distinguished career for himself as an art historian or as an archaeologist. His motto is "Duty above All."

By Arne Thorén

SWEDEN: FACTS AND FIGURES

THE COUNTRY
Bounded by Finland on the northeast, the Gulf of Bothnia and the Baltic Sea on the east, the Skaggerak and Kattegat Seas on the southwest, and Norway on the west. Total area, 173,378 sq. mi.; population, 7,290,000.

GOVERNMENT
Constitutional monarchy. Executive power wielded by a Council of State of about 15 ministers, whose head is the prime minister. Parliament, or the Riksdag, has two houses. Members of the first house (150) are elected by members of the *Landstings*, or provincial representatives, and by electors from six towns outside the *Landstings*. The second house has about 230 members elected by universal suffrage for four years. Both sexes over 21 have the right to vote.

COMMERCE AND INDUSTRIES
Agriculture is the chief occupation. Main crops are hay, potatoes, fodder roots, sugar beets, oats, rye, wheat, barley. Mineral resources include iron ore, sulfur pyrites, fire clay. More than half the country is covered by forests, mostly pine, birch and spruce. Lumbering and the production of pulp and paper, and the manufacture of pig iron, steel, cream separators, lighthouse apparatus, telephone equipment, motors and electrical machinery, procelain and glass are among chief industries. Exports: wood pulp, paper, timber, minerals and metals, machinery. Imports: minerals, metals, machinery, raw-textile materials, animal products. Monetary unit is the krona (crown).

COMMUNICATIONS
More than 10,230 mi. of railway, main lines largely electrified and nearly all government-owned; 54,800 mi. of roads. Merchant fleet: 1,800 ships with a gross tonnage of 2,812,000. Scandinavian Airlines System operates domestic and international service.

RELIGION AND EDUCATION
The Evengelical Lutheran Church is the state religion but there is complete freedom of worship. Public elementary education is compulsory and free for 9 years. There are two national universities (Uppsala and Lund) and two private universities (Stockholm and Göteborg).

CHIEF CITIES
Stockholm, capital 786,000; Göteborg, 380,000; Malmö, 210,000; Norrkoping, 89,000; Halsingborg, 74,000; Uppsala, 71,000.

SKIS BY THE HUNDRED for the ardent Finnish athletes. Ski manufacture is one of many woodworking industries based on the country's wealth of forests. The strong ash wood makes fine skis.

PLAYTIME for Lapp children—what is more fun than a boat of one's own? Though the Lapps are a wandering people, the children go to school regularly, and are taught in Finnish and Lapp.

GAY FLOWERS, a lovely scarf inspire the young artists who are painting earthenware in a pottery at Helsinki. Finnish design, combining beauty and utility, has won international recognition in many fields.

48

The Land of a Thousand Lakes
Finland and Its Progressive People

When one reads of the achievements of the Finns, naturally one expects them to be associated with a large and prosperous people. As a matter of fact the Finns are a small nation (slightly more than four million). The people are usually tall and fair-skinned, and they speak a language similar to the Hungarian. The coast of Finland is island-fringed and no country of Europe has an equal area of land that contains so many lakes. Forest covers nearly three-quarters of the land and the abundant waterways provide routes by which lumber and its products may reach the sea. Though under Swedish domination for centuries the Finns had been under Russian control for the hundred years before 1917 when they declared their independence. There is a small Swedish-speaking population—on the southern and western coasts and in the Åland Islands. Among the many Finns who have made the world richer by their genius are Jean Sibelius, the composer, and Eliel Saarinen, architect.

ANCESTORS of present-day Finns were sailors, hunters and primitive farmers who came into the territory of what is now Finland about two thousand years ago. The Finnish language is related to the Estonian and the Hungarian. The three peoples were probably in close association before they settled in their present homelands.

The early Finns, though brave, hardy and resourceful, were conquered, in 1157, by the King of Sweden and converted to Christianity. The Finns guarded their own customs jealously, yet they adjusted readily to Swedish rule.

For the next five centuries Finland was incorporated as an integral part of Sweden. Thus it was that the Western ideals and the Lutheran faith were inculcated to survive even the later period of Russian dominance. In 1710 Peter the Great of Russia entered into a bitter struggle with Charles XII of Sweden in which his troops overran the whole of Finland. Sweden made repeated efforts to win back her lost province, and did keep the western part. Russia took over all of Finland in 1809, and Tsar Alexander entered into an agreement for the union of Finland and Russia guaranteeing the Finnish constitution. His successors did not keep the pledge, but attempted to make the country Russian. The Finns resisted stoutly. An oft-quoted saying ran, "We have ceased to be Swedes; we cannot become Russians: we must be Finns." The Declaration of Independence of December 6, 1917, was the outcome. But the Finns had to fight the Red armies of the new Russian state to make good their freedom, and it was not until 1919 that the Finnish republic was set up. Twenty-one years later, Russian troops marched again into Finland, as we shall see later in this chapter. Events seesawed from 1940 to 1945; but after the war the Finns had to cede some of their territory, and also special privileges, to the Soviet Union.

In this land of dense fir and pine woods, lumbering and woodworking are leading industries. Timber, plywood, spools, paper and pulp are by far the chief exports. Butter, cheese and eggs have also been shipped out in large quantities. Finnish factories, farms and mills produce steel, machinery, cereals and textiles. But Finland needs more of these than she can produce, so she must import a certain amount.

The great glaciers that once covered northern Europe scored the face of Finland with rugged lines of scenic hills and placid, twisting lakes. Forests spread over and between the gravelly ridges and down to the sandy shores of the lakes. When the seas rose for a time they covered the south of Finland with a heavy clay soil. Here forests are thick and farming is most productive.

The rivers, filled with rapids, are excellent for generating electric power.

A CALM LAKE IN EASTERN FINLAND, DOTTED WITH ISLETS
Not even a boat breaks the still waters at the moment. At other times, however, logs float down on the lake and barges pass laden with goods for areas without rail or road.

A FARM WIFE PREPARES BARLEY FOR MAKING MALT
The barley is soaked in water for two or three days, during which the water is replaced several times. When the grain has sprouted a little, it is dried. The result is called malt.

LAKE PAIJANNE, SECOND LARGEST OF FINLAND'S 60,000 LAKES

PHOTOS, FINNISH NATIONAL TRAVEL OFFICE

OLAVINLINNA CASTLE IN THE RESORT TOWN OF SAVONLINNA

But one, the Ulea, is navigable for any great length. Boats of considerable size can traverse its whole length.

The extraordinary system of lakes is connected with the Gulf of Finland by canals that provide about 2,700 miles of navigable inland waterways for ships. Of these canals, the most important is the sluiced canal connecting Lake Saima with the Gulf of Finland. It permits ships from the Baltic to penetrate 270 miles inland. Lake Ladoga, which is cut by the Russian border, is the largest lake.

The three main lake basins are separated first by low flat hills which finally slope to the Gulf of Bothnia. Narrow moraines of earth and stone left by the ice-sheet run across Finland from northwest to southeast, rising as forested ridges from thirty to a hundred feet or more above the surrounding country.

This labyrinth of lakes, connected by short rapid streams, covers southern Finland. To the north, nearly uninhabited tracts of hill country, the Keel (Kjölen) Mountains, stretch into a land of dark winters where the days are only a few hours long. At the headwaters of the

THE LAND OF A THOUSAND LAKES

Torneå, Finland reaches a finger into the highlands of Lapland, where flat-topped summits or *fjälls* rise from three to four thousand feet above sea level, and deep-sunk river basins make a dreary waste.

The Karelians, the people of the north and east, nearest Russia, are good musicians and accompany their singing on the national instrument, a kind of zither called the *kantele*. The Finns of the south and west, nearest Sweden, and Tavastlanders, who show that there has been some intermingling of Teutonic stock, are more serious minded and less inclined to play. The Lapps in the extreme north of Finland (as in northern Sweden and Norway) follow their reindeer herds.

The tar industry is an important one. Portions of the bark are peeled from the pine trees, a little at a time, until the bare trunks are covered with a thick yellow substance. The trees are then felled and placed in a slow kiln shaped like a goblet with a hollow stem. Down the inside of this stem the tar runs into barrels.

The tar boats which take the barrels along the waterways to Uleaborg are specially built to shoot the rapids of the Oulu River, which occur on the last stage of the journey. Only professional pilots are then allowed to take charge of these boats, for the slightest mistake on the part of the helmsman would cause the boat to be dashed to pieces.

In summer Finland is a riot of wild flowers and wild berries, particularly strawberries and raspberries. The moun-

FINNISH NATIONAL TRAVEL OFFICE

A COMBINED KITCHEN AND WORKSHOP IN A SPACIOUS FARMHOUSE

The various members of the family may cook or work at their crafts without getting in each other's way. Beautiful fabrics are created at home on such hand looms as this one.

AN INN AT IVALO, A CROSSROADS VILLAGE IN LAPLAND

Ivalo is on the Arctic Highway, the main road through Finnish Lapland. It crosses the tundra for 330 miles, from Rovaniemi, on the Arctic Circle, to Pechenga, Russian seaport.

STOWING SHEEP ON SLEDGES FOR A LONG TRIP NORTH

Though Laplanders have some permanent villages, many wander with their herds, mostly reindeer. Winters are spent in the southern lowlands but warm weather heralds a trek north.

A LAPP OF THE INARI TRIBE IN A FOUR-CORNERED CAP

The cap's points represent the winds and the blue tunic is trimmed with bands in colors borrowed from the northern lights. At the man's feet is a canoelike sleigh—a *pulkka*.

FINNISH NATIONAL TRAVEL OFFICE

A COUNTRY OF SMALL FARMS

A large percentage of Finnish people live in rural areas. This scene in Somerniemi, in southern Finland, is typical. Agriculture is the country's chief occupation, accounting for the employment of about a million men and women. However, cultivated farm land comprises only a small part of the country's land surface, and it is divided into many small holdings.

THE LAND OF A THOUSAND LAKES

tain ash is abundant and in autumn its brilliant scarlet berries add to the beauty of the countryside.

Bears and wolves, which were once found all over the country, have now almost disappeared. The elk has been saved by the game laws. Reindeer are found only in Lapland. In winter, Lapps come into Torneå with sledge loads of reindeer flesh, horns and skins.

Finnish life has to be arranged to suit the climate, which is characterized by a short, hot summer when everything grows quickly, followed by six months of winter. Torneå, at the head of the Gulf of Bothnia, has then only three hours of daylight, and the whole country is covered with snow. The lakes, rivers and canals are frozen for months.

Finnish hospitality always includes a good cup of coffee. The coffee-pot is kept on the back of the stove in constant readiness. With it one eats rye bread, smoked herring, sardines, dried reindeer meat, curdled milk, and the most excellent milk, butter, and potatoes.

The Finnish steam-bath is a peculiarly national affair. Every village and every farmstead throughout the country possesses a bathhouse. This is a large room with tree trunks fixed against the wall to form rough seats. On the floor is a heap of stones which have been heated in an oven or by a wood-fire. A pail of water is thrown on the stones, and this causes the room to be filled with steam. The bathers sit on the lowest seats at first and mount to the higher ones as they get used to the steam, meanwhile beating each other with thin birch twigs. The bath ends with a plunge into a cold stream, or sometimes with a roll in the snow.

For centuries Finland has excelled in the art of making beautiful rugs, and in olden days these rugs were part of a bride's dowry. They were used as bedspreads and as wall-hangings.

FINNISH NATIONAL TRAVEL OFFICE

CARDING, OR HACKLING, FLAX FIBERS FOR WEAVING INTO LINEN

Carding is the final step in the preparation of the fibers, before spinning. Drawing the fibers through a comb disentangles them and makes them lie side by side. For the finest linen the process is repeated a number of times, using successively finer combs. Previous to this step, the fibers have been retted—soaked in water to remove the covering of bark.

In November the Folk High Schools are opened. These institutions are found all over Finland, and now the young people who have worked the farms all summer go on with their education.

The state offers instruction in dairy farming, navigation and other matters of practical interest. There are free libraries and lectures, and a number of co-operative agricultural societies. The University of Helsinki is an excellent climax to the public-school system.

The women of Finland have almost complete equality with the men. They may enter any occupation and any profession. There are women lawyers, architects, government employees and bank officials. Finnish girls are brought up to earn their own living. Women often continue in their careers after they marry.

Ancient Songs and Chants

Before they came under the influence of Sweden and Christianity, the Finns worshiped their ancestors and the spirits of natural places and things, such as springs and woodlands. Spirits, the early Finns thought, had the power to bring or take away prosperity. For him to expect a good harvest, a farmer would have to be on good terms with the proper spirit. Often the people gathered together under the stars to sing of the deeds of their forebears and to chant magical phrases meant to call forth the favors of nature.

For centuries the songs and poems were not written down, but they passed from generation to generation, with new lines and stories added from time to time at the great songfests.

In the sixteenth century, scholars began to take an interest in the folk poems and recorded them in writing. A man of the nineteenth century made the most notable collection. He called it the *Kalevala,* which means "Land of the Giant Being," *Kaleva.* The weird rhythms excited poets in many lands. Longfellow, who studied and translated into English the folk poetry of several ancient nations, came to love the *Kalevala.* When he wrote *Hiawatha,* a narrative poem about another brave and imaginative people, the American Indians, he used the rhythms of the Finnish folk poems.

Finland's music also had its beginning in the old songfests. Like the lines of the *Kalevala,* modern Finnish music, especially that of Jean Sibelius, Finland's foremost composer, preserves the magical flavor of life in early Finland.

Wood smoke and the fragrant odor of pine trees, with the ax of the logger ringing in the cold air—that is Finland in winter. The farmhouses are often of logs chinked closely with clay, with the roof at a steep slant to throw off the snow. Within, in the big kitchen-living room, the huge wood stove blazes merrily.

The Spring Log Drive

Forestry and woodworking are Finland's principal industries and during the long winter months the loggers are busy in the woods. In the spring when the ice breaks out of the rivers and lakes, great rafts of cut logs are made, and floated down to the mills. Over the waterfalls and through the rapids they go. The short, hot summer with long, bright days is a time of planting and harvesting.

Pine, spruce and birch are the most numerous trees. Pine and spruce are the raw materials for Finland's busy paper-pulp and newsprint industries. Hardwoods, principally birch, are exported and sold as cut lumber and also made into plywood and furniture at the hundreds of woodworking plants throughout the country.

Water power and firewood long drove the mills of Finland. Today, huge generators convert the plunging water of the streams into electricity. It now turns most of the machines in the mills.

Ore Fields of Outokumpu

Wood and electricity are the principal —indeed, almost the only—fuels. There is little or no coal in the Finnish earth, but there are deposits of copper, zinc, nickel, iron and other minerals. The huge ore fields and refineries in and around Outokumpu in the southeast produce a high-grade copper as well as iron, sulfur and even some gold and silver. In the

AN OLD WINDMILL WITH SLATTED ARMS, NEAR ORIVESI

Though Finland has tremendous water-power developments which provide power for most purposes, here and there one may still see windmills. A few of them remain in use on farms.

THE LAND OF A THOUSAND LAKES

same region, at Imatra, is the leading hydroelectric plant of the country.

Farming, in spite of the severe winters and short growing seasons, occupies a large part of the population. Most farmers own their own land. When the section called Karelia was taken by the Soviet Union after World War II, many Karelians fled westward into Finland. The Government helped to settle them on new farms. It divided large estates among the landless farmers, drained and cleared fields and built homes.

Few fruit trees can survive the cold climate. Most grains—wheat, rye, oats, hay and barley—and field crops such as potatoes and sugar beets do well. Dairying and hog-raising are extensive, but there are few months when the animals can be left out to pasture.

Farmers no longer wear a distinctive dress. Men generally prefer rough tweeds and high boots in the winter, and linen blouses and light trousers secured at the waist by a leather belt during the summer. Women wear blouses, skirts and sometimes aprons, richly embroidered. The colored handkerchief, tied under the chin, is the favorite headdress.

Helsinki, the Capital

The largest city and leading port of Finland is Helsinki, the capital. It is built on a rocky peninsula, which, with a number of small islands, forms several excellent harbors. Thick ice halts all shipping for a few months in late winter and early spring.

The stone and brick public buildings are in many styles. The Parliament building is classical with a front of Greek columns. Ornate churches and cathedrals have rounded domes, statues aplenty and bright decorations. Some churches, theaters, hotels and other buildings are modern—stark and simple in design and built of near-white native stone. The railroad station is by one of the best of modern architects, Eliel Saarinen.

On a cluster of islets outside the city is Suomenlinna (Sveaborg, in Swedish), a historic fortress. Zoological gardens, beautiful parks and bathing beaches, museums and communities of lovely homes grace other nearby islands.

The short twilight of the winter day in Helsinki finds the streets silent. Traffic is light and what noises there are—from a jingling droshky, an occasional taxi, bus or trolley—are softened by the heavy cover of snow. People huddle by in deep fur coats, save on bright Sundays when some appear, in knickers and gaily colored sweaters, on skis. The frozen harbors become the scene of ice hockey and hair-raising automobile races.

Long, Pleasant Evenings

The summers present an extreme contrast, with their long evenings and magical sunsets. Restaurants are rhythmic with dance music. Some of the people swim and others sail about in agile craft. Large numbers retire to the parks on the islands. Everything and everybody are clean and tidy. Even the market place on the water front is scoured daily by men with powerful water hoses and women with brooms.

Next in importance to the capital are Turku (Åbo, in Swedish) and Tampere. Turku, on the southwest coast, is the oldest city in Finland. The harbor, free of ice throughout the year, is busy with ships to and from Stockholm. Turku was the capital of the country until 1812 and has several fine old buildings—the cathedral and the castle, both erected in the thirteenth century. Tampere, also in the southwest, is on the Tammer Rapids, which run through the city, dropping about sixty feet in a distance of less than a mile. The city has large textile and pulp mills and other factories.

Borga is a place of steep, cobbled streets twisting up and down hill, and of wooden houses, red, yellow and green, clustered about a gray old cathedral rich in wood carvings, old brass wall sconces and crystal chandeliers.

Finland's Tragic War Years

Several months after the beginning of World War II, the Russians decided that the Finnish border was too near Leningrad for Russia's safety. They demanded that

A FINE BRIDGE AND A HUGE FACTORY BUILDING IN PORI

Pori, on the Gulf of Bothnia, is a center for shipping activity and has a number of industries. There are lumber and cotton mills, nickel and copper refineries and match works.

PHOTOS, FINNISH NATIONAL TRAVEL OFFICE

THE UNIVERSITY OF HELSINKI ON THE SENAATINTORI

The Senaatintori is a great square in Helsinki with the severely classical building of the university on one side. In charming contrast are the graceful wrought-iron lamps.

FINNISH NATIONAL TRAVEL OFFICE

FINLAND—TIMBERLAND

Seventy-five per cent of Finland's land surface, or more than 60,000,000 acres, is heavily wooded with fir, spruce and birch. More than 40,000,000 acres are cultivated forest lands whose crops keep the country's sawmills humming constantly. The logs we see are floating to their mill through a series of lakes connected by canals. This is Lake Lohja, in the southern part of Finland.

ARE THESE LOAVES DATED?

Although these women appear to be hanging up moccasins, they are actually suspending dozens of flat loaves of sour rye bread from the kitchen rafters. The bread is baked in huge quantities and hung up to dry. One baking will provide a family with bread for many months to come. The people of Finland are used to working hard and for long hours on end.

the Finns give up considerable territory and lease the port of Hanko for a naval base. Finland refused, and on November 30, 1939, the Russians attacked. In spite of brave resistance, the Finns were forced to yield, after 105 days of fighting.

When the Germans attacked Russia in June 1941, the Finns entered the war on Germany's side, hoping thus to regain the land they had lost. When the Germans were driven out of northern Russia in 1944, Finland signed an armistice in Moscow with the Soviet Union and Great Britain. A treaty signed at Paris in 1947 recognized the Soviet claim to all of the land around Lake Ladoga and between the lake and the Gulf of Finland—the Karelian Isthmus including the important city of Viipuri. The Petsamo region, Finland's outlet to the Arctic Ocean, and about 150 square miles surrounding Porkkala also went to the Soviet Union.

Finland also had to pay war reparations. The last payment was made in 1952. By an agreement made in 1955, the U.S.S.R. formally gave up the Porkkala area in January 1956. All Soviet troops were withdrawn from the region.

AT FIRST GLANCE the country church at Rajamak looks strikingly modern. Yet the side windows, suggesting flying buttresses, and the soaring tower have a Gothic feeling.

WIDE PICTURE WINDOWS and balconies are attractive features of an apartment house.

CLASSIC BEAUTY in the midst of modern Helsinki—the Suurkirkko, or Great Church.

THE HANDSOME RAILWAY STATION in Helsinki was designed by Eliel Saarinen, who helped to make Finland a leader in modern architecture. The structure is of native granite.

FINNISH NATIONAL TRAVEL OFFICE

MONUMENT TO SPORTS

The huge stadium at Helsinki, dominated by its tall, modernistic tower, is a monument to the Finnish love of sports. In 1938, Helsinki was selected by the International Olympics Committee as the site of the 1940 games, which never materialized because of World War II. The stadium, completed in 1940, fulfilled its purpose when the Olympics came to Helsinki in 1952.

FINLAND: FACTS AND FIGURES

THE COUNTRY

Bounded on the north by Norway, on the west by Sweden and the Gulf of Bothnia, on the south by the Gulf of Finland, and on the east by Russia; 10% of the area is covered by lakes which are mostly in the southern part. Area, 130,119 sq. mi., including 12,190 sq. mi. of inland waters. Population, 4,249,000. According to a 1955 agreement, Russia withdrew her troops from the Porkkala Peninsula in 1956. The area had been leased to the Soviet Union, for 50 years, in 1947.

GOVERNMENT

Republic since 1919. President elected for six years and House of Representatives of 200 members for three years. Fifteen electoral districts with proportional representation. Universal suffrage at age of twenty-one. Voting system devised toward proportional representation.

COMMERCE AND INDUSTRIES

Agriculture is the chief occupation of the people, although only 7.7% of the land is cultivated. The principal crops are hay, oats, barley, rye and potatoes. Lumbering and fishing are important industries and dairy farming is increasing. The chief exports are timber, paper and pulp, and butter, and the imports are textiles, cereals, metals and machinery. Monetary unit, the markka.

COMMUNICATIONS

Railways, 3,057 miles; roads, 39,400 miles. Lakes connected with each other and with Gulf of Finland by canals. Telephones, 408,350. Air services: one domestic airline and foreign lines operate into Helsinki.

RELIGION AND EDUCATION

The national church is the Evangelical Lutheran with liberty of conscience guaranteed. Education is well developed. There are 11 training schools for elementary teachers and 3 universities (a state university at Helsinki, and a Finnish and a Swedish university at Turku). In addition there are numerous special schools.

CHIEF TOWNS

Helsinki, the capital, has a population of 404,000; Turku, 110,100; Tampere, 110,000; Lahti, 48,000; Pori, 47,000; Oulu, 44,250; Vaasa, 39,000; Kuopio, 37,100; Jyvaskyla, 33,-500; Kotka, 28,100.

Islands of Fire and Ice

Iceland's Norsemen and the Eskimos of Greenland

Iceland, so-called because the Norsemen who landed there in the ninth century found ice in one of the fjords, is rather a land of fire than of ice. The island is composed entirely of volcanic matter and more than one hundred volcanoes still exist, while there are scores of hot springs and lakes of boiling mud. The folk of Iceland are the descendants of Norsemen as well as early Irish and others. They have developed into hard-working farmers and fishermen. Greenland, a vast island the interior of which is covered by an ice-cap that breaks off in huge bergs, was colonized by Eric the Red, who sailed over from Iceland. Today a colony of Denmark, Greenland—green only in midsummer along a narrow coastal area—is inhabited chiefly by Eskimos, Danes and descendants of early Danish settlers.

ALTHOUGH Carthaginian mariners left fragmentary records of voyages into northern waters, Iceland was little known to Europe until adventurous Norsemen landed on the east coast about 850. They found a small colony of Irish already there and more Irish as well as Norsemen came later. The story of the early times is set down in the famous "Landnamabok" which may be translated "Book of Settlements." By 930 they had established good government, with an Althing or General Court of Parliament. Though largely employed in fishing and sheep-herding, they wrote sagas in the twelfth century which Icelandic children of today can read in the original twelfth-century Norse. In the thirteenth century Iceland established a personal union with Norway, retaining her ancient rights and laws; but in the fourteenth century passed with Norway under the rule of Denmark. In time Lutheranism was imposed by Danish battleships, a trade monopoly was likewise established by the stronger nation, and by the eighteenth century the handful of Icelanders had no outward independence left. By 1845, however, they were able to re-establish their Althing, and soon after a really great statesman came forward in the person of Jon Sigurdsson. In 1854, by throwing the trade of Iceland open to the world, he laid the foundation for the national prosperity of today, and in 1874 he achieved a constitution. In 1903 the Danish Minister to Iceland was displaced by an Icelandic Prime Minister, and in 1918 an Act of Union as between two independent nations was signed. In 1941, Iceland declared its complete independence.

Iceland is one of the most completely volcanic countries in the world. Indeed, in 1783, volcanic eruptions destroyed nearly nine thousand lives—an all but overwhelming disaster. The largest volcano, Hekla, in south Iceland, has made the surrounding country a desert, owing to the dust and boiling lava that it hurls out from time to time. Its last great eruption occurred in 1845. In the tableland of the interior, geysers and hot springs occur, often high in the unweathered lava of the mountain peaks amid ice and snow. The Great Geyser has a crater sixteen feet in diameter and intermittently spouts a column of boiling water over a hundred feet in height.

An island lying a little under six hundred miles to the northwest of the European mainland, it is possible that in recent geologic times Iceland was formed by volcanic eruptions along a crack in the earth's crust running through the Faroes toward Ireland. Though Iceland touches the Arctic Circle on the north, its southwestern portion is laved by the milder, fog-breeding waters of the North Atlantic drift. Of the ice-fields, Vatna, the largest, which in places rises to six thousand feet, is in the south.

Around the rugged coasts there are many islands, and on one group, called the Vestmanna Islands, the chief means of support of the inhabitants are the count-

ISLANDS OF FIRE AND ICE

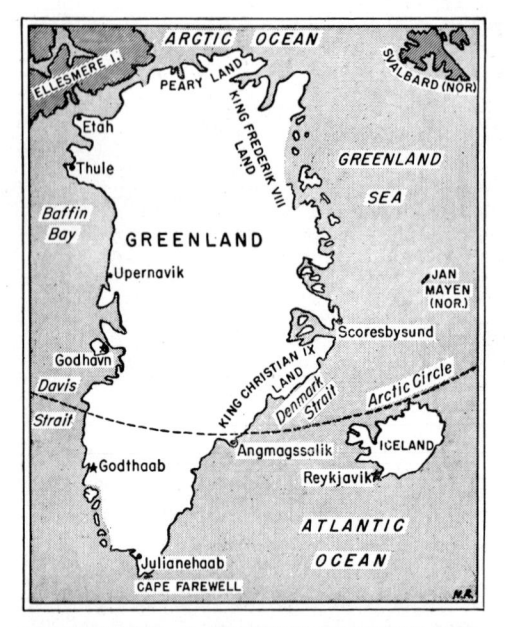

GREENLAND: A COLONY OF DENMARK

less sea birds which have made their homes in the cliffs. These cliffs are the property of the government and are hired out to the islanders, who are experts in scaling the precipitous heights. They catch one variety of bird, the puffin, in a huge net not unlike that used by butterfly collectors.

The eider ducks, from which we get the eider down used for stuffing quilts, are also found in Iceland, and the birds are so tame that they will allow the islanders to stroke them while they are seated on their nests. The ducks pluck the down from their breasts to line their nests, and it is then collected and exported. The poor birds replace the down.

Reykjavik, on Faxa Fiord, is a trade center to which once a year the outlying farmers come with their trains of laden ponies to sell their wool. The town has a cathedral and a university, a state hospital, telephones and a radio station, and to the modern harbor come the half-dozen mail steamers of Iceland's steamship company. Young people are taught English and Danish. One of the world's greatest sculptors, Einar Jónsson, was born at Reykjavik. During World War II the United States established an operations base here.

At Framnes and elsewhere on the northwest peninsula there are various whaling stations. The whaling vessels shoot their harpoons from cannon. On shore, the blubber is cut up by rotary machines and is then steamed to extract the oil, while the bones and refuse are converted into manure products for shipment to other countries.

The fishing, which is one of the most important industries, is conducted by means of steam trawlers and motor cutters. Quantities of split codfish are exported, chiefly to Spain, as is some herring and a little fish oil.

Dairying and sheep raising are important. Coal, petroleum, machinery and textiles have to be imported. There is a little gold in the country, but it has not been exploited. One interesting small export is Iceland spar, a refracting crystal used in optical instruments. In the waterfalls of the turbulent rivers, all of which flow northward except the Thorsa, there is great potential electric power and some of it has already been generated for lighting the larger towns. A much more extensive development is under way.

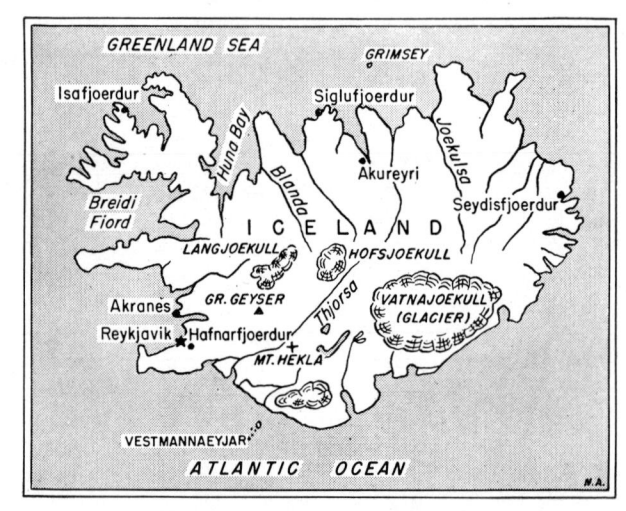

THE REPUBLIC OF ICELAND

68

DANISH INFORMATION OFFICE

FRAIL KAYAKS GLIDE BY IN THE LEE OF A HUGE ICEBERG

The kayak is said to be the lightest and most graceful boat ever invented. It is not easy to handle, however, and no other northern people are as expert as the hunters of Greenland.

Iceland's small population is increasing. Somewhat more than half lives either in Reykjavik, the capital, or in smaller towns and villages. There is a university in the capital, several grammar and high schools and institutes for special vocational training. Children from seven to fifteen years of age must attend school. The social-service program of the Government provides medical and unemployment insurance. The few factories process fish and fish products, and make woolen cloth, crates and other small items.

The real life of Iceland is not to be seen in the towns but among the little farms that are scattered over the roadless wastes. The typical Icelandic farm has a roof of turf and is surrounded by sheds and barns built of turf and boulders. The windows are usually fastened shut for the winter, though a small opening which can be closed as required affords ventilation. Kerosene is the usual lamp fuel and peat the cooking fuel.

The entire family sleeps in a large room in the upper story, where bunks filled with dried seaweed and feathers serve as beds. No one could be more hospitable than these Icelandic farmers. They give of their best. Skyr is a favorite dish—a clotted milk eaten with sugar. There is also river salmon. When

SUKKERTOPPEN—A TINY TOWN ON THE TOP OF THE WORLD

The little Eskimo town on the fringe of the Arctic Circle has less than a thousand inhabitants. It is at the southern tip of Sukkertoppen Island in Davis Strait, off the southwest coast of Greenland. Sukkertoppen has weather and radio stations and both a hospital and a sanitarium for children. The chief occupations are raising reindeer, whaling and hunting for seal.

PHOTOS, DANISH INFORMATION OFFICE

A SOD AND STONE HOUSE IN THE THULE REGION

The Eskimos of Thule and of many other small northern settlements still follow the customs of their early ancestors in building. Their houses are constructed of turf and stone, a combination that results in snug dwellings that are surprisingly warm, watertight and healthful in the rigorous Arctic climate. Only one feature is more modern today—the inner walls are of wood.

Danish Information Office

A MODERN HOSPITAL ON GREENLAND'S BLEAK SHORE

Few people live in Greenland, and those who do lead hazardous lives, fishing and hunting in icy waters or over treacherous fields of snow. This fine modern hospital is at Umanak, a hamlet of about 1,400 people on the coast of western Greenland. All the settlements on the island are along the coast, the only part that is ever even briefly green.

a visitor has finished his meal, with which delicious coffee is always served, he rises and says: "Thanks for the meal." The answer is always: "May it do you good." Their speech is the old Norse spoken a thousand years ago by the Scandinavian peoples, and their frames are tall and virile.

The farmer makes the most of the poor soil, growing turnips, potatoes, and hay. His chief occupation is the breeding of sheep and ponies. The flocks near the coast sometimes eat seaweed if grass is scarce, but a large proportion of the productive land is devoted to grass, and much hay is raised for the cattle as well as root crops.

The ponies play an important part on the farms. The roads in Iceland are few and bad, and horses are the chief means of transport. Indeed, there is one pony to every two persons. Sleighs are used in winter where the roads permit. In southern Iceland, however, good roads and bridges are being built and motorcars are becoming common.

We may often meet a girl leading a string of ponies each of which carries two cans of milk. They must go slowly to avoid churning the milk into butter.

These ponies are small and sturdy, their coats are long and their tails are thicker than those of horses. During a storm they turn their backs to the wind and their tails spread over their flanks, forming a natural protection. The ponies

U. S. COAST GUARD

PROUD OWNER

This Greenland lad's greatest treasures are his three husky-dog pups with which he is delighted to pose. The population of the island is composed of a few hundred Europeans, mostly Danes, and of non-Europeans who are called Greenlanders. Some in the less populous districts are pure-blooded Eskimos, but most of the natives are of mixed European and Eskimo origin.

72

DANISH INFORMATION OFFICE

GREENLANDERS STUDY GEOGRAPHY

The schools of Greenland are largely under church tutelage. The Danish Minister of Public Worship appoints and pays the salaries of Danish and Moravian missionaries, who foster education. Instruction in the schools is in the native, or Eskimo, language. The display board at the right shows a model of a kayak, a sixteen-foot-long canoe that is usually made of sealskins.

BLACK STAR

HOT OFF THE PRESS!

A Greenlandic newspaper, printed in the Eskimo language, is being prepared for distribution. Since 1861 there have been several monthly periodicals appearing somewhat irregularly. Textbooks, pamphlets, official circulars and books are also printed at this office. A really native literature is evolving, covering religious subjects, biographies and books of popular interest.

are sure footed and carry their loads across fields of lava with a certainty that even a mule might envy. When a visitor calls at a farm he never lets his ponies graze near the buildings. The farmer would regard it as discourteous, for every blade of grass is precious.

Some Eskimo Stories

Now let us turn to the neighboring Greenland chiefly inhabited by Eskimos, though there are a few hundred whites and more of mixed blood. The Eskimos are interesting, and so are their dogs which are harnessed like the ribs of a fan in Greenland though they are driven tandem in Canada, or in pairs in Alaska. In fact Eskimos differ widely in different regions.

During the winter nights, the Eskimos occupy themselves with various handicrafts, making their clothing and their weapons from the materials at hand. As they work, they tell one another stories. A favorite tale runs thus: One day an old woman was scraping a wolfskin to cleanse it. By and by a strange man came and asked her what skin she was scraping. When she replied that it was a wolfskin he uttered a prolonged howl and ran off on all fours, for he was a wolf-man. Next day the old woman saw a great gathering of wolves, foxes and bears outside her hut, all growling savagely. "Ah!" she cried, "come in, all of you. I am boiling berries to make a pudding. You shall taste it if you will come into my hut."

She deceived them, however. First she put a pot of water on the fire to boil. Then she laid wet wood on the fire and stopped up the smokehole so that the hut was full of smoke. As the animals coughed and choked, and felt for the door to escape, she seized her husband's harpoon and slew them all. Thus she obtained their skins, which were of great value.

The Sun Swings Around the Sky

Greenland is a vast, inhospitable island, a waste of glaciers and snow-clad plateaus, the population of which (chiefly Eskimo) is over sixteen thousand. An island eight hundred miles wide by seventeen hundred long, this region is separated on the northwest by a narrow strait from Grant Land, Grinnell Land and Ellesmere Land.

In winter, when the Arctic night has settled down over the north, Greenland is a land of silence, save for the beating of the winds across the bitter wastes and the rustle of the hard flakes, when the snow shuts out the stars. But in the swift two months of summer even the treeless tundras brighten into mats of wild flowers —the seeds of which may have been brought by birds. In all frankness, myriads of mosquitoes also breed in the pools of melting snow. The sun swings around the sky, never once dipping clear beneath the horizon for a hundred and thirty nights as seen from Northern Greenland.

Half-way down the west coast, off the Nugsuak Peninsula, the tourist approaching by steamer is charmed by a scene of high blue mountains rising abruptly from the sea, while the cliffs of the shoreline gleam pink, with streaks of gray-green lichen in their seams, and eider ducks and Arctic tern in summer residence along their tops. Beneath, in the sounding sea, mountains of ice that have broken off from the interior ice-cap float green-blue and sparkling, with all but their peaks submerged. At times they float together with reverberating booms, startling the gulls into grating cries. Seals, peering about with sleek puppy-like heads, hump themselves over the water-darkened rocks or dive as some kayak, manned by a Mongol-faced Eskimo with spear upraised, comes darting toward them.

Flowers Fringe the Ice-Cap

Only along the southern coast are there treelike growths. There, in summer, the mean temperature is 46 degrees above zero, and the ground is not frozen for several feet beneath the surface; the dwarf birches and willow bushes spread out into lush green mats and the pale yellow of Arctic poppies embroiders the mossy tundra, clear to the eternal ice-cap that gleams a few miles inland.

ISLANDS OF FIRE AND ICE

Curiously enough, the northwest coast from Peary Land to Washington Land presents a broad stretch of water nearly free, in summer, of floating ice. The water off the eastern coast, however, is so distraught by opposing currents that the warring ice-cakes prevent ships from approaching.

The better part of Greenland consists of some of the most ancient rocks on earth. Throughout geologic time, invasions of the sea have left deposits of sediment on the submerged edge of the ancient plateau. From these sands and muds of various ages now hardened into rocks, we have a record of times past.

The glaciers break off when they reach the coast and form the icebergs so dreaded by sailors. Large bergs may rise as much as four hundred feet, though only one-ninth above water. In the sunshine they appear like huge ships of cut glass, but as they drift down to the Banks of Newfoundland they gradually vanish under the melting influence of the warmer seas.

The Eskimos of Greenland are chiefly found on the coast. A merry, friendly Mongoloid people whose menfolk stand little over five feet in height, they dress in furs, harpoon fish and seals, and love to eat the nourishing whale blubber when they can get this delicacy. But they have fallen an easy prey to diseases introduced by the white man.

The life of the Eskimos is one continual struggle to obtain food. They can live only where there is game, and when

DANISH INFORMATION OFFICE

A PORTABLE SEWING MACHINE HELPS A BUSY HOUSEWIFE

The Eskimo way of life is rugged and conveniences such as a sewing machine are all the more highly valued. To this woman the machine may well be her most prized possession.

they have killed all the game in one district they move elsewhere. In the spring the tribes voyage from place to place, hunting the seal, walrus, reindeer, bears and eider ducks, and with the coming of the Arctic winter return to their villages. Their houses are usually built of stone, and the walls are covered with sealskins. A stone bench is used as a bed, dried grass forms the mattress and skins the bed clothes. Material for the windows is made from the dried membrane of seals.

The Eskimo boats are of two kinds, both made of sealskin stretched over a framework of wood. The hunter's boat is the kayak, a graceful craft propelled by a double paddle. The umiak, the women's boat, is used to transport the household goods during the spring migration. It must be greased with fat every other day to keep it water-tight.

The Eskimos depend upon seals for many things and hunt them cleverly. When the winter ice forms on the sea, the seals make breathing-holes in it. An Eskimo, having found such a hole, takes his spear and waits patiently for the seal to come up to breathe. He may wait for hours, because the seal may have many such holes scattered over a large area; but sooner or later it will come to the fatal hole, and the sound of its breathing is the signal for the patient hunter to thrust his harpoon.

In the short Arctic spring this method is not practicable, because the seals crawl on to the ice to sleep in the sun. They are so afraid of polar bears, however, that they will bob up and down in the water for a long while before coming out to enjoy their sleep. Now is the Eskimo's chance. He lies down and, concealing his spear, commences to creep toward his prey. At once the seal raises its head suspiciously and moves a little nearer the water. The hunter instantly begins to imitate the actions of a seal crawling on the ice, and, if the imitation is good, he

TRANSPORTATION, INCORPORATED

These Iceland ponies are a well-known breed, of Celtic strain, similar to those formerly to be found in the north of Ireland and in the Hebrides. They are small and sturdy, usually of a dull yellowish color. Wide use is made of them in transporting goods and equipment from the coast to the interior, and they are a most common means of transportation throughout the island.

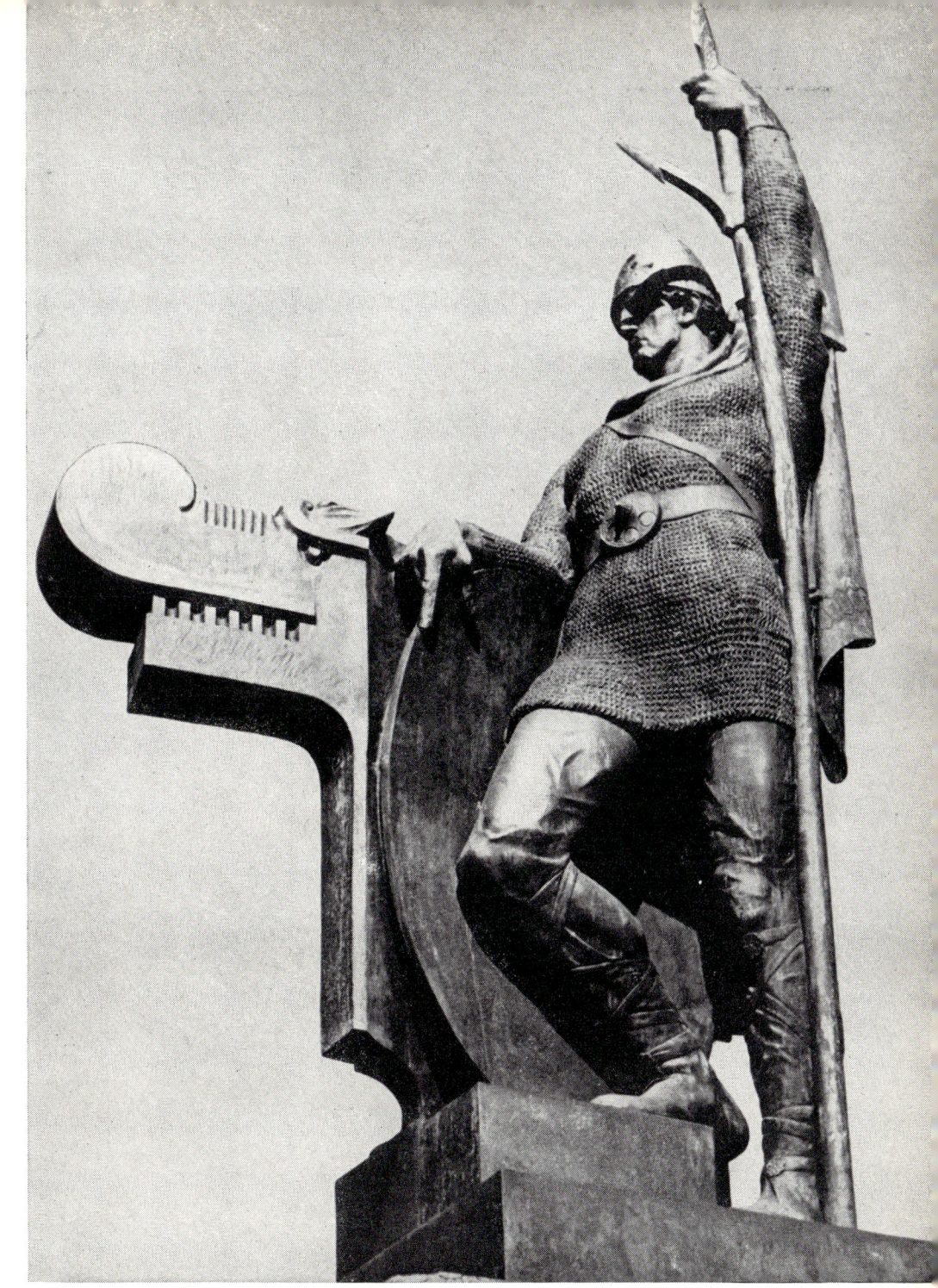

VIGOROUS STATUE OF A HARDY NORSEMAN

In Reykjavik, capital of Iceland, stands a huge statue of Leif Ericson, explorer and mariner. He was the son of Eric the Red. Leif is believed to have landed somewhere on the North American continent in the eleventh century. Here he established a community, which he called Vinland because of the profusion of vines that he found growing in the region.

BLACK STAR
NO RED HERRING IN THIS SHIPMENT
Fishing is a major industry in Iceland, where a large percentage of the people depend on it for support. Cod and herring are the chief catch, and herring oil is produced in great quantities. The Icelanders manufacture fishing equipment and crates in which the fish products are exported. The barrels on the wharf above contain herring, packed and ready for shipment.

CONSULATE GENERAL OF ICELAND
HOT HOUSES OPERATED BY NATURAL STEAM
Volcanic activity plays an important part in Iceland's history and progress. Geysers and hot springs dot the island. Although much of Iceland's water power, roughly 2,500,000 horsepower, is still unharnessed, hot houses like those above are heated by the underground waters. Flowers, fruit and vegetables, once unknown in this northern area, can be raised in this way.

THE BRIDE KEEPS HER NAME

The wedding dress of this Icelandic bride is exquisitely embroidered in gold, which harmonizes with her linked belt and jeweled bracelet. The veil is of fine lace. The bride will not assume her husband's surname as is customary in most countries. In fact, surnames are less important here than elsewhere, and even telephone directories are arranged according to given names.

will be able to deceive his quarry. Gradually he approaches nearer and nearer, until he gets within range and can plunge his spear into the creature.

The clothes of the Eskimos are made of the skins of various animals. The women, like the men, wear sealskin trousers, and over these pull the native boots, or kamiker. The skins from which the boots are made are first chewed by the women to soften them, a practice which rapidly wears down the teeth. In the more civilized districts the women wear a long blouse of imported cloth, and their coarse black hair is adorned with ribbons. The unmarried women wear blue ribbons and the widows black. The women ornament their costumes either with beads, colored leather or feathers. They carry their babies in hoods which hang down the backs of their tunics.

The Plague of Mosquitoes

The great plague of Greenland in summer is not wolves or bears. It is the mosquitoes, that rise in clouds from the swamps and make life a misery to man and beast. Once the howls of a bear attracted the notice of some hunters. It was found that the animal had been so terribly bitten about the nose, eyes and ears that it was forced to open its mouth to breathe. The mosquitoes then bit its tongue and throat so severely that they, too, swelled, and the bear was suffocated. White people cover their heads with nets of fine gauze which keep these pests at bay.

Greenland was discovered perhaps as early as 900, and its parliament began about 1000. When the Norseman, Eric the Red, sailing over from Iceland, discovered its brief summer verdure he induced a band of his countrymen to come with sheep and cattle and colonize, in 985 or 986. (The ruins of that colony, which lasted for four hundred years, may still be seen.) In 1261 the Republic of Greenland voluntarily became a part of the then powerful Kingdom of Norway, but the original Norse colonists perished. The hardy Norsemen had built several towns, and at Harjolfsnes, one of the larger settlements, there were a cathedral and several monasteries. The settlements maintained a flourishing trade with Europe, and it is recorded that they contributed a large quantity of walrus ivory to assist the Crusaders.

The Norse in Greenland

About 1300, some think that there may have been climatic changes in Greenland. It became colder, and the coast grew more and more ice-bound. At this time, too, the Norwegian shipping was suffering a decline. Early in the fifteenth century, the settlements were left to their fate. The Eskimos were coming southward, following the seals, and many encounters between the newcomers and the Norsemen are mentioned before all records cease.

Much medieval clothing was found in the tombs at Harjolfsnes, none dating later than the fifteenth century, a fact which would seem to show that this period saw the end of the Norse colonies in Greenland. Of the manner of their passing we know nothing, but, in view of known facts, it may be surmised that the enfeebled settlements were gradually overwhelmed.

Relations with Denmark

In 1721, a Danish missionary, Hans Egede, brought a Danish colony to Greenland which made several west coast settlements and established a trade with Denmark. It is now the only colonial possession of Denmark. The first data from which the north coastline was mapped were supplied by a Danish explorer, Knud Rasmussen, and by Admiral R. E. Peary of the U. S. Navy. In 1888 Fridtjof Nansen crossed the interior ice-cap on snowshoes, the first of a number of explorers to negotiate it successfully. To-day aviators can secure a bird's-eye view of a region in which inland travel was formerly a matter of snowshoes and sledges drawn by husky dogs. But the land is an unfriendly one and the largest settlement, Sydproven, has under a thousand inhabitants.

Various scientific expeditions have been

BLOWING UP a bladder. Attached to a harpoon, it keeps a slain seal afloat.

MODERN CHURCH for the Eskimos at Kanak, in the far north of Greenland.

HOLSTEINSBORG, fishing port in southwest Greenland, on Davis Strait. The town is also a boat-building center, constructing cutter-size vessels.

CAPITAL ON TOP OF THE WORLD

The coastal city of Reykjavik, capital of Iceland, is situated on the Faxafloi. Although close to the Arctic Circle, Reykjavik has a mean temperature of about 40° F. Large numbers of volcanic springs make up for Iceland's lack of fuel. The boiling hot water is carried by aqueducts to the city to heat homes, offices, and hot houses that grow fruit, vegetables and flowers.

PHOTOS, BLACK STAR

NOT PAVING STONES, BUT FISH!

This drying and salting field on the outskirts of Reykjavik is just one of many. Codfishing is a major industry of Iceland, providing employment for a large percentage of the people. The men catch and the women cure the fish. They split, clean and salt the cod and spread them in the sun to dry. At night they collect and cover the fish and respread them in the morning.

CROSSROADS FOR THREE GENERATIONS

This little square in Reykjavik presents a study in contrasts. The quaintness of the costume in the foreground is typical of a generation several times removed. It is pointed up by the informal attire of the young woman on the curb. More than one-third of the entire population of Iceland lives in Reykjavik, which was settled by Norsemen as early as the year 877.

TOWERING CLIFFS hem in the Umanak Fjord, opposite the village of Umanak, which is situated on an island off the Nugsuak peninsula. The Umanak Fjord is on the west coast of Greenland, and at its head is a glacier that sometimes advances as much as fifty feet in a day. Icebergs are continually breaking from this glacier, so that the waters are never free from masses of ice. Greenland, a colonial possession of Denmark, has a total population of about eighteen thousand, while its largest settlement, Godthaab, has about 1,300 persons.

WATERFALLS. Many small rivers made by the melting glaciers in the interior of Iceland have to leap great cliffs to reach the sea; the Seljalandsfoss, at the base of which this horseman stands, is in the district of South Land. The Norse word "foss" means a waterfall—the same word is found in Yorkshire, for Norsemen settled in both England and Iceland.

SEYDISFIORDUR, TINY TOWN IN NORTHEASTERN ICELAND, STRAGGLES ALONG THE HEAD OF SEYDIS FIORD

This tiny fishing port marks one end of the cable between Iceland and Denmark. Less than a thousand people live in this village, which is in a sparsely settled district. It is close to the Arctic Circle, and summers bring three months of continuous daylight, while the winters bring an equal period of unbroken darkness. Corrugated iron roofs keep the houses snug during the long winter months when the snows never melt. Travel during these months comes almost to a standstill, save for the little that can be done by rough sledges over the heavy snow.

made to Greenland. The Lady Franklin Bay Expedition starved at Cape Sabine the spring of 1884 because its relief ship was crushed in the drift ice. The Macmillan Arctic Expedition of 1923-24 placed a memorial to their memory.

The Dane, L. Mylius-Erichsen, explored eight hundred miles of coast in 1907, reaching Northeast Foreland, thence pressed westward to what is now Denmark Fjord, and on through the channel that makes Peary Land an island. But faced by darkness and starvation, he perished after marching 160 miles back across the ice toward his ship, as his records, found later, plainly show.

Greenland becomes increasingly important as the nations bordering on the North Atlantic prepare for the possibility of future global war. The shortest air route between New York and northern Europe is over the vast island. The fiords of Greenland—those that are free of ice—serve as excellent harbors for emergency sea patrols. During World War II the United States sent troops to Greenland. Some were there to meet any possible attack, others to search the ice wastes for downed airplane crews. The Allies also set up weather stations, airfields and a naval refueling base.

Under the terms of the treaty signed by Denmark and the United States in 1941, Denmark regained her colony at the end of the war. In 1951 the two countries signed a new agreement. The bases built by the Allies are now under Danish control, but any member of the North Atlantic Pact may man these bases or build new ones when the need arises.

Fog and menacing icebergs no longer keep ships and planes from the shores of either Greenland or its rocky neighbor, Iceland. They have both become way stations for travel between two worlds and vital sentries in North Atlantic defense.

ICELAND AND GREENLAND: FACTS AND FIGURES

ICELAND

An island in the North Atlantic Ocean, is one of the most volcanic regions on earth. It is 298 miles in length and 194 miles in breadth, with a total coastline of 3,730 miles. The area is 39,770 square miles and the population is 155,000. By an Act of Union, effective in 1918, Denmark acknowledged the island a free sovereign state with which they were united only in the person of the king. In 1944 all ties with Denmark were severed by a referendum. On June 17, 1944, the republic was formally proclaimed. Iceland has a president, a cabinet and the Althing, a two-chamber parliament of 52 members. More than a thousand years old, the Althing is the oldest parliamentary assembly in the world. All men and women over 21 may vote.

About six-sevenths of Iceland is unproductive and less than one-half per cent is under cultivation. Hay, potatoes and turnips are the chief agricultural products. Fishing is the chief industry, with cod and herring representing the greatest catch. Sheep raising, dairying and manufacturing are important industries. The exports are mainly fish, fish oil, fish meal and animal skins. Imports include nearly all essentials of living, such as grain and meal, oil and petrol, coffee, sugar, ale, wines, tobacco, manufactured wares, iron and metal wares, timber, salt and coal. There are no railways, but 3,800 miles of highways, traversed by more than 10,000 automobiles and trucks. Keflavik Airport serves several international airlines. Monetary unit is the króna. The Evangelical Lutheran Church is the national church. Elementary education is compulsory from 7 to 15 years. Besides several special schools, there is one university at Reykjavik. Approximate populations: Reykjavik, the capital, 60,000; Akureyri, 7,000; Hafnarfjordur, 5,500; Vestmannaeyjar, 4,000.

GREENLAND

Greenland is a colonial possession of Denmark, lying almost wholly within the Arctic Circle. Its area is 840,000 square miles, but most of it is under an ice sheet and only 132,000 square miles are ice-free. The population numbers 24,800, mostly Eskimos. Since 1953 part of the Danish realm. It sends 2 elected representatives to the Danish Parliament. Greenland Council consists of 13 members. Trade carried on largely with Denmark. Some coal is mined, and deposits of lead and zinc are known to exist. The world's largest deposits of cryolite, used in making aluminum, are in Greenland. Capital, Godthaab, population about 1,000.

SHOP SIGNS are a folk art in Denmark and brighten towns and cities everywhere. If you have a sweet tooth, look for the sign of a knot-shaped cake surmounted by a crown.

ART STUDENTS sketch one of the statues in Ny Carlsberg Glyptotek, an art museum in Copenhagen. It has a notable collection of works by the French sculptor Rodin.

THE DANCING of the Royal Danish Ballet fires the enthusiasm of audiences at home and abroad. Besides grace, superb technique, the dancers infuse the performances with a verve all their own.

FAIRY-TALE LAND—a quaint shop near the birthplace of Hans Christian Andersen, in Odense. To visit this section of the city is to step back into the enchanted atmosphere of the immortal tales.

"FAIR WEATHER FRIEND"

A bronze figure of the modern Danish girl with her indispensable bicycle faces the Town Hall of Copenhagen on fair days. When it rains she is replaced by a twin sister with an umbrella.

EUROPE'S OLDEST KINGDOM

Denmark and Its People

Denmark is one of the most highly developed countries of the Old World. Scientifically improved agriculture is the base of its wealth. However, due to its position by the sea, over which products of all kinds may be transported cheaply, Denmark has also developed a strong industry although it is almost devoid of raw materials. The Danes are one of the most enlightened nations in the world and they are proud of their advanced social legislation. This is, as a patriotic song puts it, a country "where few have too much and fewer too little."

DENMARK is the gentlest and most idyllic of all the Scandinavian countries. Its green pastures are dotted with brown and speckled cows, red or white farmhouses and whitewashed churches; and its quaint gardens and wind-caressed groves next to blue inlets and sandy beaches breathe a fairy-tale atmosphere of charm and undisturbed harmony. Perhaps it was not by chance that one of the world's great writers of fairy tales, Hans Christian Andersen, was a Dane.

Denmark's smiling and friendly landscape seems to invite the stranger to prolong his stay. It must have done so for thousands of years. Numerous finds and excavations indicate that Denmark has been inhabited for at least four thousand to five thousand years and possibly much longer. It is quite possible that the earliest settlers were the ancestors of today's Danes, because no relics have been found of peoples of different stock. The country's position at the entrance to the Baltic Sea, one of Europe's oldest trading routes going back to prehistoric times, favored early settlement here. At any rate, Denmark is the oldest existing state in Europe and was mentioned as united under one king as early as the eighth century A.D.

Denmark consists of one peninsula and 493 islands and islets; but only about a hundred isles are inhabited. The Danish peninsula, called Jylland by the Danes and Jutland by English-speaking people, is bigger than all the islands together. The whole of Denmark is flat. The highest elevations, one of them ambitiously called Mount Sky (Himmelbjaerget), are less than six hundred feet above sea level. The sea, of course, is the natural link between the different parts of the country, and so the Danes became a seafaring nation quite early in history. They roamed the neighboring seas and conquered neighboring lands. The Angles who colonized England, together with the Saxons, and gave that country its name, came originally from Angeln in what then was the southernmost corner of Denmark. The very name of Norway means the "way toward the north," implying that its earliest settlers came from the next-door neighbor to the south, Denmark. Centuries later, Danish Vikings founded the Danelaw in eastern England and conquered even distant Normandy (the name means "land of the men from the north"). Several Danish kings—Canute the Great among them—ruled over all England and Norway in addition to Denmark. Later in the Middle Ages, the chief area around which the Danes spread was the commercially important Baltic. This sea was practically a Danish lake in the thirteenth century. However, soon after, Danish sea power was contested first by the German cities of the Hanseatic League and later by the Dutch and by the Swedes. The struggle with Sweden for leadership of Scandinavia and domination of the Baltic lasted intermittently through many centuries. It led to the permanent loss of Denmark's foothold on the Scandinavian Peninsula, the provinces of Skaane, Halland and Blekinge, which today constitute the southern tip of Sweden but were part of Denmark until 1658.

Denmark is no longer a naval power,

STACKING HAY on Fyn (Fünen), second largest Danish island. It is a fertile lowland and its many dairy farms produce top-grade butter and cheese.

A COLONY GARDEN. A city apartment dweller usually has a tiny cottage with a bit of garden in the suburbs. There the whole family spends the summer.

BOTH PHOTOS, J. BARNELL FROM READERS DIGEST

HARVESTING A BEET CROP. The mound of ruddy vegetables will be covered with earth. This keeps the beets until needed as winter fodder for cattle.

BOTH PHOTOS, D. FORBERT FROM READERS DIGEST

WORKING on Saxbo stoneware, one of the excellent products of the flourishing ceramics industry. Some of the designs are traditional. Danish artisans also are leaders in the creation of handsome modern pieces.

93

THE KINGDOM OF DENMARK

but the Danes are still a seafaring people. The Danish straits are among the most trafficked waterways in the world, although the Germans siphoned off part of the Baltic trade by constructing the Kiel Canal through Holstein in the 1890's. In 1938 some 40,000 vessels with a total of 35,000,000 deadweight tons passed through Oresund (the Sound) alone. On the average, this is one quarter more than passes through the Suez Canal and almost twice as much traffic as passes through the Panama Canal. About half of the vital foreign trade of Denmark, which is the greatest foreign trade in relation to population of any country in the world, is carried in Danish bottoms. Most of the traffic between the different parts of Denmark and with near-by countries is carried by steamers and motor vessels and train-carrying ferries, but Denmark also has a dense railroad and highway network. The national vehicle is the bicycle, which means to Denmark what the automobile means to the United States and Canada. But there are more automobiles in Denmark per capita than in any other European countries except Britain and France. Denmark has two of the longest bridges in the world—one 10,534 feet long, between Zealand and Falster; the other, 3,860 feet, spanning the Little Belt (a strait) and connecting Jutland and the island of Funen.

Most foreigners coming to Denmark arrive in Copenhagen either by boat, by plane or by train and ferry. Copenhagen, the capital of Denmark, is the biggest city of Scandinavia. Due to its sheltered site on a small sound between the islands of Zealand (Sjaelland in Danish) and Amager, it early became the most important shipping center of the whole Baltic region. Not for nothing does its name (Kobenhavn in Danish) mean "merchants' haven." While the main part of the city is situated on Denmark's largest island, Zealand, the southern part of Copenhagen lies on Amager. On Amager is Copenhagen's Kastrup Airport. This is one of Europe's largest airports and has become the busiest air junction of the whole Continent. The Danish Air Lines, today an affiliate of the Scandinavian Airlines System, is the world's oldest commercial air line (established 1918).

The Danes call their capital "the city of beautiful towers." But the many gracious steeples in Dutch Renaissance and later styles are not its only mark of beauty. Copenhagen is an unusually appealing city. It is like a museum of exquisite samples of various styles of architecture, from the unique Stock Exchange, built 1619–40, with its grotesque spire formed by the entwined tails of four dragons standing on their heads, to the serene, unadorned loveliness of the modern Radio House. The old town has many narrow alleys and picturesque canals, but on the outskirts there are fine examples of twentieth-century

COPENHAGEN, "MERCHANTS' HAVEN"
The free port of Copenhagen is the distribution and assembly center for northern Europe. Domestic and foreign firms have plants here, and can export and import materials duty-free.

housing developments and town planning. Copenhagen is a city of many parks, and each park is used as a permanent exposition ground for sculpture. One of the most noteworthy statues is Eriksen's Little Mermaid. The figure is that of the character from Andersen's fairy tale. In the park of Langelinje, she watches the ships from a big boulder at the water's edge.

Copenhagen is often called the Paris of the North, and it is undoubtedly the gayest city of Scandinavia. Visitors from all over the neighboring countries are drawn to its opera, its world-famous ballet, its concerts and many plays and, last but not least, to Tivoli, an amusement park with old-fashioned charm and a fairy-tale atmosphere in the very middle of the city. The Danes have a gift for enjoying themselves, and in Copenhagen one can watch them give themselves to an art they thoroughly understand—how to spend hours of leisure within well-defined limitations of decorum. Here are also innumerable opportunities for indulging oneself in the culinary specialties for which Denmark is famous, the open sandwiches, or *smorrebrod*, which entice the eye as much as the palate and of which one well-known restaurant features not less than 172 varieties.

Founded in the twelfth century, Copenhagen has been the royal residence and national capital for more than five hundred years. It is also the largest industrial city of Scandinavia, with 43 per cent

WEALTHY DRAGONS
The Stock Exchange (Borsen) on a Copenhagen canal lifts a spire of twisted dragons' tails.

J. BARNELL FROM READERS DIGEST

TIVOLI AT NIGHT. The national pleasure garden, in the heart of Copenhagen, first opened in 1843. Concerts, pantomime, ballet, terrace restaurants—all await you in the beautifully landscaped grounds.

of its productive population employed in industries and handicrafts. The main industries are iron and machinery, shipbuilding, textile and clothing manufacture and food processing. These industries not only supply more than two-thirds of the products needed at home but also provide Denmark with articles for export, using imported raw materials and semifinished goods. The flourishing Danish export business is due partly to the high quality of Danish products and partly to the city's excellent port facilities. These are larger and more modern than those of any other harbor of the Scandinavian and Baltic region and include a free port of twenty-one and a half acres in Copenhagen. This was Denmark's answer to Germany's construction of the Kiel Canal.

After World War II, Danish industry made a spectacularly fast recovery, thanks to the fact that the German surrender came before the Germans had time to carry out plans to destroy Danish plants. As soon as foreign raw materials were available again, the wheels of the Danish factories began turning. Within eight months industrial production rose from 23 per cent of the prewar level, in May 1945, to 100 per cent, in January 1946, and to 168 per cent in October 1951.

Elsinore's Haunted Castle

Although Copenhagen is the only large city, there are many quaint and picturesque towns on the island of Zealand. Best known abroad is Elsinore (Helsingor in Danish) of Shakespearean fame. Here, on the real site of HAMLET, the tragedy about the melancholy Danish prince is produced every year by a different foreign theater group. The open-air performances take place within the very walls of Kronborg Castle that the ghost of Hamlet's father is supposed to haunt. Today, this jewel of a castle in Dutch Renaissance architecture is only a museum of Denmark's glorious past. But through four centuries, from 1425 to 1855, this was the place where the Danes collected the Sound tolls from passing ships. The narrows are hardly broader than a wide river at this point, and originally the toll was collected for passage through Danish territorial water in accordance with the international traditions of those days. But when the eastern shores of the Sound became Swedish in 1658, the straits became half Danish and half Swedish. Nevertheless, the Danes continued to collect what was the largest revenue item of the Danish crown for another two hundred years. Finally, American shipowners proclaimed that they would no longer stand for this antiquated interference with the freedom of the seas, and the tolls were abolished by international agreement once and for all.

Going west from Zealand, one passes another of the Danish straits. Large ferryboats carry the express trains from Copenhagen to Jutland and the rest of the Continent across the Great Belt (Storebaelt in Danish) in less than seventy-five minutes. After leaving Zealand, one

SCULPTURED SERENITY

From her rock at Copenhagen, the Little Mermaid of Andersen's fairy tale gazes out to sea.

EUROPE'S OLDEST KINGDOM

crosses the island of Funen (Fyn in Danish), which is even more fairylike than the rest of the country. There are medieval castles and Renaissance manors, dreamlike towns and villages with one-story frame houses, whitewashed cottages with stork nests on the straw-thatched roofs and crooked cobblestoned alleys. Here, on Funen, Hans Christian Andersen was born in picturesque Odense. The house he lived in is preserved intact as a museum and is one of the country's main tourist attractions. The name indicates that Odense already existed in pagan times with a shrine consecrated to Odin. Today, it is Denmark's third largest city, while still preserving many of its quaint characteristics of by-gone times. Its development is due largely to the growth of a large shipbuilding industry. Though the city is landlocked, it is connected with the sea by a fifteen-mile-long canal.

The third strait, the Little Belt (Lillebaelt), scarcely broader than a medium-sized river, separates this "garden of Denmark" from the fairly rugged Danish

FRESH FISH TODAY!

Copenhagen, once just a fishing village, retains some of its original atmosphere in the fish market along the Gammel Strand. The tower of St. Nikolaj Church is in the background.

HOME OF "THE MELANCHOLY DANE"

Kronborg Castle, setting for scenes in Shakespeare's *Hamlet*, is located at Elsinore, a seaport on the Danish island of Zealand. The Dutch Renaissance edifice dates back to 1580.

peninsula. Jutland is, in a way, the backbone of the nation, jutting out into the sea like a tremendous natural breakwater and protecting the fair and idyllic islands against the harsh western winds and the unruly waves of the North Sea.

Jutland, too, has quaint old towns, such as Aebeltoft and Ribe (birthplace of New York's social pioneer Jacob Riis), where nothing seems to have happened for centuries. More indicative of the stern Jutlanders' tenacious endurance, however, is the modern city of Esbjerg, Denmark's newest. Esbjerg, the only harbor on the peninsula's inhospitable west coast, was built after the duchies of Schleswig and Holstein were lost to Germany in 1864 and the southern North Sea port of Husum had become foreign territory. Today, with four miles of piers, Esbjerg is Denmark's foremost export center. Here, the butter, bacon, eggs and cheeses from Jutland's thriving farms are stowed into freighters that carry Danish products to England, France and overseas markets. Esbjerg is also the center of Denmark's deep-sea fishing fleet, which supplies, by means of highway trucks, the large cities of northern Germany with fresh fish.

The friendlier and more typically Danish east coast of Jutland harbors Denmark's second and third ports Aarhus and Aalborg. Both of them are busy commercial and industrial centers that have, nevertheless, preserved touch with their historic past in architecture and tradition. Aarhus is Denmark's second largest city. It has a unique open-air museum, the so-called "Old Town," with picturesque ancient buildings. Some still stand on their original sites and others have been transferred to Aarhus from all parts of the country and reconstructed in such a way that the atmosphere of an old urban community is preserved. In Lyngby, near Copenhagen, there is a similar museum of old farmhouses.

Near Aalborg is a national park of special interest for Americans. Here, in the heather-covered hills of Rebild, Danish-Americans bought an extensive tract of the heath that formerly covered a large part of Jutland and set it aside as a shrine of Danish-American co-operation and friendship. A so-called "Lincoln Log Cabin" made out of logs and shingles from all parts of the United States was set up, and each Fourth of July scores of thou-

Danish Information Office

OLD KILNS STILL USED FOR FIRING DANISH PORCELAIN

No product of Denmark is so widely known abroad as the exquisite porcelain, valued by all those who appreciate fine china. It has been developed by generations of craftsmen, working with loving care. The Royal Porcelain Factory was founded in 1775. Some of the loveliest pieces have a fluted effect with a delicate blue and creamy white underglaze.

Danish Information Office

THICK "WHEELS" OF CHEESE STORED FOR RIPENING

For its size Denmark is one of the greatest dairying countries on earth, and the production of milk each year is tremendous. A vast quantity of butter is made and is one of Denmark's chief exports. Cheese is also made although not so much of it is shipped abroad. The Danes themselves are fond of cheese and use it in a variety of dishes.

sands of Danes with kinsfolk in America meet here to celebrate the American Independence Day.

As time goes by, this national park will one day probably be all there is left of the famous Jutland heath. In the early 1950's there were still some 500,000 acres left of the original 2,000,000 after one of the most spectacular reclamation projects ever undertaken.

Like many other regions of the world, Jutland had suffered reckless deforestation during the Middle Ages when the Danish kings needed large wooden fleets to maintain naval supremacy in the Baltic. Slowly, but irresistibly, the majestic oak forests gave way to the encroaching heather, as the persistent western winds blew the denuded topsoil away. By the nineteenth century, the all-engulfing heather had become a major threat to cultivated areas and towns. After the rich farmlands of Schleswig-Holstein were lost in 1864, the slogan of E. Dalgas—"Recover at home what was lost abroad!"—finally caught on. After 1866 a large-scale attempt was made to stop the spreading of the wastelands and to turn unproductive areas into woods and arable land. It was a truly Herculean task for a small nation, because this was long before steam-shovels, power drills and bulldozers were ever heard of. Every effort to penetrate the stony hardpan had to be made by hand. But the effort was successful. More than one and a half million acres were reclaimed and converted, first into woodland, and later, when new topsoil had formed, into pastures and fields.

Here and elsewhere, Denmark has laid under the plow poorer soil than most other countries have; but within a few generations it has managed to lay on this poor soil the foundations of one of the most successful agricultures in all history.

This development started in the winter of 1881–82. A group of farmers were sitting together in the Olgod Inn, twenty miles north of Esbjerg, discussing their plight. Until some ten years earlier they had been making good money sending quantities of grain to England after the repeal of the English Corn Laws in 1846. But with improved transportation facilities by land and by sea, such as railroads and steamships, overseas countries like the

BIRTHPLACE OF IMMORTALITY

Odense is famous as the birthplace of Hans Christian Andersen, immortalized in his delightful fairy tales. The house in which he was born (below) is now a museum containing his effects.

KOSTICH

"WHEN GRANDMOTHER WAS YOUNG"

At the open-air museum of Lyngby, near Copenhagen, these two gracious young ladies pose for visitors. They are wearing the picturesque costumes of an earlier era in Danish history.

United States, Argentina and Russia started dumping huge quantities of wheat into the British granaries. The bottom dropped out of the market, and Danish agriculture, which slowly had become a one-crop system, was threatened with utter ruin.

That winter day in the Olgod Inn, a young man spoke up and the farmers listened. This young dairy assistant had an idea. If it was no longer profitable to sell grain to the British, why not try something else, say, butter? He had figured out a way to go about the venture—a way that smaller farmers, without the dairy facilities of the wealthy ones, might take. Suppose they all got together and dumped their individual batches of butter into big casks to be marketed as a unit? Another fellow had an even better idea. Instead of collecting the butter on the various farms, it would be easier just to collect the milk and have the churning done in one place, as was done in the dairies on some of the big estates. Only, this particular dairy should belong to all the participating farmers together. The principle was "one for all and all for one," similar

103

"TOWN OF THE STORKS"

Ribe, in southwest Jutland, is the oldest town in Denmark and probably in all Scandinavia. Storks, beloved birds of Denmark, seem to prefer roof-tops in this town for their nesting.

to the idea behind the consumers' co-operative societies that had begun to spread. The rich and the poor, the man with thirty cows and the little fellow with only one, would all have an equal voice in running the affair. The profits would be distributed according to the contributions of each.

In this way, Denmark got its first co-operative dairy. It was a tremendous success, and the idea spread like wildfire. Five years later, there were already 350 co-operative dairies in Denmark. Today, there are almost 1,500, and they are processing more than 90 per cent of all Danish milk.

One particular advantage of this system was that the skim milk was returned to the farmers who fed it to their pigs. This gave birth to another grand idea. The farmers also got together in regard to establishing co-operative slaughter-houses. Here, pigs raised by individual farmers—but to standard size, age and weight on a standard diet—could be slaughtered and transformed into bacon and ham for English breakfast tables. This, too, was a roaring success, and today 61 co-operative packing houses handle 85 per cent of the Danish pigs. The first was established in 1887, only five years after the first co-operative dairy.

Later came co-operative egg-collecting societies. The Danish farmers left it to their overseas competitors to supply the British with bread, but they undertook to furnish everything else that belonged on the English breakfast table. The short distance to the market gave them an advantage that was hard to beat, until modern refrigeration enabled the farmers of New Zealand and other Commonwealth countries to ship their products to London in fresh condition. But in the meantime the Danes had won a reputation for unchanging standards of excellence in quality, and this reputation is the very foundation of the country's wealth. The quality of the Danish products is supervised strictly by the Government, and there are scientific check-ups to prevent any inferior goods from being shipped abroad.

Peasants are usually a cautious folk and hard to win for costly and uncertain experiments. An idea like the co-operative scheme might never have caught on had Denmark not had, for those days, an unusually enlightened and progressive farm population. It did not take the Danish farmers a long time to figure out on which side their bread was buttered. This was mainly due to the development of a peculiar Danish institution, the so-called Folk High Schools.

The Folk High Schools are nonvocational institutes of advanced education for farm boys and girls. They admit students at least eighteen years old who have left primary school at fourteen or fifteen and have had several years' practical experience in agriculture. They are boarding schools and try to build up a strong community feeling in the students by stressing good citizenship and community activities. The main subjects taught are history, philosophy, religion, civics and literature. At the same time, they offer courses that will help the student improve his farming, such as—animal husbandry, truck gardening, chemical soil analysis, and use of fertilizers, and accounting. Oral instruction—that is, lectures—and free-for-all discussions are the main teaching methods. Tests and examinations are banned and no diplomas are given. The first school was opened in Rodding in the duchy of Schleswig in 1844, but the movement caught on only after the loss of Schleswig and Holstein twenty years

SLEEK DAIRY CATTLE BOUND FOR PASTURE

Typical of what appeals to visitors in Denmark is this peaceful little village in the central part of Jutland, with one of the quaint windmills that are all too rapidly disappearing from the scene.

EUROPE'S OLDEST KINGDOM

later. There are now fifty-eight government-supported Folk High Schools training over six thousand students yearly at nominal cost (about $20 a month, including board and tuition). It is estimated that about one-third of the rural population has at one time or another attended the schools.

Like the other Scandinavian nations, carried out after 1930 under the sponsorship of Labor governments but with the active support of most other political parties. One of the most unusual features is the so-called Danish People's Holiday. This co-operative association offers, at nominal cost, recreation facilities that enable the worker and his family to get the maximum benefit from his twelve days'

WORKSHOP OF MASTER CRAFTSMEN

In the Georg Jensen workshop, the exquisite Jensen silverware is fashioned. Originals of the sauceboat at the left and the jug at the right are in Copenhagen's Industrial Art Museum.

Denmark is one of the world's most advanced countries in social legislation. Scandinavians quite generally subscribe to the idea of the welfare state. Denmark was the first country to abolish slave trade (1798), to institute free and compulsory elementary school education (1814) and to introduce a free old-age pension system (1891). Spectacular social reforms were annual paid vacation. Such a vacation is guaranteed every Dane by law, regardless of how often he changes his employment. This venture is supported financially by the Government, the trade unions and the employers' associations.

Other outstanding features of Danish social legislation are extensive free maternity care and a municipal nurse and

106

RURAL CONSUMERS' CO-OPERATIVE

Denmark has co-operative societies for purchasing, marketing, production, insurance and banking. From ten to twelve per cent of the country's total retail trade is handled by co-operatives.

servant service to help with the household chores during a housewife's illness. By medical standards, Denmark ranks as one of the most advanced countries in the world, largely due to its excellent medical facilities which are accessible to anybody at negligible charges. Denmark is leading the world in the fight against tuberculosis and has played an important part in the extensive campaign to control the disease in war-ravaged Europe.

Ever since the eighteenth century, Denmark has tried to keep out of foreign wars, but not always with success. In Napoleonic times, Copenhagen was bombarded and the Danish fleet was captured by the British; Norway was lost to Sweden. In 1864, the duchies of Schleswig, Holstein and Lauenburg were ceded to Prussia and Austria, but the northern part of Schleswig (Nordslesvig in Danish) became Danish again in 1920 after a plebiscite. During World War I, Denmark managed to remain neutral, but its traditional neutrality broke down in World War II. Denmark proper was invaded by the Germans on April 9, 1940, and its possessions, the Faeroe Islands and Greenland, were occupied by the British and American troops to forestall German landings. Because of the underground resistance of the Danes, Denmark was recognized as a belligerent and an ally by the Western powers. It became a member of the United Nations after the liberation in the spring of 1945.

"ONE FOR GOOD MEASURE"

Butter is being weighed from the churn in one of Denmark's numerous co-operative dairies.

107

In 1918, Denmark recognized its former possession Iceland as a free and independent nation connected with Denmark by a common king, but this last tie was severed in 1944 when the Icelanders proclaimed their country a republic. During World War II, Denmark escaped actual warfare, but was impoverished by German exploitation of its resources. However, recovery was greatly speeded up by Marshall Plan aid from the United States to the tune of $266,000,000. During the cold war, Denmark felt exposed at the entrance to a sea that the Russians would like to make a Soviet lake. In view of the Russian interest in the "northern Dardanelles," through which the large Soviet submarine fleet would have to pass in case of another major war, the Danes discarded their traditional neutrality for good and joined the North Atlantic Treaty Organization. Denmark is a stanch member of the Atlantic community.

By GUNNAR LEISTIKOW

DENMARK: FACTS AND FIGURES

THE COUNTRY

The total area of Denmark is 16,576 square miles, and the population is 4,405,000. To Denmark belong also the Faeroe Islands (540 sq. mi., 30,000 pop.) north of the Shetland Islands between Norway and Iceland; and Greenland (84,000 sq. mi., 21,000 pop.). The Faeroe Islands, inhabited by descendants of Norwegian Vikings, are self-governing, with their own legislature. Greenland, according to the findings of a French expedition in 1951, is not one tremendous island but an archipelago of at least three islands. Its inhabitants are mostly of Eskimo stock. A sweeping administrative reform was carried out in 1951 in order to give the Greenlanders a greater say in their own affairs.

The Danes are, like the Swedes, Norwegians and Icelanders, of Germanic stock and speak a Scandinavian language. In North Slesvig there is a minority of less than 40,000 Germans. The Danes are soft-spoken and friendly, tolerant and adverse to all extremes. They are very down-to-earth and display what has been called an "uncommon common sense."

GOVERNMENT

Denmark has been a kingdom with a democratic constitution, with greatly reduced royal power, since 1849. In June 1953, a new constitution was adopted. It made women eligible to succeed to the throne and substituted a unicameral parliament (the Folketing) of 179 members for the former Rigsdag of 2 houses. It also lowered the voting age from 25 to 23 years and changed the status of Greenland from that of a colony to a full member of the Danish Commonwealth with representatives in Parliament.

COMMERCE AND INDUSTRIES

The most important occupation is agriculture, but more people are employed in crafts and industries. Sweeping land reforms laid the foundation for a wealthy class of freeholders as early as 1788. The typical Danish farm is seldom bigger than 40 acres and specializes in scientific dairy farming, pig raising and egg production, all for export. Denmark raises about four times as much food as the Danes eat themselves. Although Denmark's exports are mainly farm products, industrial goods account for more than 25 per cent. Main items are ships, Diesel motors (42 per cent of all Diesel motors in ocean-going vessels of all nations were Danish-built in 1939), agricultural machinery, canned foods, beer and fruit beverages, and cement. Famous export products are also objects of industrial art, such as pottery from the Royal Copenhagen Porcelain works and others, and silverware. Monetary unit, krone (crown).

COMMUNICATIONS

There are 3,120 miles of railroads; 33,254 miles of roads; 826,000 telephones; 1,327,000 registered radio receivers. The broadcasting system is government-owned and Denmark has regular television programs. The merchant fleet has over 1,585,000 gross tons.

RELIGION AND EDUCATION

The established church is Lutheran, to which the king must belong. There is religious freedom. Elementary education is compulsory for the ages 7 through 14. There are two universities, in Copenhagen and Aarhus, with about 6,100 and 1,200 students respectively. There is also a Technological Institute and an Agricultural College in Copenhagen. Standards of education, science, arts and literature are high. So is literacy. In 1938, Denmark published 15 times as many books per capita as the United States. Danish men of letters have won more Nobel Prizes in proportion to population than those of any other nation.

CHIEF CITIES

Copenhagen, the capital, 1,166,300; Aarhus, 116,200; Odense, 101,000; Aalborg, 79,900; Esbjerg, 48,300; Randers, 40,100; Horsens, 36,000; Kolding, 31,000.

The Heartland of Europe

Germany and Its People

Germany has produced many intellectual giants—Goethe, Leibniz, Wagner—to whom the whole world is indebted. In the light of their genius, Germany has sometimes been thought of as a nation of philosophers, scientists, poets and musicians. Unhappily, to their neighbors at times, the Germans have appeared as ruthless conquerors. They are the most numerous and ambitious people in Western Europe, though they have suffered two crushing defeats and though their land is cut in two. Eastern Germany is a Soviet satellite. Western Germany, however, is a free, independent nation and a member of the NATO.

ONE of the most striking features about Germany, the "heartland" of Europe, is that its border lines have fluctuated so much since about 1850 that it is hard to say which areas are truly German and which are not. A map of Germany drawn around 1850—when it was a loose league of independent states—looks quite different from a map of the German Empire established only twenty years later. In 1919 Germany lost large regions to France and Poland and smaller ones to Denmark and Belgium. During the Third Reich of the Nazis, Germany annexed Austria, the Sudeten area of Czechoslovakia, the Czech regions of Bohemia and Moravia and other bits and pieces of territory. Most of these sections had been part of the German league until 1866, but were outside Bismarck's German Empire. During World War II even larger territories came under nazi control which had never been under German domination before.

Retribution was exacted in the collapse of Hitler's "Thousand-Year Reich" in 1945. Germany not only had to give up every square mile of territory she had annexed but also lost what then was known as Eastern Germany to Poland and the Soviet Union. The German population of the old Eastern Germany was expelled. What was left of Germany was occupied by the Allied forces. Since the Eastern and Western powers could not agree on conditions for setting up a united German government, two rival German governments were eventually established.

Day by day the split between East and West became deeper, especially as Eastern Germany (the new one) followed ever more closely the pattern of a Soviet satellite. Thus two different Germanies emerged, drawing ever farther apart in government and outlook.

The bewildering shifts in Germany's boundaries have been largely due to the fact that German unity was achieved much later than that of most other European nations and took place mid the rivalry of the two only really strong German states—Austria and Prussia. This contest for power was the determining factor in German history from the middle of the eighteenth century until after a brief war in 1866. Then Austria was thrust out of Germany, and German unity was established under Prussian leadership. This outcome settled a question that had split the whole people: Should a united Germany be a Greater Germany including Austria with its many non-German peoples, as the old Holy Roman Empire had done, or should the new German state be a Smaller Germany without Austria but under the leadership of a Prussia that was vigorous, military-minded and thoroughly German? As a consequence of the decision on this question, millions of Austrian Germans were left outside the new Germany. The state became more Prussianized as time went by, while Austria's interests veered toward the southeast, to the Balkans.

When the Austro-Hungarian monarchy fell apart as a result of World War I, there was a strong feeling among Austrian Germans for union with Germany. But

GERMANY DIVIDED, WITH TWO CAPITALS, BONN AND BERLIN

Anschluss (union) was vetoed by the victors who did not want to see the vanquished Reich strengthened. Twenty years later, in 1938, *Anschluss* was carried out by Austrian-born Hitler, but this was union, at the point of a gun, with a nazified Germany, and a very different thing from the old dream. During the following years Austria lost all remnants of self-government and was ruled much like a conquered province. The Austrians were embittered, and when nazi control was broken in 1945, they severed every tie with Germany and refused to consider themselves German any longer.

All that is left today of the dream of a Greater Germany is, strangely enough, the German national flag, with its stripes of black, red and gold. Around 1850 these colors symbolized a loosely united Germany under Austrian leadership—black and yellow (or gold) were the colors of the imperial Hapsburg dynasty; and red was the predominant color of most other German states. The flag of the German Empire was black, white and red—dominated by the Prussian black and white. In 1919 the old hues were restored and were then said to be symbolic: "from night (black) through blood to golden freedom." Today black, red and gold are claimed by both the democratic Western Republic and the communist government of the Eastern zone as their national colors.

At present the German people would seem to be thoroughly reconciled to their loss of territory—except on the east. It is hard for them to accept the fact that the Polish and Soviet flags wave over Silesia, Pomerania and East Prussia and that not a single German is left in these areas.

Germany went through ordeal by fire toward the end of World War II. Whole cities were gutted as a result of Allied air attacks. Priceless treasures from bygone times, such as the medieval part of Frankfurt-on-Main and the baroque gems of Dresden, were destroyed for all time. Nevertheless, much is still left of the architectural riches of the German past. Many of the great Gothic cathedrals, such as Cologne, are still standing, a number of palaces remain untouched, and such medieval towns as Rothenburg and Dinkelsbühl and Hameln (or Hamelin, of pied piper fame) are still enchanting.

Nor did warfare ruin the pervading loveliness of the German countryside, celebrated in song and story. Many of the

WAREHOUSES ALONG THE OVERSEAS DOCK OF BREMEN HARBOR
Though some distance inland from the North Sea, on the Weser River, Bremen has been one of the chief ports on the Continent for centuries. Ships from all over the world anchor here.

A LIFELIKE STATUE PEERS FROM HAMBURG'S SMALLEST HOUSE
One of the city's oddities, the building was erected in 1871. It has only two rooms, one above the other. The street floor is a tiny shop; over it is a charming little balcony.

most famous regions, dotted here and there with quaint medieval towns, lie in Western Germany, where Western visitors may enjoy them: the lordly Rhine winding between vineyard-covered slopes, where perch the castles of princes and knights of long ago; the hilly Black Forest, or Schwarzwald, mysterious in its thick growth of dark firs, the scene of so many legends and fairy tales; the lovely valleys of the Main and the Neckar, with romantic old Heidelberg on the banks of the latter river; the shimmering white peaks of the majestic Bavarian Alps, in which Garmisch-Partenkirchen, one of the most popular winter resorts in Europe, nestles in a little valley.

Marshall Plan Aid

A vigorous and industrious people like the Germans were not likely to remain in despair very long even after such a tremendous blow as their defeat in 1945. But even so, they needed help to get on their feet. For Western Germany, the opportunity came in May 1948 with the Marshall Plan, more properly called the European Recovery Program. What overwhelming importance the program had for the economic reconstruction of Western Germany is vividly illustrated by the fact that the Western German Government, formed about fifteen months later, established a separate ministry, with Cabinet rank, "for the Marshall Plan" in addition to a Ministry of Economic Affairs. It is not too much to say that German rehabilitation dates from that time.

What Germany Needed

The Marshall Plan furnished what prostrate and starving Germany needed then above everything else: a sufficient supply not only of food but also of raw materials from abroad so that the wheels of industry might be set turning again. Within the next four years Western Germany received about $1,500,000,000 worth of this type of support. About half of it was food and the other half raw materials.

In this same period a new currency was created in the three Western zones—the German mark or D-mark. By this means

TEDDING HAY WITH A WILL

An energetic farm worker, wielding a pitchfork, helps his country to feed itself.

almost all claims and liabilities in the old Reichsmark currency were devaluated down to one-tenth or less, including savings accounts, current accounts, credits and mortgage bonds. This made the flow of money easier. Equally decisive was the restoration of a free economy—competition—to replace the strictly enforced planned economy of the Nazi Government.

Results came fast. In June 1948, Western Germany's industrial output amounted to hardly more than one-half of the production of 1936. By the end of 1948, production had already reached 80 per cent of the 1936 level. By the middle of 1952 it reached the 140 per cent mark. Agriculture—which had to feed about 20 per cent more mouths because of displaced persons and Germans expelled from the east—reached 110 per cent. As Western Germany had lost many of its natural resources—they had belonged in Eastern Germany or former territories—it had to start out with importing much more than it could export. In 1949 imports were worth 8 billion D-marks, about twice as much as exports. Only two years later, the figures for exports and imports were equal, at about 14.5 billion D-marks.

In spite of this amazingly rapid beginning, West German recovery was at first bedeviled by unemployment and a severe lack of capital. Then, about 1948, the tide began to turn. Today, Western Germany is again one of the leading industrial nations of the world. In fact, in shipbuilding and in the manufacture of chemicals, automobiles, machine tools and the like, Western Germany is leaping far ahead of most of its neighbors.

Relations with France have improved. In 1956, France agreed to let the Saar return to West Germany, though France would still get some of the Saar's wealth of coal. France and West Germany also agreed to build a canal, to cost $130,000,000. It will be cut through the Moselle Valley and link the Ruhr coal basin with the iron-rich French province of Lorraine.

German cities suffered such total destruction during the war that even more than ten years later rebuilding was still of prime importance. In housing, especially, West Germany is far in advance of East Germany. The East has some "show" apartment blocks but for every one there, there are a dozen or more in the West. Hamburg, for example, has almost literally arisen from ashes. More than 300,000 of its homes were destroyed. By 1956 about 180,000 families had been able to move into new houses or apartments.

There has been a fortunate side to rebuilding. It has presented architects and everyone employed in the building trades with a great opportunity. The memory still lived of an architectural style perfectly suited to a period of austerity when every stone is at a premium. Right after World War I, Walter Gropius had started a school of design, the Bauhaus, in Weimar (it was later moved to Dessau). There he, with the assistance of

THE OPENING OF THE PEACE BRIDGE AT FRANKFURT-ON-MAIN

The span was completed in 1951. It was the last of Frankfurt's seven bridges crossing the Main to be restored. All of them had been destroyed in the closing months of the war.

EXPORTS FROM WESTERN GERMANY AWAITING AIR SHIPMENT
Some of the boxes contain microscopes, cameras and other kinds of precision-made optical goods. This is a field in which the highly skilled labor of Germany has long been adept.

PHOTOS, STANDARD OIL CO. (N. J.)

BICYCLES BY THE HUNDREDS SPIN ALONG IN FRANKFURT TRAFFIC
In Frankfurt-on-Main, as in many other European cities, bicycles are an everyday way of getting from place to place. This wide street is in the center of the city's business section.

115

FUR EXPERTS EXAMINE PELTS OF LUSTROUS PERSIAN LAMB

The German fur industry today is centered in Frankfurt-on-Main. It has moved there from Leipzig, in Eastern Germany, where furs once were a big attraction of the famous fairs.

some of the most imaginative architects of the day, such as Mies van der Rohe, had developed a new building style. It was based on the idea of design for use—called functionalism—and was a protest against the superficial and confused styles of the preceding decades. Though functionalism influenced building almost everywhere in Western Europe, it was despised by the Nazis as un-German and "degenerate." Its leaders had had to seek asylum in the United States or Latin America. But their efforts in their homeland had not been wasted. Many of their pupils had privately held to their ideas during the nazi years. Thus after 1945 they jumped at the chance to design under freer conditions in a style they had cherished. The concepts about which they had had to keep silent for so long now burst forth with renewed vigor.

Heaps of Rubble to Be Moved

Before reconstruction could get under way, however, the piles of rubble, often as high as a three- or four-story house, had to be removed. The task was hampered by a lack of transportation. Even as late as 1953, it was far from being finished.

In the meantime, architects got busy with their blueprints. Since destruction was not limited to individual buildings, but, rather, involved whole districts or even whole cities, it favored the advocates of large-scale town planning. Under other circumstances there might have been strong objections from those who yearned for their old familiar town. However, very few individuals had the means to build new houses for themselves. Besides, when materials are scarce and funds are low, the idea of simple, practical design is particularly convincing. Businessmen and city authorities gave their architects full powers to build as they saw fit. Prize-winning plans worked out by whole architectural associations were adopted in Nuremberg, Berlin, Hamburg, Kiel, Hanover, Emden, Frankfurt-on-Main, Mannheim, Kassel and elsewhere. Legal snarls, legacies from an earlier day, handicapped the planners in some other places, however, and held up rebuilding.

The Pace of Rebuilding

Altogether, by the beginning of 1953, about 1,200,000 dwelling units had been built in Western Germany, a little more than one-fifth of what was deemed necessary. Innumerable factories, office buildings, bridges and churches had been erected. Particularly significant was the erection or reconditioning of hundreds of theaters and concert halls.

The legitimate theater has long been a popular art in Germany. Its modern history goes back to the eighteenth century, when Germany consisted of a bewildering host of tiny principalities. In those days it was a matter of prestige for a prince to have his own court theater, no matter how small his domain. Eventually many of these theaters were taken over or supported by state or town authorities. Some of the greatest names in German literature —Lessing, Goethe and Schiller among them—were intimately associated with these theaters and did much to make them appealing to broader audiences. The peak of theater art was reached in the first third of the twentieth century. Then the theaters of Berlin and Vienna were admired all over Europe. There were also a considerable number of repertory companies in smaller cities, which offered an impressive variety of good performances.

After 1933, the interference of a totalitarian regime did much to destroy this achievement. A great many of Germany's most distinguished actors and directors—such as the grand old man of the German stage, Max Reinhardt—found it necessary to leave the country.

Theaters Mid the Ruins

Almost immediately after the defeat of 1945, a rebirth of the German theater began with astonishing speed. At first actors had to manage with crude, makeshift stages, in ruins or barns, but it soon turned out that their efforts were well worth the hardships. It seemed as if the whole nation was turning to the theater for advice and solace in the midst of the catastrophe that had come down on them. Actors might faint with hunger and cold, but record-breaking crowds, in coats and blankets, jammed the unheated theaters. The more soul-searching and serious the play, the greater the demand for admission. It was notable that nobody protested against the renovation or building of theaters at a time of extreme want and housing shortage. By 1951 no fewer than 168 theaters were again operating in Western Germany, 92 of them city or state theaters. As is evident from this, the old idea of government support for the theater was still an accepted one.

The public had a strong craving for what the outside world could offer. American and British authors—Steinbeck, Tennessee Williams, Arthur Miller, Van Druten, Wilder, Saroyan, O'Neill, T. S. Eliot and Christopher Fry—French playwrights such as Sartre, Camus, Anouilh, Claudel and Giraudoux—were hurriedly translated and produced. German authors, such as Zuckmayer and Bertold Brecht, who returned from exile with plays ready in their suitcases, were staged. German and foreign classics were the next choice of a public that seemed insatiable in its desire, not so much for entertainment as for understanding. New German playwrights have since come to the fore, but the critical taste of theater-goers has not been easily satisfied.

It has been hard to find among the postwar generation worthy heirs of the prenazi actors. Lovers of the theater complain that the achievements of the German stage are often out of proportion to the untiring, feverish efforts. The break with tradition caused by nazism seems to be hard to overcome. An interesting trend is the increasing number of summer festivals patterned after Max Reinhardt's old Salzburg festivals. Often they are staged in romantic natural scenery or even in the midst of picturesque ruins, for the benefit

A CORPUS CHRISTI PROCESSION AT ISERLOHN IN THE RUHR
In celebrating the solemn festival, the procession goes from church to church. A priest walks beneath the canopy; and the girls clad in white strew their flowers in the streets.

THE BUST OF A COAL-MINE FOUNDER WATCHES OVER HIS DOMAIN

The statue looms up rather strangely in front of one of the coal mines of the Ruhr. They are Germany's most precious mineral resource, on which the iron and steel industry depends.

of the local population and foreign visitors alike.

What holds true for the German theater also holds true for another art for which the Germany of old was loved—music. The war played havoc with musical life too. Concert halls vanished. Of the big opera houses only two remained intact, in Stuttgart and Wiesbaden. Opera companies were split; scenery, costumes and props were lost. Musical scores were up in flames, instruments were broken and nothing could be bought abroad for lack of foreign currency. No music-publishing houses were functioning.

But the craving for music was still there. Perhaps it was even greater than ever. Slowly things stirred. Musicians returned from the war and sought out their old associates. Evenings of solo performances and chamber music were the easiest to organize and demanded little in the way of equipment. The public thronged school auditoriums and gymnasiums. In the meantime the rebuilding of opera houses was begun and concert halls received priority along with theaters. Symphony orchestras were reorganized, and new ones were created with musicians who had had to leave their towns farther east. The Bamberg symphony orchestra developed into an elite body from the core of the former German Philharmonic Orchestra of Prague, replenished with members of the former Carlsbad and other Sudeten German and Silesian ensembles. In addition to the exiled artists who returned, foreign conductors and singers and other musicians again toured Germany and performed for capacity audiences.

An interesting aspect of this flourishing musical life was the change in public taste. In a few years the German people seemed to be drawn more by the dramatic sweep of symphonies than by the intimacy of chamber music and recitals. In the new and often lavishly equipped opera houses, conductors and directors developed a new style. They turned away from superficial, melodramatic effects. One result is that today the musical drama no longer tries to appeal only to the emotions, as the old declamatory style did. It also offers intellectual stimulation. It uses the story of an opera as a springboard for insight into human problems and comment on them, which the music serves to make more forceful.

Even the famous opera festivals at Bayreuth, which featured Wagner operas in highly conventional patterns for seventy-five years, have changed in style. Since 1951, under the leadership of Wieland Wagner, a grandson of the composer, the productions at Bayreuth have become simpler, with less of their old air of mystery and myth.

Less quick was the recovery of other arts such as painting and sculpture. Artists were handicapped by the lack of a public with funds to buy luxuries such as pictures. The first painters to overcome the tremendous practical difficulties were the representatives of two schools of modern art that had been banned and persecuted under Hitler—expressionism and nonobjective art. (In expressionism the artist dramatizes his own feelings about life. In nonobjective art, no object appears that can be recognized; it relies for its appeal on color and form.) Both schools had been in the vanguard during the 1920's and now they attracted greater interest than ever before.

Early in the 1950's there was also a strong revival of religious art, which had been on the wane for scores of years. Church congregations were among the first groups who could afford to spend money on art again. Countless churches were being rebuilt and many new ones were being erected to take care of increased attendance. A curious result of this situation was the development of an expressionist style in religious art. Perhaps because the Nazis had outlawed expressionism as they had also harassed the churches, church-goers felt more sympathetic to a style that had outraged them thirty years before. Also light building materials were used and there were other architectural features that lent themselves particularly well to the expressionist style.

The Revival of Literature

German literature had suffered a great decline under the Nazis. They had attempted to debase it to a mere vehicle for political propaganda. Writers who refused to conform were deprived of any means of being heard. Famous authors such as Thomas Mann sought refuge abroad. Though the tyrants were overcome in 1945, they left a slough of despond behind them. Fortunately, oppression had not lasted long enough to break completely all links with the past. German classics as well as books from abroad became guides in a search for new values. The first postwar work of German poets was strongly philosophical and contemplative; prose writers were highly critical but at the same time tended to seek flight in vague themes from a much too painful reality, perhaps a natural reaction.

Background for Reconciliation

Both the strides in economic recovery and the upsurge in cultural activities offered favorable conditions for the re-entrance of a democratic Germany into the circle of Western nations. After a time it became apparent that Germany was unlikely to be united for a long time, if ever. Yet Europe could never be a stable continent as long as Germany remained an outcast. The Western nations realized that normal relations—in trade, diplomacy—would have to be resumed with the country that occupies the very center of Europe. Sooner or later, an independent German state would have to be created again.

A Proposal for Self-Government

The first change of attitude toward the conquered enemy was indicated in September 1946 by James F. Byrnes, then United States Secretary of State. In a speech in Stuttgart he proposed that the German people should be given responsibility for running their own affairs. Local self-government had by that time already been carried out successfully in Western Germany. Government of the various states had been re-established on a democratic footing.

By 1948 there was no longer any doubt that the Soviet Union was opposed to free elections. However, it could control matters only in its own zone. Consequently, the next year, representatives from the West German states met and

Text continues on page 137

BROAD TOWERS AND LACY STONEWORK OF COLOGNE CATHEDRAL

Mounting high above the Rhine Valley, Cologne Cathedral is the largest of Gothic churches in northern Europe. It was begun in the thirteenth century, completed in the nineteenth.

DOCKSIDE in the little fishing and dredge harbor of Schulau. It is a short distance west of Hamburg, where the Elbe River widens out as it nears the North Sea.

MAKING HOOPS from willow withes. The strong flexible wood is excellent for barrel staves. The scene is in the rich farming country of Holstein, in the northwestern part of Germany.

THE BIRD POND, with zebras grazing placidly in the background, fascinates young visitors to the world-famous Hagenbeck Zoo. It is in the Stellingen district of Hamburg.

A PEDDLER'S CART, heaped with gay pottery and various other utensils, tempts a housewife who lives near Haffkrug. The little port is on the Baltic Sea, north of Lübeck.

CONE-SHAPED SPIRES top the medieval Town Hall of Lübeck, once the head of the Hanseatic League. Thomas Mann, twentieth-century German novelist, was born in Lübeck.

RHEINSTEIN CASTLE, NORTH OF THE WHIRLPOOL AT BINGEN

Rheinstein was built and destroyed within one century, the thirteenth. Now restored, with a collection of medieval weapons, it is a worthy stopover for travelers on the Rhine.

AN OLD TAVERN OF BACHARACH
Timbered and steep-gabled, the house was built in 1368, in the vineyard region of the Rhine.

BLACK FOREST—STOVEPIPE HATS
Triberg villagers, in the charming dress of an earlier age, encourage a look into the past.

ALL PHOTOS, TRANS WORLD AIRLINES

BY THE SPRINGS OF THE MATTIACI—THE BATHS OF WIESBADEN
An early people, the Mattiaci, who inhabited the land about Wiesbaden, gave their name to the springs of the city. It is today one of the most popular health resorts of Europe.

TIDY FIELDS on the lovely rolling hills that rise east of the upper Rhine River. The land is cultivated with scientific care.

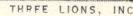

A CASTLE is on almost every crag in the winding Moselle Valley. Each was once the domain of a feudal lord. On the sunny slopes, vineyards thrive, which yield the white wines for which the Moselle region is noted.

GLOOMY AND FORBIDDING, a medieval prison tower looms over a quiet street in Rotenburg an der Fulda (on the Fulda River), in Hesse. Half-timbered houses with peaked roofs add to the atmosphere of long ago.

IN THE OLD PART of Frankfurt am Main (on the Main River), a few of the buildings erected in the Middle Ages still stand. Elsewhere the city presents a bustling, twentieth-century appearance.

THE PIED PIPER charms children again—in a performance of the celebrated legend in Hameln (Hamelin). The town has an amusing Ratcatcher's House, adorned with paintings of the tale.

ELISABETTEN TOR, ARCH IN THE CASTLE GARDEN OF HEIDELBERG
In southwest Germany is the romantic old university town of Heidelberg. Heidelberg Castle, sometimes called the "German Alhambra," overlooks the town and the gentle Neckar River.

A WOOD-CARVER'S STUDIO IN THE VILLAGE OF OBERAMMERGAU

In the green valley of the Ammer River high in the Bavarian Alps, Oberammergau preserves the art of wood-carving. The town is celebrated for the Passion Play enacted there every ten years.

FRIENDLY BARGAINING in Dinkelsbühl, Bavaria. The walled town has been left practically untouched since the days of feudal lords. Today it often has a delicious aroma from gingerbread factories.

NO VISIT to Bavaria is complete without acquiring one of the region's gay peaked hats, often made of suede. Sportsmen in other lands have adopted the headgear.

PHOTOS, EWING KRAININ

THE SUSPENSION TRAMWAY at Wuppertal follows the course of the Wupper River, a branch of the lower Rhine. Wuppertal, near Essen, in the industrial heart of West Germany, is well known for textile manufacture.

FEATHERS AND FRINGE—clothes of yesteryear in the Berchtesgaden area. The town is in the midst of rugged Alpine ranges in southeast Bavaria.

CHAPEL ON KÖNIGSSEE—ALPINE LAKE DÜRER'S BIRTHPLACE, NUREMBERG

PHOTOS. TRANS WORLD AIRLINES

UNDER THE SIGN OF THE GOLDEN ELK, AN OLD BAVARIAN STREET
Though busy with the manufacture of modern textiles and metalware, Rothenberg ob der Tauber retains a medieval air. Its old inns, churches, shops and narrow streets attract many travelers.

BAVARIAN WOMEN IN COSTUMES THAT DELIGHT THE TOURIST
A glimpse of the Bavaria of yesterday may be caught in the exquisite collector's items that furnish the room and in the richly brocaded aprons and floral adornments displayed by the women.

GARMISCH-PARTENKIRCHEN is an international winter-sports resort in south Bavaria. The highest peak in Germany, Zugspitze (9,721 feet), is nearby. One may climb it with little effort on a cog railway.

CUCKOO CLOCKS enchant a youngster on a visit to a workshop in the romantic Black Forest of southwestern Germany. A fairy-tale land, it is famous for the manufacture of toys and music boxes as well as the quaint cuckoo clocks.

INSPIRATION for an artist—the church steeple of Ramsau. The pretty village nestles in a narrow valley near Berchtesgaden. There are magnificent views on every side.

WARM WELCOME—the attractive lodge is at Schliersee, in south Bavaria, on the Alpine lake of the same name. The mountains that gird it are a challenge to skiers.

VINCENT JERMOLOWITZ FROM SHOSTAL

SHELLY GROSSMAN FROM SHOSTAL

THE NEW CASTLE, IN THE MODE OF THE PALACE AT VERSAILLES
Formal gardens enhance the grandeur of a royal palace, the Neue Schloss, in Munich. Completed in 1704, it foreshadowed the flourish of art in the city during the nineteenth century.

BAYREUTH'S FESTSPIELHAUS, HOME OF THE WAGNER FESTIVALS
Every year thousands of music lovers come to the Festspielhaus at Bayreuth to hear the operas of Richard Wagner. The festivals began in 1876, seven years before the composer's death.

adopted a constitution for a federal government, with the capital in Bonn. Later a similar assembly adopted a constitution for a somewhat more centralized set-up in Eastern Germany. Thus the split of the country into two rivaling Germanies became an established fact. Hereafter we speak of them separately, beginning with Western Germany.

Western Germany

The official name of Western Germany is the Federal Republic of Germany (*Bundesrepublik Deutschland*). Almost all its people are of the same stock—German for many centuries. It is said that the purest German to be heard anywhere is spoken in Hanover. However, there are a small Danish minority in South Schleswig and a group speaking a different language—Frisian—on the Frisian islands of the states of Schleswig-Holstein and Lower Saxony. Elsewhere in Western Germany one may hear various dialects; and customs also vary from place to place. Though the basic population has long had a feeling of firm union, this feeling has been taxed by the influx of almost ten million expelled Germans and other refugees from the east. The problems created by this immigration are among the most difficult ones the country has. So far no lasting and satisfying solution has been found, although the strain has lessened as a result of the general recovery.

The Federal Republic consists of eleven states (*Länder*): Baden, Bavaria, Bremen, Hamburg, Hesse, Lower Saxony, North Rhine–Westphalia, Rhineland-Palatinate, Schleswig-Holstein, Württemberg-Baden and Württemberg-Hohenzollern. Some states, such as Bavaria, Bremen and Hamburg, are more or less identical with old German states that had long histories of their own. Others, such as Schleswig-Holstein, are former provinces of the old state of Prussia, which was dissolved in 1945 and formally abolished in 1947. Still other states are arbitrary combinations because in some cases, state boundaries were drawn to conform with occupation zones.

The border between Western and Eastern Germany zigzags from just east of Lübeck, on the Baltic Sea, down to the westernmost tip of Czechoslovakia.

Western Germany takes in a broad fertile plain on the north, rimmed by Holland, the North Sea, Denmark and a

HICOG (JACOBY)

HUGE BOLTS OF CLOTH REELING OFF IN A MUNICH FACTORY
With thread from the spools above, the cloth is woven circularly, like knitting. This textile plant is owned by and employs Germans expelled from their former homes in the east.

137

BERCHTESGADEN: THE BEAUTIFUL LANDSCAPE TO THE SOUTHWEST

The village of Berchtesgaden is in the mountains just across the border from Austria. Nearby, on a lofty summit, Adolf Hitler built his famous retreat, now demolished.

stretch of the Baltic Sea. As one goes south through the country the land gradually rises, finally culminating in the Bavarian Alps on the southeast. The hills of the Black Forest are on the southwest. Today the Rhine River marks the western border.

Aside from the fertile northern plain, the forests and the rich coal mines of the Ruhr district, Western Germany has few other natural resources. There is some potash, lignite, iron ore, zinc, lead, copper and salt. In highly skilled labor, however, the country is wealthy, and it has been a center of heavy industry for many years. It was a boon when France, in 1950, proposed the Schuman Plan. It went into effect two years later and is known officially as the European Coal and Steel Community. By this plan, the coal and steel resources of Belgium, France, Italy, Luxembourg, the Netherlands and Western Germany are pooled. Its aims are lower costs for industries that depend on coal and steel and a higher standard of living for the workers.

Today Germany again produces more than fifty thousand different kinds of machinery and machine tools. They range from small precision instruments to powerful locomotives, for export as well as for domestic use. Western Germany is also rebuilding its once famous chemical industry.

Since more than 23 per cent of the area is forest land, timber, wood fibers, cellulose, pulp and paper contribute a substantial share to the national income. About 35 per cent of the territory—34,000 square miles—of the Federal Republic is farmland well suited to mixed agriculture. The main crops are rye, potatoes, grain, sugar beets, wine grapes and fruit. Vineyards, from which renowned white wines are made, cover terraced slopes of the Rhine, Neckar and Moselle valleys.

A new German merchant marine is being built, practically from scratch—or, rather, scrap. By the beginning of 1953, Western Germany had already reached the status of fourteenth seafaring nation.

The constitution of Western Germany is largely modeled on the "Weimar Constitution" of 1919, though it gives less power to the central government and more to the larger states. There are two

THE HEARTLAND OF EUROPE

legislative bodies: the Federal Diet (parliament), or *Bundestag,* to which members are elected directly by the voters; the Federal Council, or *Bundesrat,* made up of representatives of the state governments. The number of representatives varies according to state populations.

A special body of electors chooses the president, who must be more than forty years old. However, actual executive power is in the hands of a Cabinet of fourteen ministers, headed by the federal chancellor (*Bundeskanzler*), who is elected by the *Bundestag* on the proposal of the president. As in most other Western European countries, the Cabinet must have the support of the *Bundestag* or else it goes out of office. But in Germany, parliament can express its lack of confidence only by electing a new chancellor.

This rule is aimed at preventing frequent Cabinet crises, which otherwise could result in bewildering shifts in government.

The chief political parties are the Social Democrats; the more conservative, and largely Catholic, Christian Socialists; and the Free Democrats—a more nationalistic party of the right, which has been criticized for admitting former Nazis. There are a few other small parties, including a Communist one, but the Nazi Party remains outlawed.

More than half the people of the Federal Republic are Lutherans and about two-fifths are Roman Catholics. Since the war there has been a striking revival of religious interest.

Illiteracy is practically unknown. German education has always been thorough; and such innovations as the kindergarten

HICOG (JACOBY)

SOLACE FOR A SWEET TOOTH—CHOCOLATE BEING PROCESSED

The delicious stuff is being prepared in a candy-making factory in Bavaria. Some of the product is destined to delight German boys and girls and some of it will be exported.

have spread through the world from Germany. Its universities—Heidelberg, Bonn, Göttingen, Munich, Frankfurt, Tübingen, West Berlin—are among the most famous schools in Europe. Foreign students have flocked to them; and once their schools of medicine were without peer.

Eastern Germany

Eastern Germany calls itself the "German Democratic Republic." As a result of communist efforts to make it a soviet state, it has been losing its population. Early in 1953 about three thousand men, women and children were fleeing Eastern Germany every day.

The people of this area have mixed less with their neighbors than the people of Western Germany. Nevertheless, there is some difference in character and dialect between the middle-German inhabitants of Saxony or Thuringia and the Northern Germans of the rest of the region. A tiny minority in the Lusatia, the Wends or Sorbs, have retained one of the Slavonic languages that were prevalent in medieval times throughout the whole of Germany east of the Elbe River.

The form of the German Democratic Republic started out along somewhat the same lines as the republic of 1918–33, though less centralized. Right after 1945, Eastern Germany consisted of five states or provinces: Brandenburg, Mecklenburg, Saxony, Saxony-Anhalt and Thuringia, most of them identical with former states. One—Brandenburg—was a former Prussian province; and another—Saxony-Anhalt—was a combination of a province and a state. But in 1952 the old state divisions were discarded, and the Republic became a single state divided into fourteen administrative districts (*Bezirke*) with very little self-government and with district lines crisscrossing the old borders. This change and a num-

FARM EQUIPMENT ON DISPLAY AT THE LEIPZIG TRADE FAIR

Though the day is quite evidently cold, this open-air exhibit draws considerable attention. The fairs are still held every year, but the emphasis is on strictly practical wares.

CHARMING AND GRACEFUL PORCELAIN FIGURINES FROM DRESDEN
The cherubic little figures and the stately couples, who seem about to dance the minuet, are painted in delicate hues. Most Dresden ware is really made at Meissen, nearby.

ber of far-reaching alterations in the basic law codes had the effect of strengthening communist control. Thus the pattern of government is similar to that in other satellites of the Soviet Union. At the same time a reunion of all Germany has been made much less likely.

Eastern Germany is predominantly an agricultural region. Most of it is a continuation of the broad plain that extends across northern Europe. Only in the south, near the border with Bavaria and Czechoslovakia, is the country really hilly.

In old Pomerania and East Prussia, large or even tremendous holdings were owned by the lesser nobility of Prussia and Mecklenburg, the *Junker* class out of which the Prussian officers corps had developed. Immediately following the end of World War II, the big estates and large holdings were confiscated and divided up among German farmers who had lost their land in regions farther east. Because of this land reform, food was more plentiful for a while in the Eastern zone than it was in the Western zones,

although the Soviet occupation army lived off the land and substantial parts of the crops were shipped off to Russia. Less fortunate was the lot of the working population of the cities, because the Russians stripped factories and offices of machinery and other equipment and carried them away as reparations.

This situation was later reversed. On Soviet demand a program for making the farms collective, as in Russia, was introduced. This caused so many farmers to run for cover across the border line to Western Germany that food production sagged. On the other hand, with raw materials from Poland and Czechoslovakia, unemployment in the cities disappeared as industries were encouraged to start up again. In 1951 industrial production reached 105 per cent of the 1936 level for the area, and crops amounted to 78 per cent. An increasing amount of the manufactured goods have been exported to Russia.

Along the boundary with Czechoslovakia, in the Erzgebirge, or Ore Moun-

ROLLMOPS IN THE MAKING—CLEANING AND SLICING HERRING
The salty morsels called rollmops are rolled-up bits of herring with pieces of onion and sour pickle in the middle. This is a factory in Cuxhaven, a center of North Sea fishing.

tains, uranium was found. A new mining industry has begun there in deep secrecy.

For centuries Leipzig, Eastern Germany's best-known city, was famous for its trade fairs, held in a great square in the center of the city called the Market Place. The fairs are still held every year, though in a different atmosphere.

Dresden, too—the city renowned for its exquisite porcelain—is behind the iron curtain. Most of the dainty shepherds and shepherdesses are actually produced at Meissen, only fourteen miles away.

The political set-up of Eastern Germany tolerates a number of parties, but all real control is in the hands of the so-called Socialist Unitarian Party (*Sozialistische Einheitspartei Deutschlands,* abbreviated SED)—a forced union between Socialists and Communists, effectively run by the latter. Outward democratic forms get a great deal of publicity, but actually the territory is tightly run on totalitarian lines.

The people of Eastern Germany are overwhelmingly Lutheran, by about 80 per cent. Some 15 per cent are Roman Catholics. The relationship between the churches and the government is mutually hostile. Taking a lesson from the Nazis, however—who ran into trouble when they harassed the churches—the authorities have refrained from open warfare. The churches even continue to receive some financial support from the Government.

Education in Eastern Germany has been modeled along communist lines. All private schools were abolished and the building of more public schools was speeded up. Instruction in communist ideas is an important part of the children's studies. Russian is taught as the first foreign language.

Just what the future of Germany will be, no one can say. The division of the country is an arbitrary one. Yet as young people grow up on either side of the iron curtain—knowing only division and absorbing very different outlooks on life—union will become all the more difficult to achieve. In any case, Germany is a proving ground for the biggest conflict in ideas of the twentieth century.

By GUNNAR LEISTIKOW

GERMANY: FACTS AND FIGURES

THE COUNTRY

Germany occupies the great northern plain of Europe between the Alps and the North and Baltic seas and between the Rhine and Oder rivers. Western Germany, with its capital at Bonn, was formed from the British, French and U. S. zones of occupation; Eastern Germany, with its capital at Berlin, from the Soviet zone. West Germany: 94,719 sq. mi.; population, 49,652,000. East Germany: 41,631 sq. mi.; population, 17,600,000. West Berlin: 156 sq. mi.; population, 1,175,000. East Berlin: 186 sq. mi., population, 2,194,600.

GOVERNMENT

Western Germany: the Federal Republic of Germany, governed under a constitution adopted in 1949; has a Federal Diet of elected members and a Federal Council; a president, prime minister, or chancellor, and Cabinet. Eastern Germany: the German Democratic Republic, governed under a constitution enacted in 1949; dominated by Communists.

COMMERCE AND INDUSTRIES

Crops are potatoes, sugar beets, rye, in the main. Forestry is important and carried on along scientific lines. Country is poor in minerals except for the coal of the Ruhr; uranium mined in Eastern Germany. Important fisheries in the North and Baltic seas. Chief industries include iron and steel, electrical appliances, chemicals, textiles, beet sugar, potash, glass, pottery, clocks, toys, tobacco products, wine, beer. Monetary unit: in West Germany, the Deutsche West mark; in East Germany, the East mark.

COMMUNICATIONS

West Germany: railways, 18,966 miles; roads, 79,622 miles; inland waterways, 2,654 miles.

RELIGION AND EDUCATION

About 62% of total population is Protestant (chiefly Lutheran) and 35% Roman Catholic. Education from 6 to 18 compulsory and highly developed. There are about 25 universities.

CHIEF CITIES

Berlin (East and West), 3,369,000. *West Germany:* Bonn, capital, 134,700; Hamburg, 1,723,000; Munich, 906,500; Cologne, 670,300; Essen, 661,000; Frankfurt-on-Main, 601,800; Dusseldorf, 594,500; Dortmund, 580,900; Stuttgart, 566,000; Hanover, 494,600; Bremen, 483,600; Duisburg, 454,900; Nuremberg, 398,700; Wuppertal, 392,800; Gelsenkirchen, 355,350; Bochum, 326,100; Mannheim, 272,300; Kiel, 259,500; Wiesbaden, 240,000. *East Germany:* Leipzig, 607,700; Dresden, 510,100.

LUNCHING ALFRESCO ON THE BANKS OF THE WANNSEE
The Wannsee, a little arm of the Havel River, wends a quiet way through a park of rolling woodland in southwest Berlin. The park is one of the most popular retreats of the city.

Berlin in Eclipse

Where the Iron Curtain Is Visible

> Berlin is a city divided but one whose spirit has not been conquered. The two opposing ideologies of our era—democracy and communism—face each other directly here, each holding sway in part of the city. There are two governments, two bus systems, two electric companies, two ways of life. To step across the dividing line in either direction is to enter a different atmosphere. Yet in spite of this division and the difficulties it brings to everyday living, the people of Berlin cling tenaciously to their city and continue to hope that some day it will regain some of its former glory.

UNTIL recent years Berlin was the chief city on the continent of Europe—in industry, in commerce, in population. It was the third city of the world, with an area almost equal to that of New York City. It was the capital of a Germany that, under Adolf Hitler, was strong enough to swallow up its neighbors. Since 1945, Berlin has been a victim of two wars, one "hot" and the other "cold."

The hot war—World War II—destroyed the city to a degree that left its mark on almost every building remaining erect and totally erased countless others. Perhaps nowhere else in the world could one see such destruction. Near the center of the city vast areas of rubble and jagged fragments of walls were all that remained of homes, palaces, theaters, churches.

While energetic reconstruction goes on, reflecting the Berliners' vitality, the Berlin that survived World War II is now the victim of the cold war. The quarrels between the Soviet Union and the West have kept Germany—and Berlin—divided.

West Berlin is an island amidst communist-controlled countries. It cannot do any business with the surrounding areas of Germany. All raw materials must be shipped in over long distances, and the output of its factories must be sent to markets far to the west.

Because of this situation there was acute distress in West Berlin for some years after World War II. There was considerable unemployment, aggravated by the flood of refugees from East Germany. Refugees still pour into West Berlin but otherwise it has changed to an astonishing degree. The architecture of the old Berlin bore the heavy stamp of nineteenth-century Prussianism. It was a city of stone. Today, with funds from the West German Government and from the United States, West Berlin is becoming almost a city of glass. Thousands of houses and apartment buildings have been erected, finished in bright colors. Most striking, however, are the new steel-and-glass office buildings. The change is more than skin-deep. One may see the new spirit on the faces of the happy children who swarm into the parks.

Bicycles spin down the streets toward the parks and forests like schools of minnows in a narrow trough. Many youngsters carry guitars or other musical instruments. Picnickers on the countless lakes inside the city—relics of the ice age —can hear the strains of singing across the water from many directions.

When Berlin swallowed up its suburbs in 1920 and became one of the world's largest cities it also engulfed a great many forests and royal hunting preserves. Such was the Gruenewald where the kaisers used to hunt. With its adjacent tracts, it provides a nine-mile stretch of woodland inside the metropolitan limits. So many pines were cut there for wood during the Russian blockade of 1948-49 that large areas are now planted in seedlings.

West Berlin has fallen from its days of glory as part of a great national capital

BLEAK POTSDAMER PLATZ, A FOCAL POINT IN THE COLD WAR
The British, American and Russian zones intersect at Potsdamer Platz. The partially restored H.O., a state-owned chain store of the Soviet zone, displays a propaganda streamer.

to the sad role of a poor relative, pleading for help. Whereas East and West Germany have each been given almost complete self-government by the occupying powers, this is not true of Berlin. The four occupiers—Britain, France, the United States and the Soviet Union—have the last word with regard to what goes on in their sectors. The three Western sectors are administered by a government built on the pattern of Western democracies whereas the East Berlin government is somewhat modeled along communist lines.

The three Western powers maintain about twelve thousand troops in the city, supported by heavy tanks. The Russian troops are outside the city.

East Berlin does not labor under the handicaps of the Western sectors. It trades freely with the rest of East Germany. Thus although the population leads an austere life, there is virtually no unemployment.

Every block of downtown East Berlin bears the communist stamp. There are red flags flapping from the roofs and hanging from cornices and windows. Gigantic photos of Russian and East German communist leaders cover entire walls of buildings laid bare by the bombings. Banners carry slogans such as "Long Live Soviet-German Friendship."

On Unter den Linden, where a new crop of linden (lime) trees has been planted, special frames and billboards are erected for additional photographs and slogans. Elongated loud-speakers, set in the sidewalks like lampposts, broadcast marching songs and speeches during demonstrations.

The symbol of Berlin's transformation from a small town to a young capital was the castle that the Hohenzollerns built on an island in the Spree River, toward the end of the fifteenth century. After seizing the city with six hundred horsemen, Friedrich von Hohenzollern built the fortress and made the town his capital. The castle grew until it was a huge building, the home of Kaiser Wilhelm II, last of the Hohenzollerns, who was exiled after the defeat of Germany in 1918.

This castle, the chief link with the city's past, was badly damaged in the war and has been torn down by the Communists. In its place, spanning the entire island in the Spree, is a great square, known as Marx-Engels Platz, a reminder that the founders of communism were Germans. This is the local equivalent of Moscow's Red Square. The mass meetings so frequently used by the Communists are staged here.

Throughout East Berlin one sees over shops and even hot-dog stands the initials "H.O." This marks the government-operated stores, shops and booths. The initials stand for *Handelsorganization* or "Trading Organization." One also sees many shops marked *Konsum,* which designates the consumers' co-operatives. The communist principles are only partially applied so far and so a number of private shops remain.

The show piece of East Berlin is Stalin Allee, which the Communists describe as Germany's first "socialist street." It was built along one of the heavily bombed avenues where virtually no buildings remained. Rubble was cleared and a broad boulevard was laid out along which new housing projects and H.O. stores were erected. Here "activists," "heroes of la-

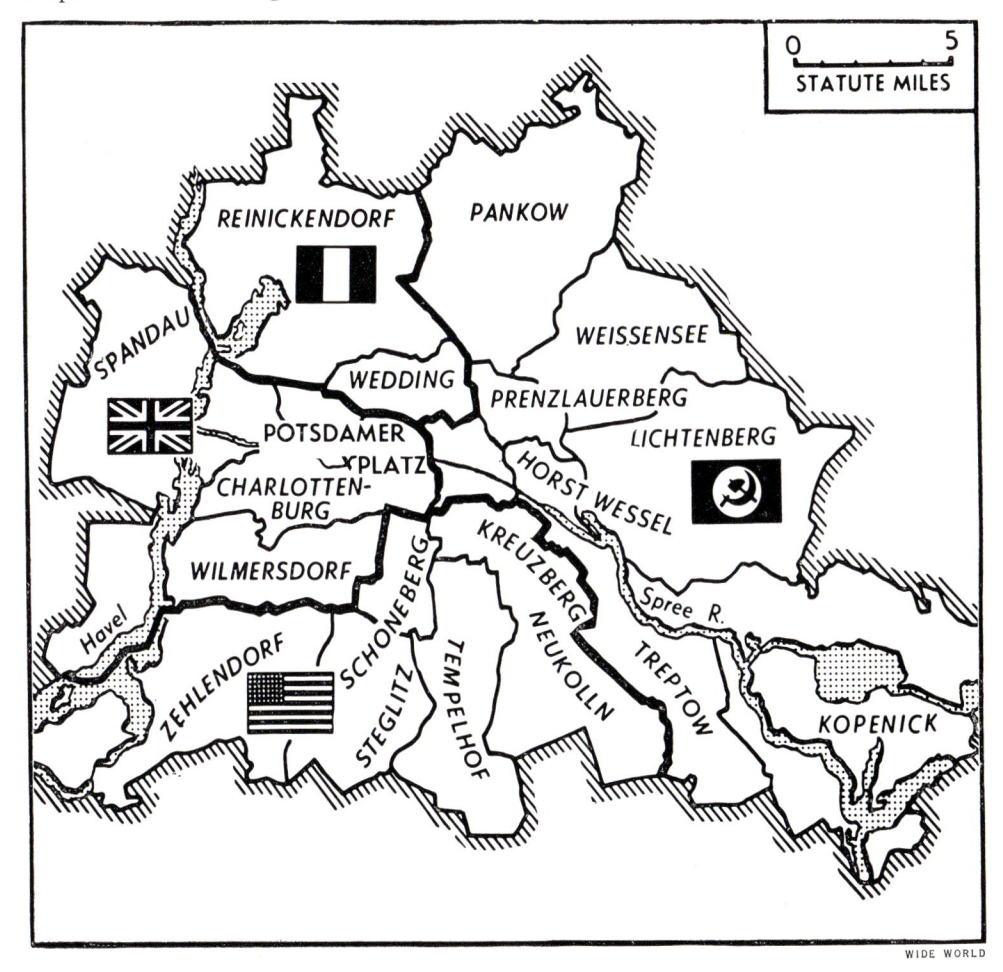

BERLIN'S FOUR ZONES: AMERICAN, BRITISH, FRENCH, SOVIET

bor" and others who co-operate with the government or who won in a housing lottery are given apartments.

Yet Stalin Allee has a queer air of being deserted. Even on a Sunday afternoon there are few strollers and very little traffic. It is as if the people fortunate enough to have an apartment there had to work around the clock in order to keep it.

Thus the Berlin of today is a city of stark contrasts. The competing systems of East and West glare at each other across the middle of Berlin at closer quarters than anywhere else. West Berlin's answer to Stalin Allee is the glittering Kurfuerstendamm, also a broad avenue. A strip in the center serves as parking space. On either side are hotels, shops, moving-picture theaters and sidewalk cafés with gay striped awnings. A steady stream of cars whizzes by, past throngs of strollers. The shops overflow with excellent merchandise including jewels and the latest fashions. In fact, the quality of the goods in the West Berlin stores and the reasonable prices bring many shoppers there from West Germany. Also, the restaurants and cafés of West Berlin serve delicious food.

Real prices in East Berlin are much higher, and for shoddy goods and tasteless food. West Berliners look smart. In East Berlin the universal outer garment is a drab beige raincoat.

Many Berliners were office workers and petty officials who turned the wheels of government in the days when Berlin was capital of an empire. Today the wheels are turning elsewhere. The West German capital is in Bonn. Headquarters of the communist-controlled East German Government is in the Soviet sector of Berlin but it attracts few of the old

A FRONTIER SIGN: "YOU ARE LEAVING THE AMERICAN SECTOR"
In times of tension in the divided city, West Berliners run the risk of being kidnaped when they enter the Soviet zone—hence the sign and the steel barrier that workmen are erecting.

A TRIM ROW OF SHOPS REPLACES THE RELICS OF BOMBARDMENT
Window shoppers take their time in passing the handsome row of stores on Fehrbelliner Platz in the British zone. New buildings and restorations of the old brighten life in West Berlin.

government workers living in the Western sectors.

As Germany is a young country, so is its erstwhile capital a young city. When Paris, London and Rome were already known the world over as great centers, Berlin was still a town.

It lies in a wide sandy plain, once nicknamed "the sandbox of the Holy Roman Empire." The region is carpeted here and there by dense pine forests such as those that stretch across Poland and the Pripet Marshes to Russia. Low ridges running east and west show where the vast glaciers of the ice age stopped their southward push.

The region was inhabited by Slavs who, in the twelfth century, were driven back toward Russia by the Saxon tribes. Two settlements then sprang up on the banks of the Spree River, which runs into the Havel River within what is now Berlin. One of the settlements, probably the older of the two, was built on an island in the Spree and called Koelln. The other, nearby on the south bank, was the village of Berlin. They were partially merged in 1307, but even combined they could not hold a candle to the great German cities of the day—bustling centers such as Cologne, Frankfurt and Nuremberg.

The cathedrals, castles and other ancient buildings of these cities tell of their glory in the Middle Ages. There are no such structures in Berlin. In 1688, when scores of other German towns were well established, the population of Berlin is believed to have been only eight thousand, barely equal to that of an average town of today in North America.

SHOW PIECE OF EAST BERLIN
A tall new apartment building provides living space for the favored few on Stalin Allee.

Nevertheless, Berlin was of sufficient commercial importance to become a junior partner in the Hanseatic League, an organization of trading cities that protected their interests in the absence of a central government.

Berlin first began to catch up with other cities in the seventeenth century when the local ruler, Frederick William, known as the Great Elector of Brandenburg, began building a canal linking the Spree with the Oder River. This helped to make Berlin the crossroads of waterways in north Germany. In those days, when there were no railways and only muddy wagon roads, such a location was a key spot.

Later, when Berlin became the chief political center in the north German plain, it drew toward itself the new highways and railroads so that today twelve main railway lines converge on the city, as do the modern superhighways built by Hitler. The iron curtain now cuts arbitrarily across these water, highway and rail routes so that the city's function as a transport center is impeded.

In its early days Berlin was too unimportant even to be an administrative headquarters for the area in which it lay. The electors, as the local rulers were called, had their capital in Brandenburg, forty miles west. It was when the Hohenzollerns moved their seat to Berlin that it began to develop, first as the capital of Prussia, and finally of all Germany.

It was during the days of the Great Elector that Berlin was swamped by its first refugees. They were Huguenots, or French Protestants, who fled persecution in France, settled in Britain and Germany and helped found new colonies in the wilds of North America. So many came to Berlin in the seventeenth century that one in every five inhabitants was French. The descendants of these refugees are now as German as their fellow citizens, sitting in Berlin cafés with their steins of beer. Their one distinguishing mark is the French names that they bear.

As the Hohenzollerns began to establish their control over the miscellaneous princes and petty rulers of the region, their capital, Berlin, likewise grew in prestige. When Frederick the Great came to the throne in 1740 the city had swelled to 70,000 people. Sixty years later, when all of Europe had learned to respect his armies, the population had more than doubled, to 172,000.

Two of the most important features of modern Berlin were established thanks to the early Prussian military spirit. One was the University of Berlin on Unter den Linden. The Hohenzollerns supported it in its early years because they thought it could turn out well-rounded army officers. In time it became one of the world's great seats of learning. The philosophers Hegel and Fichte worked there as did those beloved compilers of fairy tales and folklore, the Brothers Grimm.

Parade Grounds in an Air Age

Tempelhof airport, probably the best situated of any airport in the world, owes its existence to the love of parades, for it was once the imperial parade ground and hence the land was never built up. Here the Prussian armies displayed the goose step for many generations.

In the last century Germany burst forth into the world with the energy of a nation pent up for generations. It became a united and formidable nation and Berlin became the capital of a new empire. The city grew tenfold during the nineteenth century. There has been no such comparable growth in any other city of Europe, although there was even greater expansion in the New World.

All of the old city is in East Berlin and the Western sectors represent the growth after 1800. Their buildings bear the same ponderous stamp that is on so much Victorian architecture in Britain and North America.

As the city's expansion was so lopsided, primarily to the west, the border between East and West Berlin today lies partly along the western frontier of the old city. Potsdamer Platz, which is where the British, American and Soviet sectors come together, was once the city gate onto the road to Potsdam. It is now, in effect, the center of the city. The great colonnade gate, the Brandenburger Tor, was the gate leading toward Brandenburg; the Silesian Gate led toward the old province of Silesia, which is now administered by Poland. Yet all these gates today are on the intersectoral border.

In East Berlin some of the old palaces, museums and other public buildings dated from the days of Frederick the Great and bore the lighter, more graceful mark of the eighteenth century. A few of these have survived the war and have been restored.

When Adolf Hitler took over Germany in the 1930's, he boasted that he would build "a city that will stand for one thousand years." The Nazis erected a massive Air Ministry and other government office buildings, now being used by the East German Government. For the Olympic games of 1936 in Berlin, the Nazis built a sports area with playing fields and two stadiums, one holding 100,-000 people. But by 1939 Hitler had embarked upon a war that brought Berlin down in ruins.

Mass air raids by the Luftwaffe—the

TAUENTZIENSTRASSE, A BUSY STREET WITH A BRAVE NEW LOOK

The K. D. W., or *Kaufhaus des Westen* (Department Store of the West), at left, and other modern and newly restored buildings line one of the principal streets of the Western zone.

nazi air force—destroyed several English cities and inaugurated the era of "strategic bombing." In the end Berlin and Tokyo were the most spectacular victims. Although the younger generation hardly remembers the war they live among constant reminders of its destruction. When in sunny weather one sees scores of men and women propelling their wheelchairs through traffic, many of them lacking one or more limbs, it is easy to understand why the citizens fear a new war.

Berlin was captured by Soviet forces. It is said that ten thousand Red Army soldiers were lost in the bitter street fighting. The extent of this battle is best appreciated when one drives about Berlin in a car. Hardly a block in the entire city was not fought over; almost every building bears shell and machine-gun holes.

The Vanquished and the Victors

It is a tribute to the resilience and energy of the German people that they have risen from this chaos and have re-created the city into a living thing.

Meanwhile, the four powers who were to occupy Berlin jointly have been unable to work together. At first the difficulties were with the French, who objected to any action that they felt might help make Germany a new threat to France. It soon became clear, nevertheless, that the basic split was between the Russians and the Western powers.

As in Korea after the defeat of Japan, the Russians wanted to run things so that the local Communists, sooner or later, would get into the saddle. The Western powers, like the Russians, wanted to block a revival of nazism, but at the same time sought to prevent the Communists from seizing the reins.

From this fundamental cleavage sprang countless other difficulties. In 1948 the West gave up trying to solve the problem with the Russians and created a separate government in West Germany. In retaliation against this and against the introduction of West German currency in Berlin, the Russians imposed a blockade of West Berlin. The city government split in two in a sideshow of the central dispute, so that now separate regimes run East and West Berlin.

Since all land and water traffic to and from West Berlin has to pass through the Soviet zone it was easy for the Russians to halt the traffic on "technical" grounds. So the Berlin Airlift was begun by the West to supply the city. At times during 1948 and 1949 four-engined transport planes were landing in West Berlin at the rate of one almost every minute.

In 1952 the decision to rearm Western Germany brought new measures against West Berlin, this time imposed by the Soviet-sponsored German Democratic Republic in East Germany. West Berlin was practically sealed off from the surrounding countryside and travel into East Berlin was impeded. The thousands of West Berliners who loved to spend Sunday at some favorite spot in the country now have to make out in the city's parks.

The two great contending forces of the mid-twentieth century have made Berlin one of their battlegrounds. However, another force, that of nazism, is not entirely dead. There are about fifty neo-nazi groups known to exist in the Western sectors, most of them small and with overlapping memberships. There is also a tendency to keep alive the memory of the provinces lost to Poland. The flags of Silesia and others of those regions that for so long were part of the Prussian kingdom are flown at many official assemblies.

Despite all its woes Berlin has not lost its sense of humor. In fact the dry, cynical humor of Berlin is still famous in Germany, especially as reflected in its cabarets. Here, instead of crooners, there are political satirists who twist popular songs to their own devices. They poke fun at everything from the Communists to old Prussian militarism.

The Berliners love their city. In spite of its hazardous position, the people in West Berlin at least are finding life good again. With prosperity have come hope and cheer, and the majority refuse to migrate. Berlin is their home and they are determined to stay.

By Walter Sullivan

A State with a Glorious Past
How Poland Rose and Fell

Through the Middle Ages and the Renaissance, Poland was a great force in eastern Europe, but in the eighteenth century, Austria, Germany and Russia began whittling away at Poland's territory until there was no Poland left at all. At the end of World War I Poland emerged as a sovereign republic, only to be split up again between Germany and Russia when World War II began. In 1941 Germany opened its invasion of Russia and occupied all of Poland. When the Russian armies swept back the Germans, Poland's independence was again proclaimed. But since 1945 Poland has been closely drawn in as a satellite by Soviet Russia and independence is yet far away.

ONCE upon a time the kingdom of Poland stretched from the Baltic to the Black Sea. By the nineteenth century there was no Poland. Three great empires—the German, Russian and Austro-Hungarian—had gobbled her. Whenever Poles tried to recover their liberty, they were sent into exile, imprisoned or killed. Poles were forbidden for a time even to use their own language.

When Poland was restored in 1918 the people began to dream of making their country again a world power. It was the sixth largest state in Europe in both area and population, though only half the size of the old kingdom of Poland. The soil was rich and well-watered. The name Poland means Land of the Plains, which is descriptive of it. With the exception of that portion lying in the Carpathians in the south, the plains region presented to the traveler of yesteryear, sailing through the Bay of Danzig down the Vistula to Warsaw, the yellow of broad, ripening fields of grain, the rich earthy smell of level acres of potatoes and sugar beets. Over in the Black Country of Silesia the coveted lands still are level. The cities are less attractive, sombre with soft-coal smoke, though possessed of many buildings of historic interest.

In summer the mountain pastures of the Carpathians are musical with the tinkle of cattle-bells and the weird flute-playing of shepherds guarding their flocks. In winter the Carpathians take on a wild beauty—pines and junipers leaded with snow, the air biting, the sky at night spangled with stars. In peaceful times, it is a wonderful region for winter sports, skiing and tobogganing.

The Poles are hard workers who love the soil and till it diligently. They combine the qualities of many stocks, though they are largely of Slavic origin.

THE REPUBLIC OF POLAND

153

A STATE WITH A GLORIOUS PAST

They have produced some of the great artists and scientists. Copernicus, who wrote a famous book in which he suggested that the earth actually moves around the sun and not the sun around the earth, was a Pole; so was Chopin, the composer; and so was Paderewski, the pianist, who was chosen prime minister of the Polish republic. Madame Curie (Marie Sklodowska), discoverer of radium, was born at Warsaw. Poland is the land of Ladislas Reymont and the birthplace of Joseph Conrad, to name only a few of her great ones.

Five out of every ten people in Poland live on the land. A Polish farmer can do wonders with a small tract; however, some of the very large estates were

THE DANCE FESTIVAL, A RED-LETTER DAY FOR POLISH VILLAGERS
Embroidered aprons, white linen dresses and fancy hair-do's for the girls and handsome cavalry jackets, breeches and boots for the men add a large measure of vivid color to a country festival. The lively dances of Poland, the mazurka, the kuyawiak, oberek and krakowiak, call for sure, nimble leg work—much stamping and kicking, bowing and twirling about.

SKIERS ENJOY THE STEEP, SNOWY MOUNTAINS NEAR ZAKOPANE

In southern Poland, close to the border of Czechoslovakia, is the resort town of Zakopane. It is about three thousand feet above sea level in a section of the Carpathians called the High Tatra. The town was founded in the sixteenth century and in later years became a fun and health center, with sanitoria and hotels for convalescents, sportsmen and vacationers.

A STATE WITH A GLORIOUS PAST

as large, in olden days, as little countries, and their owners ruled over them like princes. The size of some of the old estates can be imagined by the fact that the largest two were together as big as England. All the peasants were the serfs of the nobles. Although no longer serfs, Polish farmers have little freedom under the communist system of state control.

The Poles originated in the ancient pagan tribe of Slavs that made its way from the northern grasslands to the Vistula. Christianity came to Poland from Rome in 965 and the country has remained predominantly Catholic.

Boleslaus the Brave was the first King of Poland. He came to the throne in 1025 determined to withstand German aggression, but the Teutons gained a foothold two centuries later. In the thirteenth century Poland played an important role in preventing savage hordes of Mongolian Tatars from entering the green lands of Western Europe. On account of helplessness against the Germans, she became for a time united with Lithuania when her nobles persuaded Hedwiga to marry Jagiello, the Grand Prince of the more powerful country to the north. As King of Poland, he changed his name, in 1386, to Ladislas II, and together the two countries defeated the Knights on the field of Tannenberg (Grunewald) in 1410. In the sixteenth century Poland, under the leadership of John Sobieski, stopped the Turks on their way across Europe to make converts to Mohammed by the sword; and in 1683 came gloriously to the rescue when Austria was on the point of losing Vienna to the Turks.

Now came a time when the rulers of Poland's three most powerful neighbors were unusually covetous of Poland's mines and forests and her vast agricultural estates, which were held by a few nobles and worked by many serfs, with

TO MARKET, TO MARKET! TOWARD THE TOWN OF MINSK MAZOWIECKI
Not to be confused with the much larger city of Minsk in White Russia, Minsk Mazowiecki is not far from Warsaw. The hard-working peasants of this town see few automobiles. They carry their products to market in primitive wagons drawn by plodding horses. Once the majority of Poles were farmers, but the advance of industrialization is changing that.

THE CLOTH HALL IN THE MARKET PLACE OF KRAKOW

Planned and built in the thirteenth century, after the Tatars had laid waste nearly all of the old city, the famous Cloth Hall (Sukiennice) has been altered in some ways through the years; but it has retained its Moslem design. Krakow is a very ancient city, and this cobblestoned square still has an air of the Middle Ages about it.

A WOMAN OF THE FIELDS WITH MANY CHORES TO FILL HER DAY

A woman of a Polish farm leads a rickety donkey and rig back from the fields. The Government has made considerable efforts to equip the farms with tractors and other machinery.

TRAFFIC CONTROL WITH THE FEMININE TOUCH IN WARSAW

The policewoman is a familiar sight in Warsaw. The pistol strapped at her waist emphasizes her authority while the deep cuffs over her hands are meant to call attention to her directions.

no middle class whatever. Alarmed, Poland made the mistake of asking aid of non-Christian Turkey. Outraged Austria, Russia and Prussia sent troops into Poland and in 1772 divided a third of her territory among themselves.

Twenty-one years later Prussia and Russia again decided to help themselves to Poland. Within two years Poland was again divided, this time ceasing to exist as an independent state. Her national feeling persisted, however, despite laws forbidding even the reading of Polish literature. When World War I broke out, though entire regiments refused to fight and were shot down, other Poles were forced to fight in both the Russian and the German armies. Some Poles managed to escape to the Allies.

The Republic of Poland was proclaimed on November 9, 1918. In 1920 Bolshevik invaders burned the harvests, but their drive finally was repulsed. Poland had been fought over until fields were pitted deep with shell holes.

Negotiations at the Versailles peace conference granted Poland the provinces of Posen and West Prussia, with the exception of Danzig, which was set up as a free city. These territories were taken from Germany. From Russia and Austria, Poland received Vilna (eastern Lithuania), Galicia and part of Silesia.

A New Constitution

The government, based on the constitution of 1921, was democratic; there were two Houses of Parliament elected by all citizens over twenty-one years of age, and a president elected by Parliament.

Unfortunately the democratic constitution did not solve Poland's many difficulties. The German mark, which at that time was rapidly losing all value, was the standard national currency. The entire new republic suffered from the same inflation that was causing so much misery in her defeated neighbor to the west.

There were as many solutions to the financial ills of Poland as there were parties in Parliament, and these numbered from eight to ten. There were people favoring close co-operation with France. Others looked to Russia for help in spite of the fact that the new rulers in Russia —the Communists—were known to encourage attacks on Poland's eastern border. Public feeling in Poland had always tended to regard Russia with hate and fear. The most powerful party at the time was that of Joseph Pilsudski, who had led an army that fought with Germany and Austria during World War I against Russia.

Dictatorship and Inflation

Although his ruthless methods alarmed many people, Pilsudski had followers among both rich and poor and was able to take over the government as dictator in 1926. In solving Poland's first problem, inflation, Pilsudski felt that it would be necessary to weaken the constitutional rights of other parties. He planned to strengthen Poland's currency by withdrawing German marks and backing up a new exchange with revenues from high taxes. It was also necessary to place merchants, farmers and manufacturers under the tight control of government.

For a time he succeeded in his plans. He balanced Poland's budget; he reduced the nation's indebtedness to other countries and to people within Poland. Indeed, for three years before 1930, his treasury showed a surplus, and Polish products found markets throughout the world. Profits from exports paid for needed improvements within the country. People were not so drastically affected by the seasonal ups and downs of farm life. In days of plenty Pilsudski stored food. In days of scarcity he dipped into storehouses and distributed food to the needy. During this time of stability the dictator's opponents were seldom heard outside the halls of Parliament. But, because Poland depended on the stability of France and the other nations with which she traded, her prosperity was short-lived. She went down to ruin with France in the depression that swept the world in 1930. Pilsudski's government went deeply into debt. The former surplus was used up.

Another cause of unrest was Pilsudski's inability to get along with other nations.

THE CHIMNEY SWEEP ON HIS TRADITIONAL ROUND IN KATOWICE

Katowice on the Rawa River, where ancient practice and modern ways go hand in hand, is one of Poland's large cities. It is a manufacturing center situated in the vital coal-producing region of Silesia. Poland is richly endowed with coal deposits. The marked increase in coal mined in recent years has been an important factor in her industrial advance.

READY FOR A HOLIDAY IN THE SHADE OF A LACE BRIM
Costumes such as this are carefully treasured and donned only for special occasions. An embroidered satin and moire scarf is draped from beneath the brimmed hat with its tall crown.

He knew that Germany would never give up all control of Danzig, and that Lithuania would never allow a Polish corridor through that land. Yet he needed both Danzig and a port on the Baltic in Lithuania. He bargained at gunpoint and across the diplomatic council table to gain both ends. He failed; and as a result, his control of Poland was weakened. After his death in 1935, the nation was torn by violent strife and diplomatic indecision.

A Troubled Horizon

Each political party wanted to steer Poland in a different direction, at a time when a settled course was of the most vital concern. Hitler had gained control in Germany. He had forces massed on Poland's border, threatening to move in and capture Danzig.

Poland's eastern provinces, Galicia especially, were peopled by Ukrainians and White Russians—people who were never happy under Polish rule. Russia threatened to take up the cause of these peoples and annex a third of Poland. With Russia and Germany crowding her from east and west, Poland was doomed.

Hitler attacked in September of 1939 and shared the unhappy land with Russia, which moved in at the same time from the east. The Cabinet of Poland escaped first to Rumania and then went on to Paris and finally London. During World War II, the Cabinet organized those Poles who, like the members of the Government, had fled to France and England. It set up a fighting force to help defeat Germany and thus bring nearer the return of Poland's freedom. The Government-in-Exile also negotiated with Russia, once that nation had been invaded by Germany, to have Polish troops fight alongside the Red Army.

During the war, whether living in that part of their country controlled by Germany or by Russia, the Poles who remained at home had a hard time of it. Many were conscripted into the German army, most Jews and underground fighters were killed in purges, and many Poles were taken to work in German war plants. Those who escaped these terrors watched their property destroyed and lived in constant fear.

Poland was scarred deeply by the war. Her means of producing coal and iron and steel were completely ruined. Without the products of heavy industry she could not rebuild her cities and trade with other nations for the money that was needed to farm her rich but gutted land.

At the Yalta conference, Allied leaders granted the country the southern portion of East Prussia and the free city of Danzig, and took from her the troublesome lands bordering White Russia and the Ukraine. The western boundary was to be fixed when a peace treaty with Germany should be made. Awaiting that treaty, Poland was given the rights to all German territory east of a line formed by the Oder and Neisse rivers, including the important Baltic port, Stettin, which the Poles now call Szczecin. Actually, as a result of postwar arrangements, Poland has moved several hundred miles to the west. In the move she has gained the plentiful coal fields of Silesia, and a broad coastal front on the Baltic.

The postwar Government was set up by Communists and Socialists who either had stayed at home or had worked and fought with Russia. Following the usual communist policy, the Government has encouraged industry, somewhat to the neglect of agriculture. Most of Poland's money goes to building up the coal and iron and steel industries. This emphasis has resulted in a large movement of people from the farms to big cities.

Government Ownership

The Government, being thoroughly communistic, followed its model, the Soviet Government in Russia, and planned, at first, to bring all agriculture under its control. It intended to do away with private ownership of farms, placing all small holdings under collective management. This program has gone forward, but at a halting pace. Peasants have resisted the Government at almost every turn. And they resist because the one-party system that has kept the Government in power leaves them with no voice in Parliament.

A STATE WITH A GLORIOUS PAST

The parties that once represented the interests of the peasant class in the parliament no longer exist. Any member of these once powerful groups, as well as members of even the Communist Party, who refused to follow the orders sent out from the Russian Government, was liquidated—sent to prison, exiled, or silenced in some other way.

Though the war, communist rule generally and the build-up of industry in particular have virtually turned life in Poland upside down, many of the customs of country life have not changed.

Working in the fields, the peasant wears denims and tough leather shoes made by the thousands in Poland's many new factories. Yet he still dons the traditional, bright-hued costume for Sunday strolls or for festival days on the village green. In winter evenings the peasant women weave strips of colored cloth—orange and blue, or green and purple—then join the strips into coats of many colors.

Old-time merrymaking is still a part of harvest time in Poland; a corn-shucking or a barn-raising is the occasion for a feast and square dance, perhaps outdoors round a bonfire. The mazurka and polka, favorite Polish dance tunes, and others like the krakowiak, oberek and kuyuwiak send the couples whirling with a zest and flourish that are by no means confined to the young folks.

Of all the many holidays observed by the people of Poland, the most joyous

HAM AND BACON STILL ON THE HOOF AT A COUNTRY MARKET
A stockyard attendant looks over some of the hogs earmarked for slaughter in the busy Rawa Mazowiecka market. The town, twenty miles east of Lodz, is in a flourishing farm region.

QUAINT WINDMILL NEAR RADOM, ONE OF POLAND'S OLDEST TOWNS
Radom was supposedly founded in 1350 by Casimir the Great, although it is said that its first church was built in 1187. It was frequently the seat of Polish diets (parliaments).

Polish Research and Information Service

THE ORNATE TOWN HALL OF POZNAN

Both outside and in, the Town Hall is rich with reminders of the past. The structure was begun at the end of the thirteenth century, but in the years 1550–60 it acquired a late Renaissance appearance at the hands of John Baptist Quadro, an Italian architect. It contains one of Poland's most valuable collections of historic objects.

ASSEMBLING TRACTOR ENGINES IN A FACTORY NEAR WARSAW
Manufacturing plants like this have increased Poland's production in recent years. Out-of-date methods of peasant farmers are gradually giving way to modern machinery.

A QUIET MOMENT ALONGSIDE A PIER AT SZCZECIN
Formerly the German Stettin, Szczecin is one of Poland's main ports on the Baltic Sea. It lies at the head of the Oder River and is connected with Berlin by ship canal.

REMINDERS IN WARSAW OF THE OLD KINGDOM OF POLAND

The building was once the royal palace (Zamek Krolewski). It faces on Sigismund Square, which is a central point in the city. There were several kings of Poland named Sigismund; and this monument is to Sigismund III. Four main thoroughfares radiate from the square. One of them, called Krakowskie Przedmiescie, is considered the finest boulevard in the whole city.

AN APARTMENT HOUSE FOR WORKERS IN PRAGA

Praga is the industrial section of Warsaw, on the right bank of the Vistula River. The suburb has assumed greater importance in recent years as every effort is being made to industrialize Poland. With the increase in manufacturing, workers are drawn from the country, crowding such centers as Praga. Apartment houses like this help fill the need for dwellings.

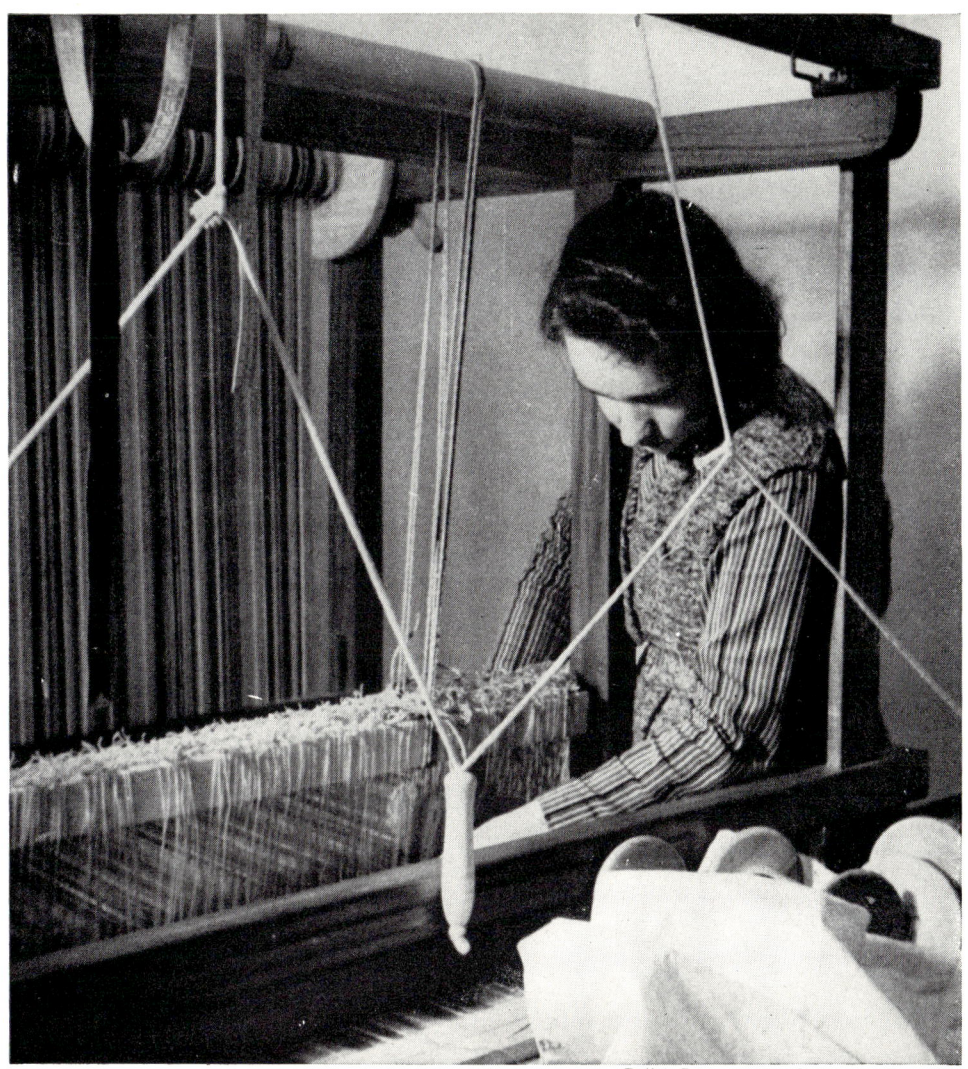

LEARNING THE ART OF WEAVING
This girl is acquiring a highly useful skill in a trade school in Warsaw. The loom is a rather old-fashioned one but it requires a higher degree of craftsmanship from the worker than would a more modern type. The Polish Government is bending every effort to industrialize the country and sets high value on the skills needed in factories.

feast is on Christmas Eve, starting sometimes at four in the afternoon, sometimes a little later. Beforehand, the mother will have made a little manger in an outbuilding, with perhaps a beautifully dressed doll in it, to show where Christ was born. At the feast a little wisp of hay is put under each person's dish as a symbol.

St. John's Eve was celebrated in old days by the country folk to drive away the evil spirits. Nowadays great bonfires are lit, and the young people gather around them, dressed in their brightest, to dance and sing. After a time the dancing becomes more and more rapid, the young men jump over the bonfire, to show how brave they are, and they pick up buckets of water and try to throw them over the girls, who run away.

All Poles love sport. The Polish countryman is a born horseman. The

COPERNICUS, HOLDING A SYMBOL OF HIS GREAT ACHIEVEMENT
Outside Staszic Palace in Warsaw, the seated figure of the Polish astronomer Nicolaus Copernicus holds out a small, simplified model of the solar system. His theory, first made known to the world in the year of his death, 1543, set forth the ideas that the earth revolves on an axis and that it and the other planets travel in regular orbits around the sun.

EASTFOTO

DANZIG, OR GDANSK, retains its medieval architecture in spite of time and destruction. At the end of the street is the graceful spire of the fourteenth-century Gothic city hall.

Uhlans, the famous German cavalry, were originally Poles, and Napoleon's Polish Lancers were well known.

There were large forests in parts of Poland in which once the lynx and beaver were to be found. A few bison are still seen, but the elk and wild goat have gone farther north. Sometimes brown bears are met, game birds there are in plenty, and wolves lurk in lonely woods, keeping out of sight unless they are driven by cold and hunger into the villages, to steal what animals they can. Wild boars are still brought in by huntsmen. Most of the country folk fear the wolves. Peasant women will whisper tales of how wolves came down to a village one bad winter and attacked and ate children; men will warn a stranger not to wander out alone at night without his shotgun; they will tell how packs have overwhelmed sleighs going through the forests, and have eaten first the horses and then the people. A favorite sport in northern Poland is to entice the wolves out of their hiding-places to kill them. A party of men starts out in a cart, the men concealing themselves as well as they can under hay. They hang a young pig in a sack from the rear of the cart, and its loud squeals attract the attention of the wolves which creep up to seize it and are then shot by the men.

The rivers play a big role in Polish life. Poland's greatest river, the Vistula, flows through the heart of the country from the Carpathian Mountains to the Baltic Sea. The Vistula and its tributaries drain the major portion of Poland and form its natural and historical pathway to the sea. The many tributaries of the Vistula keep the country fertile and enable the people to travel easily from one part to another. The rivers abound in fish; and in winter, when they may be frozen over for six months, they make fine roads for sledges.

To the south, in the foothills of the Carpathian Mountains, the flowing streams provide sources of water power. Before World War II, work on dams was begun, to use this power; and construction is going forward again. The center of this activity is where the San River flows into the Vistula. Around the junction of these two rivers, the Polish Government has started to build a vast industrial region that eventually will cover about 24,000 square miles.

POLAND: FACTS AND FIGURES

THE COUNTRY

This country of central Europe is bounded on the west and north by Germany, the Baltic Sea and Lithuania, east by Russia, and south by Rumania, Hungary and Czechoslovakia. It is drained by a number of important rivers, including the Vistula and the Dniester, while in the south the wooded range of the Carpathian Mountains forms a natural boundary. Total area is 120,359 square miles, compared to 150,433 in 1939. Total population is 28,000,000, compared to 34,775,698 in 1939. Poland is about four-fifths as large as it was in 1939, as it lost eastern Poland to Russia at the end of World War II.

GOVERNMENT

The Republic of Poland has been governed under a 32-article interim constitution, called "the little charter," since 1947. Power is divided between the president, executive (council of ministers), the Sejm (a one-house parliament) and the Council of State. In 1955, 3 new members were added to the latter which is composed of the president, 3 vice-presidents of Parliament, the head of the Supreme Control Board and 3 other members. Poland is communist-dominated; Politburo holds the real power. Resistance to Russia, however, broke out in 1956.

COMMERCE AND INDUSTRIES

Chief occupations of the people are agriculture and, since World War II, industry. The main crops are potatoes, rye, sugar-beets, oats, wheat, barley, hemp, hops and chicory. The Polish state placed a limit on the size of holdings. Stock-raising is important also. Over one-fifth of the area is forest-covered. The minerals include coal, iron, salt, petroleum and potash. Other industries are manufactures of textiles and paper, chemicals, timber, iron, and oil-refining and sugar-refining. The principal exports are cereals, dairy produce, timber, sugar, flax, coal, iron, steel, petroleum, chemicals and textiles. Imports: fertilizers, machinery, and foodstuffs. Monetary unit, the zloty.

COMMUNICATIONS

There are 17,500 miles of railways, state-owned; 66,875 miles of roads; 21,250 miles of telegraph wires; 947,500 miles of telephone lines. There are about 3,089 miles of navigable waterways.

RELIGION AND EDUCATION

No established church and ostensibly all creeds tolerated. Roman Catholicism is the religion of the majority. Education free and elementary education obligatory. There are 74 colleges for teachers and 764 professional and technical schools. There are 26 universities and other institutions of university rank.

CHIEF TOWNS

Warsaw (capital), 965,000; Lodz, 670,000; Cracow, 400,000; Poznan, 372,000; Wroclaw (Breslau), 374,000; Szczecin (Stettin), 209,000; Gdansk (Danzig), 226,000; Katowice, 200,000; Bydgoszcz, 200,000; Czestochowa, 145,000; Chorzow, 142,000; Zabrze, 133,000; Gliwice, 128,000; Bytom, 121,000; Gdynia, 120,000; Lublin, 129,000.

In Three Baltic Countries

People of Esthonia, Latvia and Lithuania

On the eastern shore of the Baltic Sea there are four countries which, until after World War I, were just provinces of Russia. The largest of them, Finland, we deal with elsewhere. Three—Esthonia (also spelled Estonia), Latvia and Lithuania—appear in this chapter. The people of these countries kept their ideas of freedom during the years of Russian rule; they became free at last as a result of World War I. They maintained their independence for a little more than twenty years. In 1939 Russia compelled them to allow their ports to be used as Russian naval bases. In 1940 she occupied them; they soon became sovietized in the Russian fashion. When the Germans attacked Russia in June, 1941, they invaded Esthonia, Latvia and Lithuania. After Germany's defeat, the three little republics again became members of the Soviet Union.

CENTURIES ago strange tribes from the northern grasslands of Asia came driving their flocks and herds before them and settled along the eastern border of the Baltic Sea. At that time Western Europe was still primeval forest, and these people long known as Letts, Esthonians (or Estonians), and Lithuanians, were sturdy fire and sun-worshipers. The Letto-Lithuanian languages were the oldest in Europe—older, even, than Latin—in fact, allied to the Sanskrit of ancient India. The Esthonians pastured their herds in the marshy, green lakelands between the Gulf of Finland and the Gulf of Riga; while the Lithuanians appear to have settled between the rivers Salis and Vistula, and the Letts between these two peoples. They did not voluntarily accept Christianity until near the end of the fourteenth century.

About the middle of the fifteenth century the federal state of Livonia was founded. It included the Esthonia and the Latvia of to-day. It is interesting to know in this connection that the word Livonian means sword-bearing and that the Livonian Knights of about 1200 formed the nucleus of the Teutonic Knights and in 1237 united with them, but separated in 1521. Russia, Poland and the Scandinavian countries contended for control of the region, and finally Lithuania was combined with Poland. With the partitions of Poland, all of the region fell to Russia. However, many of the great landowners were Germans, and in the cities the leading people were rich German tradesmen. The real rulers of the country were the German barons who, from their castles, kept the people serfs and almost slaves. Even when Russia declared that all serfs were free, the Germans managed to keep them in subjection, by propaganda in school and church.

In World War I, the German armies invaded the Baltic provinces, and there was much fighting, in the course of which many of the castles and estates of the old barons were destroyed, and many cities and villages burned. Not until the end of the war did the peasants obtain arms that enabled them to fight for their freedom. Driving out the Russians, in 1918 they declared their independence as three separate countries.

They succeeded in retaining their independence until World War II. In the year 1939 Russia had forced them to allow her to establish naval bases on their shores. In the following year the Russians occupied all three countries, claiming that their governments were decidedly unfriendly to Russia. In 1940, the three republics voted to become a part of the Soviet Union. From 1941 to 1945 German troops occupied the area; after the defeat of Germany Soviet Russia once more took possession of Esthonia, Latvia and Lithuania.

During the long period that they were under czarist rule they had not been allowed to learn their own languages in the schools. In Lithuania, for forty years the people had books printed abroad and smuggled across the border. Several thousand men were at one time sent to Siberia for using a prayer book that had been so smuggled. From 1918 until 1940, when the three countries were independent republics, each revived its mother tongue. Their languages are so difficult for foreigners to learn, however, that most townspeople, especially those engaged in trade, had to be able to speak one or more other tongues.

The Baltic peoples are still multilingual. Today, as one might expect, the second language is Russian. Street signs display both the native tongue and Russian.

Geographical location no doubt was one of the reasons the Soviet Union so eagerly seized the three countries again in 1940. They lie along the Baltic Sea, Estonia being the northernmost and Lithuania the southernmost, with Latvia in between. On the north, Estonia is separated from the republic of Finland by the Gulf of Finland. Russia proper and Poland form the boundaries on the east and south.

Before 1940 most of the people were either farmers, fishermen or lumbermen. Estonia and Latvia are still largely agricultural and practically all the farms are collectivized. Rye is the grain best adapted to the northern climate. Potatoes also grow well and form such a staple food of the people that Estonia, for example, used to be called the Potato Republic. Lithuania also has its share of collective farms but has forged ahead to a considerable extent in industry.

Large tracts of the Baltic states are thickly forested to this day, chiefly with pine and fir. As for minerals, Estonia has shale of high quality, which yields gas and synthetic liquid fuel. The gas is carried by pipeline as far as Leningrad. About 10 per cent of the total area of Latvia is covered with peat bogs.

In general the Balts are tall, blond and energetic. Just how many are left in their native lands no one knows. In Riga, Latvia, it is thought that about 40 per cent of the present-day population is Russian, compared to only about 4 to 6 per cent before the war. Actual living conditions in the Baltic states are also hard to determine, as no Western visitors were permitted there for a long time. In 1956 a Swedish warship was allowed to stop briefly at Riga and her crew reported appalling stories of squalor and cruelty.

Then, in 1957, the same city was opened to a few Western correspondents. There seemed to have been some changes in Riga at least. According to one writer, the Letts had not lost their pride in their old capital and still spoke of it as "another Paris." But the charming little medieval shops were barred with iron shutters and their artisans were engulfed in Soviet factories. And the city was strangely quiet.

Living quarters, as elsewhere in the U.S.S.R., are depressingly cramped. The ordinary person has neither space nor privacy. Central heating is rare indeed. A family may consider itself lucky if it has a room containing one of the old-fashioned stoves, which stretch from floor to ceiling.

In winter the waters of the Gulf of Finland and the Baltic Sea freeze. Once upon a time it was dangerous and lonely for the crews when ships were frozen in and held fast. No one knew where they were and they could not send for help. Sometimes the men starved to death. If a ship is icebound today, messages can be sent by radio. If food runs short, an airplane can drop supplies. The crew can also wait more easily, listening to the

SOVFOTO

CLOTH BY THE MILE streams from a textile mill in Riga, the capital of Latvia.

A WOMAN OF LATGALE IN THE TRADITIONAL DRESS OF THE REGION
The old-time costume of Latgale, a province in southeastern Latvia, includes a voluminous, beautifully embroidered mantle and a modestly decorated bonnet of white linen.

STUDENTS OF THE ZITHER, A POPULAR INSTRUMENT IN LATVIA

The zither is often played to accompany folk songs as its twang is as homely a sound as that of a banjo though it sometimes can be made to produce an extremely eerie tone. Four or five of the zither's strings, which carry the melody, are plucked with a plectrum worn on the thumb. The twenty-five to forty other strings are thrummed with the fingers of the other hand.

PHOTOS. SOVFOTO

A DREAM OF APPARENT ABUNDANCE IN A LATVIAN MARKET

The shop displays a huge stock of sausages and bologna, a ham and other meats and assorted delicacies as well as rows upon rows of bottles in the showcases. Though the Soviet Government announces periodic price reductions, many items of food are scarce and others, such as good cuts of fresh meat and good butter, are so expensive that few people can afford them.

RIGA'S SKYLINE FROM THE RIVER

Behind Riga's new embankment on the Dvina (Daugava) River rise the spires of her famous Gothic churches. Riga was a member of the Hanseatic League—a confederacy of cities in the Baltic area, Germany and Holland that flourished in the thirteenth and fourteenth centuries. Some of the old Hanseatic storehouses and granaries still stand in the old section of Riga.

A COLLECTIVE FARM, LATVIA

Most of Latvia's individual farms have been thrown into large collectives and are managed according to the Soviet pattern. Agricultural implements move from farm to farm, from a central tractor station. Latvia is an agricultural country, raising barley, rye, wheat and other grains, flax and potatoes. The raising of livestock is important, and there is much timber.

wireless concerts broadcasted from different stations.

The Baltic sailors have always been renowned for their courage, and in olden times they were famed for something less creditable, for there were many pirates among them who raided coast towns and attacked lonely ships. One of the most terrible of these Baltic pirates and the last of them all was Baron Ungern Sternberg. He was the lord of an island, and from his house he would, on winter nights, hang out false lights to lure passing ships on to the rocks where they would be wrecked; whereupon he would kill their crews and seize their cargoes. His deeds were discussed the world over, and even in the streets around the London docks notices were posted as a warning to sailors, saying, "Beware of Ungern Sternberg the Sea Robber."

For years no one dared stop him, but at last he was seized; and when his house was examined, vast quantities of goods that had been taken from lost ships were found under the floor. He was put in

ALONG THE WATER FRONT OF ONE OF TALLINN'S TWO HARBORS

The city, which is on a small bay in the Gulf of Finland, ships large quantities of lumber and is also a shipbuilding center. Though it is so far north, the harbors are frozen for only about forty-five days a year. The name "Tallinn"—which means "Danes' city"—dates from the late Middle Ages when Estonia was a Danish dominion. Today the Russians call the city Revel.

178

SCHOOL CHILDREN AT THEIR DAILY LESSONS IN PARNU, ESTONIA

School attendance is required for seven years in the small Baltic country. Education is on the Soviet pattern, but there is still a strong urge within Estonia to preserve the old culture.

A HERD OF COWS AT A MODERN CATTLE-BREEDING FARM, ESTONIA

Blessed with sufficient rainfall and with a moderate climate because of her nearness to the sea, tiny Estonia is predominantly a farming country, and dairying is an important occupation. Dairy factories are often co-operative, and the majority of farms are organized on a collective basis. The raising of poultry, sheep, pigs and horses rivals the cattle industry.

TEACHING A NEW GENERATION HOW TO REPAIR FISHING NETS
Though this man earns his living chiefly from the sea, he is fortunate in having a little coastal farm besides. Cow and chickens add up to considerable comfort for an Estonian family.

A BAND OF CHORISTERS OFF TO AN ESTONIAN SONG FESTIVAL
Down a broad boulevard of Tallinn swing files of grinning girls on their way to a gigantic national songfest. The costumes show the Estonian love of color and rich decoration.

A WATCHTOWER THAT LOOKED INTO THE KITCHENS OF OLD TALLINN
Kiek in de Kök, which, in an old German dialect, means "look into the kitchen," is a round tower built in the early sixteenth century as part of the walled fortifications of old Tallinn.

A BIRD'S EYE VIEW OF VILNIUS, LITHUANIA'S OLD CAPITAL

The city lies partly on the banks of the Vilija River and partly in the hills. Postwar building has greatly changed the appearance of this picturesque city dating from the tenth century.

PASSENGER MOTOR SHIPS CHUG ON THE NEMAN RIVER, LITHUANIA

The Neman River is the most important inland waterway in the country, and 266 miles of its course, about half of it, are in Lithuania. One of its many important uses is to float timber.

PHOTOS, SOVFOTO

ON THE ALERT IN A PAPER FACTORY IN PETROSHUNY

The two major resources of Lithuania are timber and agricultural products. Its more than two million acres of forests produce timber for export and also for pulp for the paper mills at home.

183

prison, dressed as a peasant and brought to trial with chains around his hands and feet, for people still feared him. He was then sent into exile in Siberia, and his name was struck off the roll of the nobility.

In the old days, when there were few roads in the Baltic States and the peasants could not easily get from one place to another, they spent much of their time in winter carving beautiful furniture and embroidering fine apparel. Pictures show the Baltic people of other days with embroidered shoes, the women with embroidered white linen bodices, dark striped skirts and high hats of many colors. They had to wear short skirts in winter because the snow was so deep.

Value a Good Education

The villagers, even when they were serfs, valued schooling, and now that they are their own masters, these Baltic peoples mean to have their children well educated. Therefore these countries spend a proportionately generous amount on good schools and universities, some of which, like that of Dorpat, are hundreds of years old.

Black Rye Bread the Staple

Black rye bread is the mainstay of the peasants and a favorite even with wealthier people, as are strong cheeses. One Baltic specialty is an elaborate cake decorated with colored sugar. Fish from the rivers have ever formed an important article of diet, whether eaten fresh, smoked or pickled.

The long winter of the Baltic lands is so cold that most of the country folk wear valenka—high felt boots made in the Russian style. These are exceptionally warm, though not waterproof. Those who can afford to do so dress in furs; those who cannot have clothing padded with wool. In winter the people get from place to place by means of horse-drawn sleighs; and a sleigh ride over the snow, with the harness bells tinkling, is a jolly experience.

Spring sometimes brings disaster, because when the river ice begins to thaw, pieces float down stream and often get jammed together, forming dams. Then the rivers overflow, sometimes flooding whole villages. To prevent these floods the ice-dams are often blown up with charges of dynamite; but there is still the risk of the broken ice tearing down the river and perhaps sweeping away bridges and damaging buildings on the banks.

The port city of Reval, now called Tallinn, is the capital of Esthonia. It was originally a large castle, one of the biggest in Northern Europe. It was built upon a hill and surrounded by strong walls. The castle still stands and much of the walls remain. Just below them come ancient streets on which one sees horse-drawn droshkies, the drivers of which wear red sashes. There are almost no motor cars. There are houses with steep roofs of red tile and churches with round towers and narrow steeples. Around the market place one sees arched entrances and high-walled courtyards reminiscent of four hundred years ago.

Reval, a Walled City

Reval has had need of its castle and strong walls, for there has probably been as much fighting around this city as anywhere in Europe. For hundreds of years armies have fought for and tried to capture it. What is true of this fine city has been true of the country as a whole.

In our century it has changed masters many times. Before the first world war it was a part of the old Russian Empire. It was occupied by German troops during World War I; then it had about twenty years of freedom. Germany again occupied it during World War II. Esthonia became a member republic of the Union of Soviet Socialist Republics in 1940.

In Esthonia's great epic, Kálevi Poëg (The Son of Kálev), by Frederic Rheinhold Kreutzwald (1803-82), have been preserved no less than two thousand legends centring around a twelfth-century hero.

Riga, the capital of Latvia and the largest port of the Baltic States, is modern, but it has an old quarter where women sweep narrow, cobbled streets, deliver

ESTONIAN LEGATION

THE ESTONIANS are related to the Magyars of Hungary. Their native dress is characterized by a durable long skirt and sleeveless woolen bodice worn over a launderable guimpe. The embroidered sleeve bands in bright colors, with cuffs, belts and hems to match, and the clean white aprons are not so individual as the heavy silver necklaces.

185

MARKET DAY IN MEMEL, A BALTIC CITY WITH A STORMY HISTORY

Memel, long a German city, went to the new state of Lithuania after World War I. Retaken by Germany in 1939, it was returned to Lithuania, now a part of Russia, in 1945.

cans of milk and shove wheelbarrows. The old city is a remnant of more prosperous days. Riga was once a member of the Hanseatic League. As such it thrived in the trade between the Scandinavian countries and the Byzantine Empire. During the nineteenth century, Riga grew to greatness. Under Russian rule, German traders and manufacturers built up the industry of the port. At the brink of World War I, it was the third largest city on the Baltic Sea, having more than a half-million residents. Only Stockholm and St. Petersburg (present-day Leningrad) then overshadowed Riga. Almost a quarter of the exports of tsarist Russia left its docks. After World War I, Riga flourished as the capital and industrial center of the new Latvia. As the hub of many railroads and as the terminus for the pine timber that floated down the western Dvina from the forests of the interior, Riga grew in industrial wealth. It produced fine radios and telephone sets. There were factories making electric railway engines and cars, and others producing electric parts for autos.

Riga is built on both banks of the Dvina, ten miles from the river's entry into the Gulf of Riga. Within the city limits, but at a considerable distance from the heart of the city, is a lovely stretch of sand spits on the gulf. In summer these beaches used to attract thousands of visitors.

Another important Latvian port is Liepaja (better known as Libau; and Libava, in Russian). Unlike Riga, which is clogged during cold months, Liepaja is usually free of ice throughout the year. It, too, belonged to the Hanseatic League. Lithuania, Poland, Sweden, Germany and Russia have all controlled the port at various times. Today it is one of Russia's naval bases.

Lithuania's Old Capital

Vilnius (or Wilno, or Vilna), the capital of Lithuania, is one of the oldest cities in the Baltic region. Today it is third in size after Riga, and Tallin, in Estonia. For many centuries Vilnius has been the center of northeastern Polish, western Russian and Lithuanian trade. A university was established in the sixteenth century.

During 1920 in her drive against marauding Bolsheviks, Poland captured Vilnius. Lithuania demanded the return of its historic capital, but Poland refused to give it up even at the command of the League of Nations. An unwise treaty in 1923 granted the city to Poland. From then till 1939 Vilnius was a trouble spot. In 1939 Poland was invaded, defeated and divided by Russia and Germany. By the terms of the German-Russian non-aggression pact, which preceded the division of Poland, Russia occupied the Vilnius area and immediately returned the city to Lithuania. The Lithuanians hurriedly moved their capital from Kaunas, but they could not enjoy the gift for long. In 1940, Russia made Lithuania and its neighbors, Estonia and Latvia, a part of the Soviet Union of socialist states. Russian military leaders soon took control of both the Parliament and civil affairs in Vilnius and the other capitals.

The capital of Estonia is Tallinn (or Revel). It is also an important old city of the Baltic area. It has a fine harbor on the Gulf of Finland across the water from the Finnish capital, Helsinki, called Helsingfors in Swedish.

The Baltic People

The people of the Baltic states live in an area that awards mixed blessings. The ports and cities are crossroads of the important routes of north European trade. Except for the brief period of Lithuanian greatness in the Middle Ages, the Balts have never moved from their borders in order to strengthen the position at home. They have, instead, stayed within the frontiers to work, sometimes as slaves, for foreign overseers that have come to tap the wealth. The one opportunity—their twenty years of independence—to build and prosper was stopped short by the second World War. Today there is slim hope for a return of independence for many years to come.

A scattered barbarian population roamed over the lands of Latvia, Lithuania, Estonia and Russia during the first

OLD-TIME COSTUMES of the Letts are very rarely to be seen, save in the districts remote from the influence of the towns. A loose cloak, secured by a large, round metal brooch, is one of the most distinctive features of the national dress. The ornamentation varies according to the taste of the wearer and also according to the district.

THE WOMEN OF RUCAVA are especially noted, in Latvia, for their needlework. In this photograph we can see some of the beautiful embroideries and homespun clothing that they produce. The peasant women lead a hard life, for they start to work at the age of seven, and when they are fifteen they are supposed to undertake adult responsibilities.

millennium of the Christian Era. The Slavs pushed to the coast the relic peoples speaking primitive Indo-European tongues, who became Lithuanians and Latvians. They also drove westward into their respective territories the Estonians, Finns and Lapps from their northern Russian hunting grounds.

In old Russia the Baltic area was officially designated as the "Western Territory," which from Peter I onward served for commerce with the west. It comprised what became known as Peter's famous "window on Europe." Through a window, however, one can smile amiably at a neighbor, and also stick out a menacing rifle.

These windows now seem to be boarded up forever. Very little of what goes on behind them is known by the nations outside. Since 1940, when the republics became part of the Soviet Union, many natives of the unfortunate countries have wisely escaped westward.

Many who could not leave in time were sent from their homes to work in the interior of Russia. Large naval, air and army bases now fortify the Baltic coast.

ESTHONIA (ESTONIA), LATVIA AND LITHUANIA: FACTS AND FIGURES

ESTHONIA (ESTONIA)

The most northern of these three countries has Russia on the east, Latvia on the south, the Gulf of Riga and the Baltic Sea on the west and the Gulf of Finland on the north. The total area is 17,370 square miles and the population is 1,100,000. At the time of the Russian Revolution in 1917, Esthonia declared her independence of Russia and by the Treaty of Tartu in 1918, Soviet Russia recognized it as an independent country. In 1940, after ten months of Russian occupation, Esthonia's communist government voted to join the Soviet Union.

Agriculture and dairying occupy about 33% of the people. Potatoes, oats, barley, rye and wheat are the principal crops and the dairy factories, 87% of which are co-operative, produce a large amount of butter, which is the chief export. Forests cover 21.5% of the area and timber is also exported. The other industries are oil-shale mining, shipbuilding and manufacture of electrical machinery. Giant hydro-electric power station on Narva River. Most of the population are Lutherans, the rest Greek Orthodox and Catholics. Elementary education is compulsory. There are universities at Tartu and Tallinn. Chief towns: Tallinn (Revel), capital, 146,500; Tartu (Dorpat), 60,000.

LATVIA

Bounded on the north by the Gulf of Riga and Esthonia, on the east by Russia, on the south by Lithuania and White Russia, on west by Baltic Sea and Gulf of Riga. The total area is 25,000 square miles and the population 2,000,000. From 1918, when Latvia gained her independence from Russia, until 1940 a democratic republic. In July 1940, Latvia became a member of the U.S.S.R.

The people are occupied mainly with agriculture but industrial life is increasing. Rye, barley, oats, potatoes and flax are the principal crops. Stock-raising is carried on extensively. Other industries: electrical machinery and machine-tool manufacturing, shipbuilding and fishing. Lumber is chief export.

There are 1,863 miles of railway and 2,775 miles more of navigable inland waterways. Telegraph lines, 2,265 miles and telephone lines, 24,879 miles. Fifty-six per cent of the people are Protestant and the rest Roman Catholic and Greek Orthodox. Elementary, secondary and higher education. Academy of Sciences with 16 research institutes; university at Riga. Chief towns are: Riga, the capital, 600,000; Liepaja (Libau), 100,000; Daugavpils (Dvinsk), 45,200.

LITHUANIA

Bounded on the north by Latvia, on the east by White Russia, on the south by White Russia and Poland and on the west by the Baltic Sea. Total area, 25,000 square miles; population, 2,700,000. The independence of Lithuania was proclaimed in 1918 and was formally recognized in 1922. The constitution adopted that year was democratic, but in 1926 Parliament collapsed and a dictator controlled single-party elections and Parliament from then until 1939 when Russia occupied Lithuania. In July 1940 the new communist Parliament voted to join the Soviet Union.

Agriculture and industry are the chief occupations. Wheat, barley, oats, potatoes, peas, and flax are grown. Poultry-raising, goose-farming, stock-raising and bee-keeping are important. 16.3% of the land is forest-covered. Exports consist of timber, foodstuffs, flax and linseed; and the imports are textiles, food and agricultural machinery. There are 1,917 miles of railway and 397 miles of navigable waterways. The majority of the population is Roman Catholic. There are about 1,300 schools. Universities at Kovno and at Vilnius; there is also an Academy of Sciences. Chief towns: Vilnius (Vilna) 160,000; Kaunas (Kovno), 150,000; Klaipeda (Memel), 47,000. Ruble is monetary unit of these countries.

CZECHOSLOVAKIA

Land between Yesterday and Tomorrow

"He who holds Bohemia commands Europe," says an old proverb. The Victory of Austerlitz, a town in Moravia, gave Napoleon command of central Europe. In our century the fortunes of Czechoslovakia—which consists of the old provinces of Bohemia and Moravia, and of Slovakia and part of Silesia—have twice affected the fate of the world. Hitler's seizure of the borderlands, under the Munich Pact, 1938, was the prelude to World War II. Ten years later, the Communists' sudden grasp of power in Czechoslovakia ushered in the cold war. Today the once free country is shrouded in the gray pall of communism.

IT is perhaps a sign of the sad times that today Czechoslovakia's most important railroad line runs eastward from Prague—by way of Zilina, Slovakia—to Cierne at the border of Czechoslovakia and the Soviet Union. Since 1945, when the Russians annexed the former eastern province of Ruthenia, or Carpatho-Ukraine, Czechoslovakia and the U.S.S.R. have had sixty miles of common boundary. Beyond the frontier the railroad continues, by way of Lvov, to Kiev. It is one of the oldest lines in Czechoslovakia, built in the 1880's when the country belonged to the Hapsburg monarchy. Then the railroad was a single-track line, little known. Few travelers went east.

In 1955, a new double-track line was opened on this route, after more than a billion koruny, or crowns (about $140,000,000), had been spent. Tunnels were cut, new embankments, viaducts and steel bridges were built, more than nine million cubic yards of rock were removed, and thirty-three housing projects were constructed along the route. The rulers of Czechoslovakia considered the money well spent. Traffic volume with the Soviet Union had risen thirty times between 1947 and 1955. It is over this route that Soviet raw materials are brought to the factories and armament plants of Czechoslovakia and returned as finished products to the Soviet Union. At the same time, the once important double-track lines between Prague and the western borders are little used. Between Prague and Vienna, the capital of Austria, only a couple of passenger trains go every day.

The foregoing facts point up the tragedy of Czechoslovakia's recent history. Of all the countries that today lie in the Soviet orbit, Czechoslovakia was the most Westernized. Its history, traditions and standards of education, the habits and the mental and emotional make-up of its people were linked with the Western world. Millions of Czechs and Slovaks went abroad, to the United States, Canada and South America. It used to be said that the largest Czechoslovak city was Chicago, Illinois. This was an exaggeration. Nevertheless it was true that the emigrants kept close ties with their homeland. Many, after winning success in the New World, came home to retire and to die in their native country. After World War I the largest railroad station in Prague was named for President Woodrow Wilson.

The land is beautiful. On the west the plateau of Bohemia is encircled by mountains—the Sudeten, the Erz (Ore) and the mountainous Bohemian Forest. On the northeast, the great ranges of the Carpathians, including the High Tatra, reach toward the sky. Part of the southern border is formed by the Danube River, winding there through low hills. Men have cleared the plains and the valleys, but the mountains remain covered with the thick growth of coniferous woods.

Among other differences between western and eastern Czechoslovakia is one of climate. The country lies astride the climatic divide of Europe. In the west, extreme temperatures are fairly rare. Prague, for instance, has a January average of 27° F. and a July average of

SHEEPSKIN JACKETS, worn woolly side in and with the outside gaily ornamented, are the outdoor wear of both men and women in the mountainous Carpathian region. This sturdy peasant, with his leather satchel and ribboned hat, is ready to go to market. Shoes are a luxury, but the trails are stony, and he has bound his feet, layer upon layer, with cloth.

FLORENCE FARMBOROUGH

IN THE EASTERN part of Czechoslovakia the women don their sheepskin coats and tie gay kerchiefs around their heads when they carry their farm produce to market. Market day is always a good gossip day, and many such groups of peasants may then be seen chatting by the roadside, with their wares, chiefly onions, on the ground before them.

THE SMETANA MUSEUM (left) in Prague overlooks the Vltava (Moldau) River. It is a fitting location as one of Smetana's most justly celebrated compositions is called *The Moldau*.

CZECHOSLOVAKIA, combination of ancient provinces—Bohemia, Moravia, Slovakia, Silesia

67° F. This section gets about twenty inches of rain a year, mainly in the summer. However, Bohemia and Moravia do have dense fogs in winter, when the weather can be acutely uncomfortable. Slovakia is hotter in summer and colder in winter.

Though the population of Czechoslovakia is largely Slavic, there are several different groups, of which the Czechs and the Slovaks are the largest. They are a strong people, with well-proportioned bodies, rounded heads, round faces, blond to brown hair and blue or brown eyes. Sharp profiles with upturned noses are common. The western Czechs usually are more fair in coloring than the eastern Slovaks.

The languages of the Czechs and Slovaks are similar. Most people who speak one understand the other though they may not be able to write it. Too, there has been so much intermarriage among Czechs, Slovaks, Germans, Jews and Hungarians in this part of Europe that many people are really a healthy mixture of many stocks. German tribes of Bavarian, Saxonian and Silesian ancestry have lived here since the Middle Ages. Traces of this medieval background may be seen in small towns, where traditional styles in buildings and in costumes have survived through the centuries.

Among the smaller, still distinct groups is the Chod tribe in southern Bohemia, whose tongue is a dialect called Chodsky. The Wallachians, Slonzaks and Water Polaks of Moravia speak a special argot, a mixture of Czech and Polish. In southern Moravia there are several villages of Croats, who have kept their ancient tongue.

Not so many years ago some eighty thousand gypsies wandered in Slovakia. They earned an uncertain living as peddlers and entertainers. No country fair was complete without gypsy musicians. The gypsies were a familiar sight, their horse-drawn caravans followed by dirty, unkempt children, prowling dogs and dark-haired women trying to snatch a chicken or a goose along the road. No amount of effort by the authorities could make them settle down. The present Government has finally achieved the impossible: today a great many gypsies are reluctantly going to work in factories and mines.

Relations between Czechs and Slovaks never were happy. Bohemia and Moravia have a proud history, fertile soil and thriving industries. Slovakia, dominated for centuries by the Magyars (Hungarians), has always been poor. Its poverty-stricken people attained neither the educational nor the economic standards of

HOLIDAY CLOTHES are brightly colored and embroidered in the land of the Czechs. The skirts are short to show the high leather boots worn by mother and daughter alike. The child's flowered muslin looks very simple beside her mother's finery, but perhaps she has not put on her best frock. Yellow ears of drying corn are seen hanging from the eaves.

PAINTED BANNERS are borne high in the air by these six Slovak men who head the procession which, to celebrate the name-day of its patron saint, winds through the streets of a village in the present Slovakia. The men wear their gala clothes—sleeveless jackets with many buttons, full-sleeved white shirts and white embroidered trousers.

A SQUARE FOUNTAIN marks the center of a cobblestoned village in the Sudetenland. A mountainous region bordering on Germany, it had a large German population before World War II.

their Slav cousins in the western provinces.

Visitors to Bohemia and Moravia were rarely encouraged to go to Slovakia, and with good reason. Mountainous Slovakia is mostly a rural section, with only about 180 persons to the square mile (compared to almost 300 in the western parts of the country). During the centuries of Hungarian domination the rich landowners lived in feudal state while the peasants often worked under medieval, serflike conditions. By law, each son inherited an equal share of his father's property; each received equal shares of good, bad and indifferent land. It is for this reason that, seen from an airplane, Slovakia's farming areas looked like crazily patterned carpets. Often a poor farmer might own a dozen tiny patches of land, each so distant from the others that he would be unable to work all of them. When he died, his land was divided still further. Shortly before the second World War, about 30 per cent of all Slovak landowners were dwarf holders and 20 per cent owned no land at all. Their best course was to emigrate toward the western parts of the country—or even farther west, to North America.

The old Slovak villages were never very cheerful sights. The small thatched houses had no chimneys. Livestock lived under the same roof, often in the same room, with the family. In some regions, tobacco, wine grapes and maize (corn) were grown. By and large, however, the farm products of Slovakia were of lower quality than in the western provinces.

Such contrasts helped to keep old resentments alive; they still persist. Even when the Republic was formed after World War I, the Czechs wanted to run Slovakia from Prague and the Slovaks were afraid they would be swallowed up by the Czechs. The friction was eased at certain times when great statesmen—Masaryk, Benes, the Slovak leader Milan Hodza—managed to bring about a temporary state of cordial relations.

The earliest inhabitants of Czechoslovakia on record, however, were neither German nor Slav tribes but two Celtic groups, the Boii and the Cotini. The Boii lived in the Bohemian basin and gave it the name that still remains. The first Czech tribes appeared in the middle of the fifth century, in the valley of the Elbe. During the following five centuries, various Bohemian kingdoms were established, among them the kingdom of the Premyslides near the junction of the Vltava (Moldau) and Elbe rivers.

The land knew little peace, however. It was constantly being contested among Slavs, Germans and Magyars. It is Bohemia's tragic fate to be landlocked. Attack could come from any side.

CZECHOSLOVAKIA

The Premyslide house died out in 1306. Four years later, a German prince, John of Luxembourg, was elected king of Bohemia. The most brilliant chapter in Czech history was written by his son, Charles. About the time he became king of Bohemia, in 1346, he also became the Holy Roman Emperor, as Charles IV. For a time, Prague was the empire's capital. The city's architecture still reminds one of this great era in its history. Charles rebuilt the two great defensive settlements of the Hradcany and Vysehrad. Hradcany's main palace was designed and built by Matthew of Arras. This architect also rebuilt the Gothic cathedral of St. Vitus, which had been planned in the reign of King John to replace an earlier Norman basilica. A number of Holy Roman emperors and Bohemian kings are buried in the cathedral, including "Good King Wenceslas."

The most famous of Prague's many spans across the Vltava, Charles Bridge, was completed, in 1357, by Peter Parler, a German architect. With its tower gateways and statues of saints, among them John of Nepomuk, the patron saint of Bohemia, it is a magnificent structure. It connects the Old Town, which grew up in the fourteenth century, with the New Town, where a great many Czech artisans settled. Charles Bridge and the Gothic silhouette of Hradcany Castle still dominate the timeless beauty of Prague.

Charles was patron of a Prague school of painting, ordered the making of a Latin-Czech dictionary, and founded Charles University of Prague, one of the oldest on the Continent. It stood between the two parts of the city. One of its colleges was named for Charles—Carolinum. The university student body was very large, made up of Czechs, Saxons, Ba-

MARIANSKE LAZNE (Marienbad), among the mountains of western Bohemia, has been a famous health resort since the sixteenth century. The houses bespeak the splendor of an earlier day.

EASTFOTO

GOLD, RED AND BLUE are colors always found in the holiday attire of a Czech peasant girl, and part of her dress is likely to be spotlessly white. She does not usually wear silks and satins, but works on the commonest of materials with a needle and gold thread until she has a dress so rich that it enhances her peculiarly vivid beauty.

varians and Poles. Scholastic standards were among the highest in Europe. The schools of philosophy and theology at Prague provided the background for the following centuries of Czech history. One of the greatest Czechs of all time, John Huss, was elected rector of the university in 1402. He was a religious reformer and his teachings brought on a long struggle, partly religious and partly political, called the Hussite wars.

Two outstanding leaders of the Hussites were Jan Zizka of Trocnov and George of Podebrad. George was king for a time. After his death, in 1471, the fortunes of Bohemia took a turn for the worse.

By this time the Hapsburgs, the German-Austrian ruling family, were becoming ever stronger. They had held sway in Austria since 1282 and had taken over the reins of the Holy Roman Empire in 1438. Thus the Hapsburgs were on the side of the Roman Catholic Church when, early in the sixteenth century, various groups began to split off and form Protestant churches. In history this period is called the Reformation. Combating it was the Counter Reformation of the Catholics. As we have seen, the Hussites were the Reformation leaders in Bohemia.

A Tragic Day in 1620

On November 8, 1620, the Hussite armies were defeated by Hapsburg forces in the Battle of the White Mountain, at the gates of Prague. That day the provinces of Bohemia and Moravia lost their independence, not to be regained for almost three hundred years. The battle was one of the first engagements in the Thirty Years' War, which wracked Europe from 1618 until 1648. It ended with the complete degradation of the Czechs. Not until 1848 did they regain their self-respect. That year was one of revolution in many parts of Europe, including Bohemia. The Czechs did not win all they hoped for, but out of their revolt a strong middle class emerged. Personal liberty and dignity were restored. From this position, bitterness against the Germans and Magyars was felt even more keenly.

The situation was brought into still sharper focus by the creation of the Austro-Hungarian Empire (the Dual Monarchy) in 1867. Relations between Austria and Hungary had long been confused and, at times, quarrelsome, though Hungary also was governed by Hapsburgs. As we have indicated, Bohemia and Moravia were under Austria; and Slovakia, under Hungary. Now Czechoslovakia was brought under one monarch.

When World War I broke out in 1914, various groups of Czech intellectuals and other leaders immediately closed ranks. Several of them were sent to prison, which did not help matters. The Czechs saw their opportunity and were determined to take it. Large numbers of the Czech troops, who had been forced to fight in the Austrian Army on the Eastern Front, escaped into Russian territory and formed the Czechoslovak Legions.

Masaryk, Beloved Leader

The greatest leader of all was Tomas Garrigue Masaryk (1850–1937). His wife was an American and he adopted her maiden name as his middle name. Their son, Jan, grew up speaking English, Czech and German equally well.

During the war, Masaryk and his pupil Eduard Benes worked actively in Canada and the United States for the liberation of their country from the Hapsburg yoke. Their efforts were crowned when, in Washington, D. C., on October 18, 1918, the independence of Czechoslovakia was proclaimed. Masaryk became president of the new Republic.

Life in what is now called the First Republic was pleasant. In general, the Czechoslovaks were a nation of middle-class people who understood the meaning of democracy and liberty. Unrest, civil war and dictatorship plagued Czechoslovakia's neighbors after the war. Czechoslovakia alone in central Europe had emerged from the ordeal as a healthy, democratic republic. Its constitution combined the best features of the constitutions of France and the United States.

There was no excessive wealth in the cities but there were no slums either.

A FAR CRY from grandmother's spinning wheel—a modern loom in a textile mill. The textile industry is part of a state trust organization, as are almost all Czech industries.

The people looked well-fed and well-dressed, and they faced the problems of life with vigor and cheerfulness.

One of the problems had to do with agriculture. Czechoslovakia is one of the richest farming regions in Europe. The old castles near the towns and on wooded promontories remind the traveler of past days, when large areas were ruled by landed lords. When these rich barons grew tired of living in the country, they would move to their baroque palaces and mansions in the cities. So the land was left to be tilled by people who could not own it. Consequently, one of the first actions of the new Government, in 1919, was to divide all large estates into smaller holdings and distribute them among the people. In due course more than two million acres either were given away in small lots to families who owned no land or were added to farms that were too small to be profitable. As often happens in such reforms, however, those who received the land were chosen for political reasons rather than on the basis of need. Among the favored groups were Czech Legionnaires and disabled servicemen, who were not always happy to leave the cities and become farmers.

The Free First Republic

In spite of these and other difficulties, the years of the First Republic today seem like a wonderful dream to a great many people in Czechoslovakia. There was freedom of expression and of thought. Although there were seventeen political parties in Parliament, always having noisy debates, the arguments were carried on in the healthy, democratic atmosphere of a free nation. No one was sent to prison for saying something that others did not like.

Education was there for all. Prague had a Czech as well as a German university. Music, plays, books and ideas were imported from both West and East. There were three opera houses in Prague and music lovers had the choice of several concerts every night. Prague had always been a music-minded city. Mozart, who wrote his *Don Giovanni* for the Old Guild Theater in Prague, where he conducted the first performance, once wrote that in Prague the people understood his music better than anywhere else.

Schweik, the Good Soldier

Prague had dozens of theaters: German and Czech, conservative and advanced, serious and satirical. The Czechs have always loved making fun of politics. One of the greatest Czech books of the past generation, *The Good Soldier Schweik*, is a devastating satire on narrowness and pettiness in both military and government life. Written by Jaroslav Hasek, a Czech journalist, the book relates the adventures of a Prague dog catcher. He is drafted into the Austrian Army during World War I and successfully disrupts army life on all levels, from privates to generals, by stubbornly carrying out stupid orders to the letter.

Before 1938, Prague was a favorite stopping place for visitors in Europe. Its beauty is not so dazzling as that, say, of Paris. Prague's beauty must be sought out. The façades of the ancient houses are irregular, and the old, cobblestoned streets are crooked. Among the city's landmarks is the oldest synagogue in Europe, with its strange, mid-thirteenth-century Gothic architecture. There the seat of the great Rabbi ben Joseph is still shown. Behind it is a Jewish cemetery founded in 1420. The Prague ghetto, a medieval settlement of Ashkenazic (northern European) Jews, was surrounded by walls and the entrances were locked by heavy chains from Friday sundown to Saturday sundown—the Hebrew Sabbath —so no one could get in or out. It was said that the golem, an artificial man of Hebrew legend, had come to life and was haunting the streets.

There were great palaces of baroque splendor, romantic squares with quaint stone fountains, mysterious byways, and old churches with tombs sunk deeply in the ground. Yet at the next corner there would be a modern office building made of concrete and glass, and by merely crossing the street you could move from the fourteenth to the twentieth century.

It was these medieval and modern features side by side that gave Prague its allure.

The shops were as beautiful as those of Paris and Vienna and Rome, and the restaurants were among the best of Europe. It is typical of the Czechs' healthy temperament that they have always been concerned with the pleasures of the table. Prague's automat buffets were as popular as the *halles* (markets) are in Paris or the fish restaurants in Genoa. The automats were open twenty-four hours a day and almost always crowded, forming a genuine sandwich democracy. Everybody went there, cabinet ministers and cabinetmakers, sales girls and wealthy women. Vast shelves held sandwiches in dozens of varieties besides sausages, hams and assortments of hot dishes, sweets and beverages. Businessmen conducted conferences at the automats, young couples held hands as they munched garlic-toasted bread and would-be politicians made spur-of-the-moment speeches there.

Lean Parky and Fat Vursty

Hardly less popular were Prague's smoked-sausage shops, often combined with a butcher shop. Sausages, hams and various other smoked meats were sold in the front room, fresh meat in the back room. Some citizens favored long, lean sausages called *parky,* and others preferred short, fat ones called *vursty.* They could argue for hours about the qualities of a particular sausage shop, and they would eat sausages all day long, beginning with breakfast. Prague's famous hams were the best in the world, perfectly cured, almost unsalted, delicious and tender. They were eaten hot. Ham eaters were considered a socially higher class of people than the sausage lovers!

The Czechs took a common-sense attitude toward the troubles and problems of life. This and their robust sense of humor have helped them to survive many trials. They went about their business with sober steadiness, less easy-going and charming than the Viennese, not so romantic as the Poles of Warsaw or so amusing and worldly as the citizens of Budapest.

Czechoslovakia's spirit is expressed perfectly by the music of its two foremost composers, Smetana and Dvorak—a beautiful mixture of homesickness, happiness and melancholy. Smetana's *Ma Vlast* (*My Country*) is Czechoslovakia's musical life story. There is music in the air. People love the moody folk songs, and on Sunday afternoons they used to go to small inns in the suburbs or to gardens to listen to Czech music.

Orchestras and Brass Bands

All over Europe, Bohemian musicians are found both in great symphony orchestras and in obscure dance bands. In fact, Bohemian musicians are as well-known exports as Bohemian glassware and beer. There was, and is, hardly a Czech family without at least one member who plays an instrument. Small villages have their brass bands, small towns their orchestras, and cities with a population of more than forty thousand have an opera house, performing ten months out of the year. Even the spas, the mineral-springs resorts, have their orchestras.

The great Bohemian spas of Karlovy Vary (Carlsbad), Marianske Lazne, Frantiskovy Lazne and Jachymov have given relief to countless people from all over the world who came there suffering from gout, chronic arthritis and a variety of other afflictions. The most famous spa, Karlovy Vary, was popular with people who had lived too well and not too wisely during eleven months of the year and went there for the twelfth month to atone for their gastronomic sins. At neighboring Marianske Lazne, the overweight could lose pounds fast by drinking the waters and taking long walks.

One of the loveliest and smallest of the resort towns was Jachymov (Joachimsthal) which has been known for more than five hundred years for both its mineral deposits, including silver, and its mineral waters. It was popular with Indian maharajas and North American millionaires who wanted to avoid the gala evenings and fashionable events of larger spas nearby. Along the quiet streets stood brightly painted and quaintly named

STAR IN METAL—an enormous part for a power generator. The shed is part of the Skoda factory, the vast metallurgical works in Pilsen. Today the plant is a communist arsenal.

MODERN LOOMS ARE SET for weaving cotton. The up-to-date factory is in the Liberec region of northern Bohemia, an important textile center since the early nineteenth century.

TO TEASE THE EYES and tempt the palate—boxes of sweets in gay wrappers. The candy factory is in the industrial city of Bratislava, in southwest Slovakia on the Danube River.

villas. It was pleasant to stroll the woods to small cafes in the Erzgebirge (Ore Mountains), where the air was crisp with the aroma of pines and the prices were reasonable.

For centuries, the Ore Mountains, running astride the border between what today are Germany and Czechoslovakia, have yielded valuable minerals, not only silver but tin, lead, bismuth, zinc and antimony. In 1727, large deposits of pitchblende, a greasy-looking ore that ranges in color from dirty brown to asphalt black, were discovered there. Pitchblende contains uranium and radium. It was from Joachimsthal pitchblende that the Curies, after years of experimentation, at long last extracted radium.

Czechoslovakia is rich not only in such natural resources as minerals and good soil but in its industrial capacity. The skill and inventiveness of the Czechoslovak people have a reputation that goes back over a long period. In the fifteenth century, glass vessels were made from the quartz sand of the Sumava mountains, in small forges that were stoked with charcoal. Throughout Europe, Bohemian glass was as famous as the glass from Venice. And the porcelain from the Karlovy Vary district has been known equally as long. These industries were developed further by two enlightened Hapsburg rulers, Maria Theresa and her son, Joseph II.

In northern Bohemia and in Moravia, textile mills began to hum at an early date. Liberec (Reichenberg) made woolen cloth and Trutnov made linen. Silk weaving started in Moravia, not far from the markets of Vienna. In the nineteenth century, the wool and flax were superseded by cotton. By the early twentieth century there were over three million cotton spindles in the country.

The textile mills of Bohemia and Moravia supplied the cloth for the uniforms of the old Austrian Army which was better known for its elegant color combinations than for its fighting qualities. During the Battle of Königgrätz, in 1866, many Austrian officers were killed be-

A JUMBLE OF PEAKED ROOFS in the midst of the Bohemian Forest—the town of Prachatice. Besides its beautiful location, the town has the charm of many quaint old buildings.

EWING GALLOWAY

cause they had strict orders to wear bright yellow bands across their chests which made them easy targets for the Prussians. Another outstanding target, the red trousers of the Austrian cavalry, was the result of an accident of history. The mills of Bohemia and Moravia had manufactured large quantities of red cloth for the army of Emperor Maximilian of Mexico. After the absurd failure of the Hapsburg dynasty there, the Bohemian mills were caught with their supplies. To avoid bankruptcy in the textile centers, the Austrian War Ministry bought up the red cloth and assigned it to the cavalry.

Glass, Shoes and Woolens

After World War I, Czechoslovak industries began to build up world-wide markets for their products. Their glassware and porcelains, shoes and fabrics were sold everywhere. A curious feature of the textile trade was that large quantities of Czech woolens were sent to England by certain dealers, returned from there as "English products" and later sold at import prices.

The depression of the 1930's hit the country hard. At one time there were almost a million unemployed persons in a country of sixteen million. But recovery started soon after 1934. Coke, iron and steel production, chemical and cement enterprises began to thrive again. Their names became known all over the globe: the Poldi Works, in Kladno; the Vitkovice Steel and Iron Works; the Skoda armament factories, in Pilsen. Czech plants produced anything that can be made of steel, from railroad rolling stock to machine tools. The Bata shoe factories in Zlin, Moravia, became the largest enterprise of the kind in Europe, selling inexpensive mass-produced shoes to many countries. Czechoslovak engineers were building power plants in India, sugar refineries in Indonesia and factories in Africa. Czechoslovakia began to produce and export automobiles: the Skoda, Tatra and Aero automobile factories were marketing their small, powerful cars in Holland, Switzerland, Poland and Austria. "Made in Czechoslovakia" became a trade mark of quality and precision.

Another problem came to the fore in the 1930's. There was a large German minority—three million persons—who were hostile to the Czechs and made every effort to cause trouble for the Government. Most of these Germans lived near the German border, in the Sudeten region. Though they were prosperous and enjoyed personal freedom, they looked across the boundary and considered Berlin, not Prague, their capital. It was bound to happen that they should be encouraged by the Nazis. It was just as certain that appeasing Hitler, by granting him the Sudetenland in 1938, would not bring peace. A few months later, German troops entered Moravia and Bohemia. Czechoslovakia became a "protectorate" under the Germans. The Slovaks made a partial break in March 1939 when they became an "independent" republic under the "protection" of the German Reich. Again a few months later, the second World War started.

Misery under Nazi Occupation

The German occupation of Czechoslovakia wrecked the economy of the highly industrialized country. In the Sudeten-German areas, all factories belonging to Czechs and Jews were taken over by the invaders, as well as their stocks and raw materials. All over the country, Czechoslovakia's industrial resources were mobilized by the German war machine. Czech workers were deported as slave laborers; Czech engineers were arrested; Czech managers were fired. The Germans took over the banks, factories and mines and installed their officials and puppets there. When the war came at last, there were food shortages which had a paralyzing effect on the workers. Passive resistance and silent opposition spread everywhere. The people pretended to misunderstand German orders, and "Schweikism" became a way of life. In many plants there were sabotage units. Machines broke down mysteriously, electric power failed, supplies got lost, freight cars disappeared from sidings. As the war went on, there was scattered damage from air raids.

OLD COSTUMES and old customs still prevail in some parts of Slovakia. The shepherd is playing a fuyara, an oversized pipe. At his side is a decorated cane with a hatchet on the end.

Eduard Benes had been elected the second president in 1935. In 1938 he went into exile, beginning all over again to work for his country's freedom. A Czechoslovakian government-in-exile was set up soon after the war broke out, and Benes became its head.

His efforts were not to have happy results as had happened after World War I. In 1945, in the closing months of the struggle in Europe, when the Germans were being pushed back on all sides, Soviet troops poured into Czechoslovakia. Thus the U.S.S.R. was in on the ground floor almost before the Czechoslovaks had a chance to draw a free breath. Benes and his Government came back but were soon forced to grant concessions to the Soviet Union, including the loss of Ruthenia. Also, at least partly as a result of the wartime alliance with Russia, there was now a strong Czechoslovak Communist Party. In the free, general election of 1946, it won 38 per cent of the votes.

Soon after the end of the war, almost three million Sudeten Germans were expelled from Czechoslovakia. Among them were the skilled craftsmen who had produced the country's glass and chinaware, textiles, costume jewelry and musical instruments. In the towns of Kraslice and Schönbach, tens of thousands of violins, cellos, trumpets and other instruments had been produced by manufacturers who farmed out piece work among the inhabitants. Some artisans made only the bodies of fiddles, while others cut scrolls and fingerboards or chiseled pegs and bridges. Others put parts together.

Although the Czechs hated to admit it, the loss of the German workers was a heavy blow to Czechoslovakia's industries. In any event the Czechs rolled up their sleeves, started to work harder than ever and tried to rebuild their factories and regain their markets. They received valuable help from the UNRRA. Because of Soviet influence, however, they were forced to refuse Marshall Plan aid.

The Uranium Mines

Now Russian visitors, who had never appeared before in Joachimsthal, showed up in large numbers and proved to be tireless sight-seers. They liked what they saw. Soon the spa and the region were sealed off by the Russians, the native population was moved away, into the interior of Bohemia, and the "sight-seers" began to develop the region. Jachymov ore has a very high pitchblende content. The fifty thousand miners in the region produce more uranium than the Russian-operated mines in East Germany, to the north, where ten times as many people are working. For a while, the Czechs tried to stall negotiations with the Russians. Eventually, however, they had to sign agreements giving the Soviet Union exclusive rights to the uranium mines—and to most other mines in the country.

In 1946 a two-year plan was set up to increase the production of household goods and basic industrial equipment. It also started the country on the road toward nationalization. The railroads had always been owned by the state. Now it was decided that the Government should take over certain mining and food-processing enterprises and all factories and firms with more than five hundred employees.

In spite of these and other efforts to satisfy the demands of the left, the country was being drawn irresistibly into the Soviet sphere. The final blow fell on February 9, 1948. That day, the Communists, led by Klement Gottwald, took over the country in a fast, well-organized, bloodless *coup d'état*. A Soviet-type constitution was adopted quickly. President Benes was forced to resign, and Gottwald became president. Jan Masaryk, the son of the country's founding father, was retained as foreign minister. On March 10, he died after a fall from his office in Prague's Czernin Palace. Masaryk's death sealed the fate of the country. There was no armed opposition. Newly formed communist "action committees" began to rule the country's life.

What has happened in Czechoslovakia since reflects the pattern in all countries in the Soviet orbit. All industries and businesses have been nationalized. Private ownership is a thing of the past. Even small tradesmen such as hairdressers and hatmakers have become tiny cogs in the state-run wheels. Small stores are merely parts of large combines. For instance, all food stores are run by the giant Prämen organization. The former owners—if they were lucky!—were given clerical jobs. Some groups have been wiped out altogether, in an economic sense. There is no longer a prosperous middle class of doctors, lawyers, engineers, managers. Such people were given the choice of becoming poorly paid white-collar workers or of going as well-paid laborers into the steel mills and coal mines. Many have chosen to become members of the new working class. At the same time, numbers of former manual workers and miners have become managers and directors and are forming a class of new-rich people. Life is regulated by norms and quotas, the figures of the "Plan." A doctor may be required to see up to one hundred people a day, in fulfillment of the quota that has been set him. Firemen pledge to fight "more fires than last year," and street-car conductors must resolve to sell "as many fares as possible."

An Arsenal for the Communists

Because of its industrial capacity and the skill of its people, Czechoslovakia is one of the arsenals of the communist world. Arms manufacture is dependent on coal mining and steelmaking. Consequently, in order to attract workers to these industries, high salaries are paid and many benefits promised. As in the Soviet Union, the successful coal miner is among the country's highest paid working men. A miner with strong arms, a sense of organization and skilled helpers earns more than a cabinet minister.

In Ostrava, the country's most important coal-mining and steelmaking city, the

TONS OF SUGAR BEETS ON THE WAY TO REFINERIES

Sugar beets are an important crop in most of the countries of north-central Europe. When beet sugar has been highly refined, it can hardly be distinguished from cane sugar.

PHOTOS, EASTFOTO

PRIVACY FOR WELL-BRED CALVES—EACH HAS ITS OWN BARN

The calves are being raised on an experimental stock farm in southern Bohemia. They are given a special diet; and by keeping the animals separate, individual feedings can be controlled.

miner is king. Production has gone up in the mines and new equipment has been put in. To make life even more attractive for the miners and their families, the Government has built several new cities around the old town of Ostrava which eventually will become a relic. The new cities show the face of one possible future: large, white-walled apartment houses, drab even in their fresh paint; schools; wide avenues; power plants; and community centers. Havirov ("miners' town"), which was started in 1949 on the site of a forest south of Ostrava, in 1956 had a population of 25,000. By 1966 it is expected to have 75,000. To get one of the clean apartments with central heating, elevators and kitchen, you must be a miner, construction worker or steel laborer.

Control through Education

A new sort of people is growing up in such cities. These people know little of the outside world and even less of the meaning of freedom and free enterprise. Education is controlled by the Government. The children are told that it is more important to love the state than their parents and are encouraged to spy on their parents. The children spend their first years in government-run nurseries. In elementary and secondary schools, the emphasis is on political education—that is, communist teachings. When the boys and girls leave school, the state sends them to factories, farms or colleges. In other words, the state decides a child's future, not his parents or the child himself. To be admitted to a university, a boy or girl must come from a proletarian (laboring-class) family.

Outside of the large cities, in the villages and small towns, the changes are less noticeable. Half the country's population are farmers tilling the soil much as their forefathers did hundreds of years ago. Sugar beets are planted in the Elbe Basin, northwest and east of Prague, and in Moravia. Wheat and barley are grown in these regions, and there is much dairy farming. In Moravia and Slovakia, wheat and barley are the chief crops below about 1,300 feet; rye and oats take over on the higher slopes. Grain and potatoes are grown in southern Bohemia, and in the mountains surrounding the country there is livestock farming. In Silesia, country folk raise cattle and pigs. Roast pork with dumplings and sauerkraut is the national dish in many homes.

A typical, middling-to-small farmer may have six acres of land—not in one piece but in a series of narrow strips scattered all over the countryside, marked off by stones. There may be a vineyard and an orchard. Somewhere nearby stands the white- or blue-walled house, with running water and electricity. On his six acres the farmer grows wheat, oats, barley, rye, potatoes, maize (corn), sugar beets, apricots, apples, plums, nuts, red currants, vegetables and possibly some grapes, from which he makes his own wine. He may have four cows, a sturdy white ox, a horse, a few calves, pigs, hens, geese, ducks. Horse-drawn plows are still common and sowing and reaping are done by hand, though even on small farms there are often a machine for milling grain, a separator for the dairy, a clover cutter and a thresher.

The farmers in Bohemia and Moravia work hard but they live fairly well. Before World War II the living standard there was as high as in the countryside of western Germany and neighboring Austria. The farmer and his family had plenty to eat—milk, eggs, vegetables, fruit, geese and chickens. They would sell their red meat (beef and veal) and goose livers, which fetched high prices in the cities. There were no distinctions between rich and poor farmers because the "rich" had only three times more land than the "poor." Almost every farmer had hired hands, unmarried men and women, who lived in his house.

The Life of a Farmer

"The farmer's life is a round of griefs but he bears his burden lightly," a native folk song says. The Czech farmer is hard-working and is modest in his demands on life. After a day's hard toil he returns for supper and a glass of beer. Social life is confined pretty closely to the

NEAR THE END OF A PATTERN IN BOHEMIAN BOBBIN LACE

It takes endless patience and many hours to make a piece like this. The thread is very fine, and each tiny knot made by the bobbins must lie flat and in a precise position.

SKILLED HANDS MAKE A FINE ADJUSTMENT TO AN ACCORDION

No village wedding or festival in Czechoslovakia is complete without the music of accordions. There is a steady demand for the instruments, supplied by a few factories such as this one.

family. Sometimes he may go to the village inn to meet his friends and talk over common problems. Everybody knows these problems; even the village blacksmith and the local policeman are part-time farmers. On Sundays everyone meets inside or in front of the church. The men stand on one side, the women on the other. Sometimes the women wear their traditional costumes, beautifully embroidered, with white blouses and colorful aprons. Not much has changed in these villages in recent decades. Wars, occupation and crises have left fewer scars there than elsewhere. You can still see picturesque dog carts or women binding barley into sheaves or age-old harvest festivals. The people are fond of their ancient customs and of their homes. This fondness is evident in their literature and music—their poems and folk songs.

New Ways for Slovakia

In Slovakia, however, the picture is somewhat different. Soon after the war the Communists began to industrialize the region. Many farmers were tempted to take jobs in newly built factories. Others found employment on state and collective farms. There, today, they are working with tractors and other modern agricultural implements never seen in Slovakia before. In villages that once were so poor they could afford not even a single doctor, there are lumber camps and state farms. New houses have been built. The lot of the children has improved physically. Village boys and girls now wear shoes, get hot meals at school and receive medical care when they are sick. At the same time these advances have had no political effect on the people at large. The Slovaks are conservative and prefer to stay aloof from the rest of the world. They are also devout Catholics who are more inclined to follow the leadership of their priests than the orders of the communist officials in Prague. The Slovaks accuse the Czechs of having learned nothing from the war. This stems partly from old resentments. The Slovaks have always felt that they were being patronized and were considered to be an inferior people by the Czechs.

Czechoslovakia offers ideal conditions for winter sports. Every year, from December to April, thousands of people spend vacations in the High Tatra. A magnificent range, it culminates in the 8,737-foot Masaryk Peak. Among the rugged granite formations lie shimmering, deep blue lakes, clear trout streams and lovely valleys. Charming chalets stand in the midst of vast primeval forests. Today many of the chalets belong to various trade unions (practically arms of the Government) which also have built large recreation centers nearby. Such a center consists of a hotel, a group of small villas around it and skating rinks and other facilities. The cost of a holiday at a center is low since part of the cost is paid for by the national insurance system. The problem is—how to get sent there. This depends on political reliability and one's standing with his political superior.

A few villas are set aside for the use of paying guests, mostly foreign diplomats who want to spend a holiday in comparative privacy. All other places are run by the state. Free skiing instruction is provided, and skis and boots are lent free at all centers.

On Ice Rinks and Ski Runs

Winter sports have always been popular in Czechoslovakia. Ice hockey is the national sport, comparable to baseball in the United States and soccer in England. Many cities and smaller towns have natural skating rinks. Large factories have their own teams which they support on a big scale. Tournaments and international games are followed with nation-wide interest. For past decades, Czechoslovak ice-hockey teams have been the best on the Continent. Canadian and American teams come to Prague frequently and there is as much excitement then at the city's Winter Stadium as at Yankee Stadium, in New York City, during the World Series baseball games. Some schools have special winter holidays, when whole classes and their teachers go to the mountains. The Tatras abound with ski lifts and banked runs for bob-

POTTERY AND FOLK DESIGNS—SLOVAKIAN WALL DECORATIONS
A village housewife proudly points to one of dozens of plates that decorate her spotless, white plaster wall. Brilliant colors—red, blue, green, yellow—mix in joyous contrast.

sledding. Above six thousand feet, conditions are perfect for skiing until late in spring. The most popular skiing competitions are not slalom (on a zigzag, downhill course), as in Austria, but cross-country racing, as in Russia.

No one can say what the future holds for Czechoslovakia. Most of its people were and still are Western-minded. They talk wistfully of the days when everybody was free, working and living in peace. Even many young people who have already been trained in the communist schools still cherish at least some aspects of life in the West.

The Czechs are an individualistic stock; when they are told to walk on the right side of the street, a great many of them walk on the left. They like to grumble and crack jokes about their leaders, and they are critical of bureaucrats generally and people in authority. Many have again resorted to the sly technique of Schweik, the only method of opposition they dare. Moreover, the people are religious and it is significant that the churches are always crowded on Sundays. They say, "We've survived other dictatorships and we shall survive this one, too." Their sturdy sense of humor remains unimpaired and helps them to live through the dreary years of regimentation and meeting norms—the rigid standards set for just about every activity.

One thing is certain. The country is becoming more industrial than ever and the people have to work harder than before. Every year new buildings rise—coke plants, steel mills, cement works, brick works. The people are getting television stations, more railroads, power dams, motion-picture theaters, libraries, washing machines, refrigerators. Yet there is less happiness in this beautiful country with its romantic past. There is less laughter and there is tension in the air, as if the people were all waiting for something to happen. They know that the fate of Europe, and of the whole world, may once again be decided in their country in the heart of the Continent.

By Joseph Wechsberg

CZECHOSLOVAKIA: FACTS AND FIGURES

THE COUNTRY
A communist-controlled "people's republic" of central Europe, Czechoslovakia is bounded on the north by Poland, on the east by the U.S.S.R., on the south by Hungary and Austria and on the west by Germany. The area is 49,354 sq. mi. and the population is 13,020,000.

GOVERNMENT
The Communists seized control of the Government in 1948. According to the constitution of that year, the Government consists of a unicameral National Assembly, of the Presidium, the highest legislative body when the assembly is not in session, and of a cabinet. The assembly elects the president of the republic for a term of 7 years.

COMMERCE AND INDUSTRIES
Czechoslovakia is not only a highly industrialized state but it also possesses great natural resources. About 40 per cent of the population is engaged in agriculture and forestry. Wheat, rye, barley, oats, corn, potatoes and sugar beets grow in abundance. Hops is an important crop and supplies the brewery industry. The mineral resources furnish both hard and soft coal, graphite, garnets, silver, copper, lead and rock salt. There is large-scale mining for uranium. The great Skoda works, outside of armaments, manufacture locomotives and heavy machinery. There are also textile and paper mills, glass, furniture, metal and chemical factories. Czechoslovakia exports textiles, heavy tools, boring and milling machines, high-speed lathes, forging presses, cranes and suction dredges, and imports grain, cotton, wool, nonferrous metals, iron and manganese ores, chemical fertilizers and agricultural machinery. The bulk of Czechoslovakia's trade is with Russia. The monetary unit is the koruna (crown).

COMMUNICATIONS
Czechoslovakia has over 8,000 mi. of railroads and over 44,000 mi. of roads. Several airlines serve the country.

RELIGION AND EDUCATION
Three-fourths of the population is Roman Catholic. A law of 1949 makes the clergy civil servants of the Government.

The entire educational system is under government control; 8 years of schooling are obligatory. The principal universities are Charles University of Prague and the universities of Brno and Bratislava.

CHIEF CITIES
Prague, the capital, population 922,500; Brno, 273,200; Bratislava, 185,000; Ostrava, 181,000; Pilsen, 118,000; Olomouc, 59,000. Of the total population, 67% are Czechs, 25% Slovaks, the rest Germans, Magyars, Poles and Jews.

AUSTRIA

"A Land So Fair..."

"Where have you seen a land so fair? Look round you! Where your eyes may rest ... its meadows living green, its harvests gold, a rich bouquet of blossoms everywhere, tied with the Danube's bow of silver ribbon. Higher it climbs to hills all clad in vines where golden clusters swell and ripen in God's sparkling sunshine. While capping all, dark woods rejoice our hunters. That's why the Austrian is blithe and frank and wears both faults and pleasures in the open. He envies none, and what he does is done with cheerful heart." From a play by Franz Grillparzer, famous nineteenth-century Austrian dramatist.

THE scream of the workman holding the smoldering oil lamp had given the officials of the salt mine quite a jolt. They had come down, deep into the Kaiser Josephberg mine, on this first day of April 1734, to inspect the damage caused by a broken sluice gate. Now they were staring at the body of a man, still partly encased in a block of rock and salt. Clothing and boots, as well preserved by the salt as the body was, were quite different from anything these men had seen before. They quickly concluded that this must be the remains of one of those people whose primitive tools and burned-out torches were found so frequently in the abandoned galleries. Surely this miner must have been crushed by falling rocks at least four hundred years before.

Actually he had been killed two thousand years earlier. He was an Illyrian, one of a group of early people. Graves of Illyrians have since been uncovered by the hundreds above the little town of Hallstatt, in Upper Austria. The graves contained a profusion of articles, so many that they indicate Hallstatt must have held a key position during the early Iron Age, about 900 to 500 B.C. Thus the town has given its name to a distinct culture, the Hallstatt epoch of the Iron Age. Hallstatt itself perches precariously on a steep mountainside, by a waterfall. The site forms a small promontory on the eastern bank of a deep, dark lake. It is one of a number of lakes in the Salzkammergut, a lovely mountain region. Salzburg is the area's most important city. *Salz* means salt, from the old salt mines.

In 1908, work on the railroad that was to connect Vienna with the Wachau section of the Danube Valley had reached the hamlet of Willendorf. The foreman and an engineer had just joined a group of workers who, a few minutes before, had been busy digging a cut through the thick layers of loess, a rich soil. Now they were poking at some objects half buried in the loam. A glance at the crushed bones and pieces of flint, and the dark, gray streaks—the traces of campfires—told the engineer what had been discovered, a prehistoric camp. Only a few hundred feet away was the brick yard where, by 1883, the remains of countless camps of palaeolithic mammoth hunters had been found.

Among the remains the Venus of Willendorf was found. It is a small, skillfully executed limestone statue, though anything but a Venus by our standards. Nevertheless, the little idol, perhaps sixty thousand years old, proves dramatically—as do the cave paintings found in Spain and France—that the cave dwellers, who fashioned tools from stone and antlers, could express themselves artistically.

As recently as 1956, in digging the foundations for a house in the center of Vienna, workers laid bare the remnants of the bath of the Roman camp Vindobona. The camp was one of the empire's outposts on the northern frontier.

Incidents like these have been so numerous that they would fill volumes. Through such findings, besides the old monasteries, churches and castles, and the treasures that fill their museums, modern

MARGARET DURRANCE FROM RAPHO-GUILLUMETTE

SKIERS' PARADISE—Lech, on the Arlberg. This mountain in the Tyrol was the birthplace of Alpine skiing.

PETUNIAS AND ROSES froth from the balconies of a Tyrolese house, sheltered by jutting eaves.

CHARMING FIGURINES and amusing masks are created by a skilled Tyrolese wood carver.

J. BARNELL FROM CAMERA CLIX

HANS HANNAU FOM RAPHO-GUILLUMETTE

HEILIGENBLUT is cradled in a magnificent mountain valley of Carinthia, in southern Austria. From the town a highway, the Grossglocknerstrasse, twists and turns, toward Italy, over the Hohe Tauern, a range of the eastern Alps.

Austrians are constantly reminded that they have inherited a soil on which history has been made for thousands of years.

Not far from the site of Vienna lay the crossroads of prehistoric Europe, the place where the Amber Route crossed the Danube. Along this route amber, the fossil resin, highly prized by the ancients, was transported from the Baltic to the Mediterranean. Amber has been found in Egyptian tombs.

Herders, Settlers, Invaders

The Danube River flows through Austrian territory, skirting the fringes of the eastern Alps. Between these ranges and the Bohemian-Moravian Highlands, the waterway is the only great natural route from central to southeastern Europe. Next to the Volga, the Danube is the Continent's longest river. Through the Danube Valley, Aurignacian man (an extinct type) followed herds of mammoth and reindeer. On the Danube, Illyrian traders shipped their salt. A medley of peoples followed the same path at various later times: Teutonic tribes, Huns and Avars, Slavs and Magyars, German settlers and Turkish invaders.

Where the Danube enters the Hungarian Plain beneath the last foothills of the Alps, Charlemagne, in 803, secured the eastern border of his empire against the Avars. They were a people who had broken forth from the vastness of Asia. The march (border territory) that he founded stretched from the area now called the Vienna Woods upriver and occupied parts of the modern provinces of Lower and Upper Austria. This Eastern March was destroyed by the Magyars, cousins of the Avars and their successors in what was to become Hungary. Later the territory was restored by the German Emperor Otto I. In 976, it was given as a fief to the Frankish Babenberg dynasty. After the last scion of this house had died in battle, the able and ambitious Ottokar Premysl, king of Bohemia, seized the Eastern March together with the duchies of Styria and Carinthia. By then the Eastern March had also become a duchy, with the name of Austria.

Ottokar could take this action because the German empire had begun to fall apart. Konrad IV, the last German king and Holy Roman emperor of the Hohenstaufen dynasty, died in 1254. The German princes chose then to do without a real ruler for almost twenty years. In 1273, they selected as king a relatively unknown Alsatian landgrave, Rudolf of Hapsburg. The new king sensibly accepted conditions as he found them. He realized that without greater personal power he could not revive any real kingly power. So he devoted his energy to improving the fortunes of his own family.

Rudolf's opportunity arose when Ottokar Premysl refused to recognize his accession to the German throne. Ottokar's fiefs were declared forfeit and Rudolf took the field against him. In 1278 Ottokar was slain in a battle northeast of Vienna, and Rudolf gave to his two sons the vacant duchies of Austria, Styria and Carinthia. Thus was established the Hapsburg dominion on the upper Danube. It lasted until 1918.

The greatest expansion of this dominion occurred during the fifteenth and sixteenth centuries. Through a series of arranged marriages, Burgundy, Spain with her American possessions, Bohemia and Hungary came under the sway of the Hapsburgs.

Hapsburg Losses and Gains

In the course of time the Hapsburgs lost their possessions on the Rhine, Burgundy with the Netherlands, and Spain. They acquired other territories, however —Galicia, Dalmatia and, as late as 1878, the former Turkish provinces of Bosnia and Herzegovina. The Hapsburgs were at the height of their power after the Turkish tide—halted once before at Vienna, in 1529—was turned back for good at the gates of the city in 1683.

Until 1914 the sprawling Dual Monarchy—Austria-Hungary—where eleven major languages were spoken, preserved some measure of peace and order in one of the world's most sensitive areas. Then the first World War broke out, sparked by the murder of the Austrian Archduke

Franz Ferdinand at Sarajevo. On the losing side in the conflict, in the end the old empire was torn apart. From its ruins new states were created—Czechoslovakia, Hungary and modern Austria. The rest of the territory fell to Poland, Rumania, Italy and the new Yugoslavia.

Thus modern Austria began its history impoverished by a lost war. It had little industry and only a fifth of the land was arable. There was the additional burden of trying to support Vienna, a city with almost 2,000,000 inhabitants. Before, Vienna had had an empire of more that 50,000,000 people on which to draw. The new Austria was immediately gripped by economic crises and shaken by internal strife. Sick, as most of Europe was between the world wars, and written off by the big powers, the First Republic of Austria fell victim to Hitler's schemes in 1938.

Again, 1939–45, Austria was ravaged by the scourges of war. Some 195,000 men, women and children were killed; 76,000 were listed as missing. At the end of the war, Austria was occupied by France, Great Britain, the United States and the U.S.S.R. Austria was a pawn in the struggle between the East and the West, and the occupation was prolonged until 1955. Yet during that time, with gratefully received aid from abroad, the Second Republic was launched and became a living reality, truly independent. Austria became a nation!

On the map, modern Austria has the shape of a ham, with the bone pointing west. It measures 362 miles from east to west, and its widest north-south distance is 182 miles. At its narrowest part, in the Arlberg region in the west, it is only about 20 miles wide.

As we have indicated, the Alps occupy the major part of Austria south of the Danube and the Bohemian-Moravian Highlands form most of the country north of the river. So almost three-fourths of Austria is mountainous. About two-fifths is 3,000 feet or more above sea level. Grossglockner, between the Tyrol and Carinthia, the highest peak, towers to 12,461 feet. The loftiest permanent settlements, the Rofenhöfe in the Tyrol, are at about 6,500 feet. Toward the east the land is low and level.

Wise Care of Forest Wealth

Though there are many barren summits, crowned with glaciers, in the Alps, 37 per cent of the country is wooded. Centuries ago the mountain farmers recognized that the forests gave them more

COUNTRY WEDDING. The ceremony has just ended and the bridal party, in all its finery, forms a procession.

MARGARET DURRANCE FROM RAPHO-GUILLUMETTE

THE GOLDEN DACHL (roof), Salzburg landmark, is on the balcony of a fifteenth-century town house.

HANS HANNAU FROM RAPHO-GUILLUMETTE

J. BARNELL FROM PHOTO LIBRARY

WATER SPOUTS from classic figures into the fish basins of Kremsmünster Abbey, in Upper Austria, founded in 777.

MARGARET DURRANCE FROM RAPHO-GUILLUMETTE

AN OLD GENTLEMAN of Mondsee proudly wears a traditional costume of the Salzburg area. Such costumes are brought out for the performance of *Everyman*, the medieval play, given in the town of Mondsee every year.

than lumber with which to build houses and logs for fuel. For the forests protect the villages and farms in the narrow valleys and on the steep mountainsides from avalanches and landslides. The forests also help to regulate the water cycle and this prevents erosion. Through the years, careful management of the woods, mostly evergreens on the higher slopes, has spared Austria the fate of some Mediterranean regions, where there is barely enough vegetation left to provide fodder for sheep and goats.

In Austria's forests roam the noble stag—a close relative of the North American elk—the graceful roe deer, the wild boar and, at breath-taking heights, the sure-footed chamois. In some areas there are fallow deer (imported from Asia in the Middle Ages) and a species of wild sheep that originated in Sardinia and Corsica. There are a few small colonies of the magnificent ibex. The huge capercaillie, largest of the grouse, and its relative, the game black cock, are coveted hunters' trophies. Hare, rabbits, partridges and other small game are abundant. During their migrations, thousands of ducks and geese come down on the many lakes and streams. These also teem with fish, offering good sport to the angler. Excellent laws and, above all, the sportsmanship of Austria's hunters and fishermen will preserve this rich wildlife for coming generations.

The Beautiful Brown Danube

Rivers and brooks rush down from the mountains, swelling the Danube. Along its course it carries tremendous quantities of silt. The sky must be very blue indeed for the color to be reflected in the Danube at Vienna. When Johann Strauss wrote *The Beautiful Blue Danube* he must have seen the river on such a clear day. Actually, the Danube is usually brown. On its lower course, at least, the mighty stream is a work horse, laden with river craft. Northwest of Vienna is a lovely stretch rivaling the Rhine. This section is the Wachau. Along its banks are vineyards, fairy-tale castles, historic fortresses and magnificent abbeys.

TEN THOUSAND FEET HIGH in the Otztal Alps of the southern Tyrol. The hotel commands a superb view of Seelenkögl Peak. Its summit is loftier still, by fifteen hundred feet.

Water is Austria's "white coal," her most important source of power. Hydroelectric plants harness the swift streams tumbling down from the mountains. Of a possible forty billion kilowatt hours, Austria is producing about one-fourth. Plans are under way to develop the water power further.

Unique among Austria's many bodies of water is huge Neusiedlersee (*see* means "lake"), on the Austro-Hungarian border. It is slightly salty and so shallow that one can wade through it for almost its entire length, more than twenty miles. About every seventy years it dries up completely. The dense thickets of reeds, in some places three miles wide, that rim its shores teem with rare birds and other wildlife. Since the lake waters store summer warmth, the climate of the surrounding region is moderated. Vineyards, producing excellent wines, thrive.

If a visitor is ambitious, he may ski on the glaciers of Grossglockner in the morning and swim in one of the warm Carinthian lakes in the afternoon. Because of the mountains, Austria's climate has considerable variety. The warmest areas are east and northeast of Vienna and south of Graz. There the average annual temperature is about 50° F. Above 6,000 feet the average is below freezing point.

224

Since the winds blow from the west most of the year, rain or snow falls heaviest on the western parts of the country. There and on the northern rim of the Alps as much as 72 to 120 inches a year of rain and snow fall. The drier areas, which get only 20 to 24 inches, are in the northeast.

Incredibly beautiful valleys lie within the folds of the Alps. Charming little villages nestle on the valley floors or cling to the mountainsides. Sometimes for days they are cut off by winter snows from the rest of the world. Perhaps partly because of their isolation, the mountain villagers tend to hold to the ways of the past. It is on the edge of the Alps, in the foothills and where the valleys open wide that Austria's principal cities stand: Vienna, Graz, Linz, Salzburg, Innsbruck, Klagenfurt.

Vienna, Gay and Bustling

Most glamorous of all is Vienna, for centuries the center of the Holy Roman Empire and, later, of the Dual Monarchy. For some years after 1918, the city that was once Europe's gayest capital endured great suffering. It seemed to go into eclipse under the Nazis and during the long occupation that followed World War II. Nevertheless, contrary to gloomy predictions, Vienna is not dead today but as lively as ever. Smoke billows from busy factories on the eastern and southern fringes of the city. Theaters and music halls are crowded. The shop windows dazzle Austrians and visitors alike with clever displays of domestic and imported goods, the museums proudly show their famous treasures, and in the streets there is all the hustle and bustle of a modern metropolis.

Although there are a number of magnificent medieval churches—among them Vienna's landmark, St. Stephen's—the architectural character of the city is set by the many baroque churches and palaces. They are proof of the vigorous life that welled up in the city during the eighteenth century.

Small though Austria is, there is great variety in the styles of villages and towns. The lay of the land, the materials used, the origin of the builders and military considerations—all have had an influence. Thus, in the areas that were exposed to frequent invasions or feuds, the older houses huddle together, often around a castle or fortified church. Outlying farmhouses sometimes look like castles themselves, with strong walls and small windows like loopholes. It is surprising that in such a richly forested land few even of the oldest houses are built entirely of wood. The builders felt that with stone and brick they were providing for future generations. As a matter of course a house was to be kept in the family.

Where space and climate permit, farmhouses are surrounded by orchards and tidy vegetable gardens. Flowers nod at the windows. As if this were not enough color, the artistic Tyroleans and Salzburgers cannot resist the invitation of the whitewashed walls. These are often decorated in vivid hues with scenes taken from religion or folk tales or daily life. Also in the Tyrol and in the province of Salzburg a kind of house that dates back to the dawn of history has persisted to this day. Its living quarters, barn and stables are all under one roof. The hand-cut shingles of the roof are weighted down and kept in place by large stones.

Traveling in a train or bus we pass fields, pastures, orchards and, in the warmest sections, vineyards alternating with woods. Especially in eastern Austria we are struck by the narrowness of many fields, some no wider than a few furrows. They show how farmers divided their land among several children. Modern agricultural methods cannot be applied to such narrow strips, so the situation is being remedied. By exchanging fields and pastures of similar quality and equal size among owners, larger holdings are being created.

Limited Land, Rich Harvests

The provinces that form modern Austria were once chiefly agrarian. Today more than 50 per cent of the country's products come from industry and only about 15 per cent from agriculture. Although cultivable land is limited, Austrian

REARING HORSES and a mass of foliage in stone—the ornate fountain that is one of the best-known meeting places in Salzburg.

HANS HANNAU FROM RAPHO-GUILLUMETTE

THE OLD QUARTER of Salzburg is a fascinating maze of cobbled streets. Over them loom tall narrow houses dating from the 1500's.

J. BARNELL FROM CAMERA CLIX

A SWAN PREENS itself beside Traunsee, a lovely lake east of Salzburg. Towered Castle Orth hugs the opposite shore.

J. BARNELL FROM PHOTO LIBRARY

THE UHRTURM, a quaint clock tower at the Schlossberg. This castle is near the Styrian city of Graz, in southeast Austria.

EYE-FILLING VISTA—the Mirabell Gardens in Salzburg. Shrubs, lawns, flower beds are laid out in an elegant formal design.

AUSTRIA

farmers are able to supply 81 per cent of the nation's food. Wherever possible they have adopted modern methods. The tractor is more and more replacing the horse.

Yet there are some areas where man's labor still is all that counts. At heights where the climate is so rough and the soil so poor that no grain will grow, the farmers must rely on husbandry for their livelihood. Every fistful of grass is needed to get the animals through the long winters. So when summer comes and the last snow has melted, many a mountain farmer—the *Bergbauer*—harvests with scythe or sickle the precious grass growing on ledges and steep slopes. There a slip could be fatal and he wears crampons on his shoes. The hay is stored in little log barns and in winter is hauled to the farms in sleighs.

KOSTICH

Since there is only sparse pasture in the narrow valleys, the cattle, sheep and goats are driven to the high alpine meadows in summer. On the approach of winter the return of the animals is celebrated with colorful pageants. The sound of cowbells fills the air as the gaily bedecked creatures wend their way down the narrow paths. On the backs of their herders, coming home after lonely months, are huge cheeses. These have been made in the mountain dairies.

It is not an easy life that the *Bergbauer* leads; but he is hardy and proud. He clings to his inherited soil. Since 85 per cent of Austrian farms are of less than

HAY-MAKING TIME in the Alpine valley of the Inn River. Beyond the field is Innsbruck, charming capital of Austrian Tyrol.

PRACTICE at the Spanish Riding School, in Vienna. The horses, all white, are trained to go through extremely intricate maneuvers.

fifty acres, they cannot, as a rule, support all the children. Industries absorb many of those who must leave home. Thus Austria's farming population is the source from which the nation's industrial man power is constantly fed.

The farmers' conservatism has preserved many ancient customs. In some parts of Austria at the advent of spring, the demon of winter is burned in effigy, and the forces of life, still slumbering in the earth, are wakened by cracking whips and other noise-making instruments. The summer solstice—Midsummer Eve—is still observed throughout Austria by huge bonfires that light the mountain tops as far as the eye can see.

Love of old ways also shows in the farmers' dress. On festive occasions such as a wedding, particularly in the Tyrol, one may see many a farmer and his family wearing costumes that go back to baroque or even medieval times. The Tyroleans use much red. In the Middle Ages only free men were allowed to wear it. With the Swiss and the Friesians (of the Netherlands), the Tyroleans are among the European farmers who were never serfs.

We have already spoken of Austria's forests and of her "white coal." Another important resource and basis of many of Austria's industries is iron. The Erzberg, the "mound of ore" in Styria, was mined by Celts and ancient Romans. Today it accounts for three-fourths of Austria's production of iron and steel. Besides iron and salt, the country is also rich in graphite and magnesite and has a sufficient supply of lead, zinc, copper, molybdenum and antimony. While there is not enough coal, Austria produces enough oil to satisfy her own needs and to export crude oil and oil products. The Zistersdorf fields yield about 3,500,000 tons of crude oil a year.

Iron and steel heads the country's manufacturing industries. The well-known Böhler works produce some five hundred special kinds of steel, which are exported to many parts of the world. From other major industries come aluminum, paper, chemicals, textiles, all sorts of machines and machine tools, vehicles, building materials and electronic equipment. Austria's most important exports are lumber, iron, steel and paper. The country's location in the center of Europe is ideal for big trade fairs.

Flourishing Arts and Crafts

With all the efforts being bent on raising the standard of living through mass production, the Austrians have not neglected the arts and crafts for which they have long been noted. As in the Middle Ages, an artisan still must serve as an apprentice for three or four years before he can become a journeyman and, eventually, perhaps a master craftsman. One result of this thorough training is that Austrian quality products, such as blown and cut glass, leather goods, pottery and ceramics, wrought iron, custom-built guns and rifles, jewelry, lace and petitpoint, are in demand in many foreign countries. The dingdong of hammer upon anvil can still be heard in the village smithy. The wheelwright still can make a wheel; and the cooper, barrels. The carpenter still knows how to handle broadax and adze, and the shoemaker earns his name.

Austria has a dense network of railroads and highways. There is hardly a community that cannot be reached by a public means of transportation. Some roads still follow the Roman highways that reached to the frontiers of the empire. However, the hills and narrow streets of

IN VIENNA—the imposing Parliament Building, a classic Greek design, on the wide Ringstrasse.

IMPERIAL GRANDEUR—the formal gardens and the vast pile of the Schönbrunn, Vienna. It was once the summer palace.

THE SPIRE of St. Stephen's Cathedral thrusts skyward from among the gabled roofs of the oldest part of Vienna. Construction of the landmark began in 1137.

BURG THEATER in Vienna, as rebuilt since World War II. The traditions of the famous national playhouse go back to the 1770's.

DREIMÄDERLHAUS (House of the Three Maidens), Vienna. It is associated with Franz Schubert.

231

the centuries-old towns are often quite a problem for modern automotive traffic. While engineers and city planners try to keep in step with time, they are anxious to preserve the old beauty and charm. Not long ago it became necessary to make room for the growing traffic along the narrow left bank of the Danube in the Wachau. It was decided not to widen the main street and tear down picturesque old houses but to build, at great expense, a tunnel through the mountainside.

This is the mountain on which the quaint little town of Dürnstein nests. In its castle, in 1193, Richard the Lion-

THE GREAT COMPOSER Mozart was born in this house in Salzburg. Today the house is a museum filled with mementos of the genius.

EWING GALLOWAY

hearted was kept prisoner. According to legend, Blondel, his faithful minstrel, set out to find his King. He went from castle to castle, playing the melodies that Richard loved. In Dürnstein, at last, Blondel heard, from a narrow window in the impenetrable castle, Richard's voice taking up a familiar tune. Blondel hurried back with his tidings to England. There the King's loyal subjects soon raised the ransom that freed Richard.

The first great mountain railroad was constructed in Austria, over Semmering Pass, fifty-four miles southwest of Vienna. Other pioneer work was done with the building of cable, or aerial, railways. Dozens of them, and hundreds of ski lifts, make remote summits more accessible.

In fact, Austria has become one of Europe's favorite playgrounds. She offers beautiful scenery, lovely resorts, including numerous spas, and splendid opportunities for outdoor sports. Other lures are music and theater festivals, a rich folklore and magnificent art treasures. Last but not least is the hospitality of the Austrian people.

Burgenland to Vorarlberg

Modern Austria consists of nine provinces. Farthest east is Burgenland, literally the "land of castles." This old border territory had to take the brunt of many invasions and so was heavily fortified. Lower Austria, for all its name, is actually on the northeast. Here are the romantic Vienna Woods—west and southwest of Vienna. Vienna is a province as well as the nation's capital. Styria is called the "green land" because of its wealth of forests. Upper Austria is noted for its fertile farms. It has also some of the most important industries of the Republic. The province of Salzburg has the same name as its capital. It became a part of the Hapsburg domain only after the end of the Napoleonic wars. Before 1816 it was an independent archbishopric. Carinthia is the land of lakes. The Tyrol is world famous for its magnificent alpine scenery. The Tyrolean costumes are recognized almost everywhere. The Vorarlberg is the most western province. Its

A FESTIVAL BAND toots a merry way through Zell am Ziller. The pretty village, in Zillertal Alps, Tyrol, draws many visitors.

name means the land before the Arlberg. This is a mountain, and also a pass, the watershed separating Vorarlberg from the Tyrol. On the Arlberg's slopes, modern alpine skiing was born.

These provinces (officially called states today) form a federation. Powers are divided between the provinces and the national government. However, government in Austria is centralized to a considerable extent. There are, for instance, no state judiciaries. On the national level, the legislative, executive and judicial branches of the government are strictly separated.

Parliament consists of two houses, the *Bundesrat* and the *Nationalrat*. The provinces are represented in the *Bundesrat,* whose members are elected by the provincial legislatures. The actual lawmaking power is vested in the *Nationalrat*. Thus it is something like the British House of Commons. Its members are elected by popular vote. Executive power is largely in the hands of the chancellor and several ministers, who form the cabinet. They answer to Parliament and must have the latter's confidence. Only a cabinet composed of members of the majority party or parties can stay in power. The position of the president of the Republic is like that of the French president.

A supreme court takes care that the constitution is not violated and that there is justice under the law. Like other Continental legal systems, Austria's excellent civil and criminal laws are codified and largely based on Roman law. Capital punishment has been abolished.

Austria's colors are red, white and red. The story goes that the Duke of Austria, Leopold V, fought so valiantly in the battle of Acre during the Third Crusade that his white surcoat was drenched in the blood of enemies he had slain. After the battle was over, Leopold took off his broad belt in the presence of the flower of European knighthood. The part of the coat that had been covered by the belt

WIDE WORLD

shone white between the red. Then the mighty lords from France, Germany and England loudly proclaimed that henceforth these should be Austria's colors.

Who are the Austrians? We have already mentioned some very early people, the Illyrians. There were also Celts. Eventually, these people came under the influence of Roman culture. Later, Lombards and other Teutonic groups settled in the land. Traces of all these were found by the Bavarian, Frankish and Swabian settlers who followed Otto I's hosts in the tenth century, after the Magyars had been repelled. In the north and southeast there were Slavs. Then, after the Turkish wars, Croats came to the ravaged eastern areas. During the latter part of the 1800's, Czech and Slovak immigrants swelled the populations of Vienna and nearby industrial sections.

All have blended. There are no minority problems to speak of in modern Austria. In a recent census, 99 per cent of the population gave German as their mother tongue. Since the overwhelming majority are Roman Catholic by birth, religion is not an issue. Religious freedom is guaranteed by Austria's constitution. Not all Austrians practice their religion but they may be called a religious people. In the countryside, where the farmers for the success of their toil are so dependent on God's mercy, you will find many little shrines and crosses at waysides or atop the mountains. In the cities and towns are countless awe-inspiring churches and cathedrals. Monasteries, some of them dating back to the eighth century, are practically everywhere.

The Austrians are a gay people and they know how to live. One expression of this joy of life is their fondness for music and the theater. Austrian taxpayers willingly support the Vienna State Opera and four other Viennese stages operated by the Government. More people attend theater performances than spectators watch sports. The reconstruction of the Opera House in Vienna, which had been destroyed in World War II, and its reopening in November 1955, were the concern of every Austrian.

Tradition-loving Austrians also maintain the Spanish Riding School in Vienna, which was a court institution in Hapsburg days. Since 1565 the white stallions have been taught there the art of dressage, that is, the classical maneuvers executed by the mounts of medieval knights.

With such beautiful surroundings, the Austrians are naturally lovers of the outdoors. They are marvelous skiers and, when warm weather comes, enjoy hiking.

PHOTOS, AUSTRIAN STATE TOURIST OFFICE

RAILROAD BRIDGE spanning the little Trisanna River in the Paznauntal, a deep valley in the Tyrol.

STATE OPERA. The handsome building is the pride and joy of the music-loving citizens of the capital, Vienna.

As in other European countries, soccer is the chief spectator sport.

Austrians appreciate good food. The influence of their Germanic, Slavic, Hungarian and Latin neighbors shows in the many delicious dishes that make up the Viennese cuisine. The city's pastry shops are the delight of foreign visitors. The rich *torten* (cakes)—not to speak of the coffee with whipped cream—are justly famous. Wiener schnitzel (breaded veal cutlet) appears on menus in other lands.

To some extent, Austria's social structure still reflects the feudal past. Yet class distinctions no longer have any real significance. The Austrians solve their problems in a democratic manner. All careers are open to the gifted. Elementary education has been compulsory since the days of the Empress Maria Theresa, who ruled from 1740 to 1780. All children must attend school until the age of fourteen. Numerous secondary schools (*Mittelschulen*) give young men and women a well-rounded general education. It enables them, if they so choose, to attend one of Austria's fourteen institutions of higher learning. The oldest, the University of Vienna, was founded in 1365. Almost all schools are public. Illiteracy is practically nonexistent.

Austria has produced great musicians—Haydn, Mozart, Schubert. Though perhaps Johann Strauss and his son were not "great," their lilting waltzes have set people dancing the world over. There are also many brilliant Austrian scientists. At last count, twelve of these had won Nobel Prizes. Among the prize winners are Karl Landsteiner, who established the fact that there are blood groups, and Victor Hess, who discovered cosmic radiation.

The Austrians are proud of their traditions and have never lost their relish for life. But they are not idle dreamers. They work hard for their happiness and they want to live in peace and friendship with each other and with their neighbors. They are equally willing to defend their freedom, which they have gained only at great sacrifice.

By Wilhelm Schlag

AUSTRIA: FACTS AND FIGURES

THE COUNTRY

Bounded by Germany and Czechoslovakia on the north and northwest, Hungary on the east, Yugoslavia and Italy on the south, and Switzerland and tiny Liechtenstein on the west. Consists of 9 provinces, or states: Burgenland, Lower Austria, Vienna, Upper Austria, Styria, Carinthia, Salzburg, Tyrol and Vorarlberg. Area, 32,369 sq. mi.; population, about 7,000,000.

GOVERNMENT

A sovereign and independent republic, with a president elected by popular vote. Has cabinet headed by a chancellor. Parliament consists of two houses: *Bundesrat,* with 50 members elected by the state legislatures; *Nationalrat* (lower house), with 165 members elected for 4-year terms by popular vote. Women have the vote and may be elected to office.

COMMERCE AND INDUSTRIES

Agriculture is still the chief occupation of many of the people, though the country is rapidly becoming industrialized. Farm products: potatoes, turnips, rye, oats, wheat and barley. Cattle, hogs, sheep and goats are raised. Mineral resources: salt, iron, magnesite, lead, zinc, copper, molybdenum, antimony and graphite. Water power is important. Manufactures: iron and steel, aluminum, paper, chemicals, textiles, machines and machine tools, automobiles, electronic equipment. Exports: lumber, iron, steel, and paper. Imports: grains, and some other foodstuffs, cotton. Monetary unit, the schilling.

COMMUNICATIONS

3,727 mi. of railways; 55,000 mi. of roads; has a number of aerial railways. One domestic and at least 12 foreign airlines service the 8 major airports.

RELIGION AND EDUCATION

Almost all the people are Roman Catholics; constitution guarantees freedom of worship. More than 5,000 primary and secondary schools, mostly public; 14 institutions of higher learning, including universities at Vienna, Graz and Innsbruck.

CHIEF TOWNS

Vienna, capital, 1,625,000; Graz, 227,000; Linz, 185,000; Salzburg, 103,000; Innsbruck, 95,000; Klagenfurt, 63,000; St. Polten, 40,000; Wels, 38,000; Steyr, 37,000; Leoben, 36,000.

LOOKING DOWN ON PEST FROM THE HEIGHTS OF BUDA
Buda is built on hills, which in places are a thousand feet above the Danube. This view is from the plateau on which the Royal Palace stood. Little but the statue remains.

A Link Between East and West

The Magyars and Gipsies of Hungary

Hungary has led a long and varied existence of alternate freedom and oppression. Hungarians, who call themselves Magyars, are descendants of Finno-Ugrian tribes that came in the ninth century and for centuries held the plains against the Turks—not always successfully. For less than fifty years, Hungary was a part of the Austro-Hungarian Empire; between the two world wars she was a kingdom without a king. After the war a republican form of government was adopted, and Hungary came within the Russian sphere of influence. The gipsies who are dealt with in a feature article, have long roved the plains. Hungary has been termed the gateway of the East, and the people still retain many Eastern characteristics. Indeed, the influence of the East is everywhere manifest.

THE Hungarian plains and sun-baked steppes are sheltered on the northeast and southeast by the Carpathians, and on the west and southwest by a long arm of the Alps, known as the Bakony Wald. This mountain encircled basin contains an area of wide treeless steppes where graze vast herds of horses, cattle, buffaloes, sheep and swine. Rich fields of wheat flourish on cultivated land, and the hill slopes are fragrant with wine grapes. The mountain slopes of the Bakony Wald are heavily forested. The Danube and the Theiss (Tisza) afford water transportation. The Danube is navigable in its entire course through Hungary.

The division of land for the past thousand years—two-thirds of it into large estates—had preserved feudalism; and until Hungary procured independence from Austrian oppression there was little incentive to manufacturing. For over a thousand years this fertile land has been occupied by an Asiatic people somewhat related to the Finns. According to legend, hordes of nomads came in 895 or 896, led by Khan Arpád, and drove out the Slavs; and these Magyars are still the dominant race, though varied peoples long menaced national stability. Hungary's charter of liberties, the Golden Bull, is older than Magna Carta and she celebrated her thousandth anniversary in 1896. Early in the eleventh century King Stephen knitted the tribes into an organized state and established Christianity. Hungary then became a bulwark against the Asiatic invasion of Europe: for in 1353 the Ottoman Turks crossed the Hellespont and for three centuries terrorized all of Europe. In 1443 John Hunyadi became a national hero when he defeated the Sultan before Sofia. In 1526, however, the Turks made murderous onslaught at Mohács, securing central Hungary; and soon after, the Hapsburgs secured the throne, with supremacy in western Hungary. The Turks were finally driven out in 1683 by the kings of Austria and Poland.

Though the Magyars strove desperately in 1711 to regain their freedom, thirty years later they made a gallant sacrifice for the young queen, archduchess Maria Theresa of Austria, when she asked aid in repelling the invasion of Austria by the French. Wearing the iron crown of St. Stephen, she addressed the Hungarian Diet at Pressburg (Bratislava). In reply, the hall re-echoed to the sound of sabres half drawn, then thrust back into scabbards, and with one voice they cried: "We consecrate our life and blood to your most sacred majesty!"

During Maria Theresa's reign a pontoon bridge was built across the Danube to connect Buda and Pest. The two ancient cities had long been rivals. But not until 1873, under the Dual Monarchy, that the law was passed decreeing that they should henceforth be one. Some twenty-one years later Budapest became a royal city, equal in rank to Vienna. Famed as a center of beauty, entertainment and culture, it was soon attracting visitors from all parts of the world.

During World War II, it suffered severely from bombings and a fourteen-week

MAP OF THE GREAT PLAINS OF HUNGARY

siege by the Russians. A program of rapid rebuilding has restored its seven bridges and many famous landmarks.

The Dual Monarchy was established in 1867 when the Austrian emperor Francis Joseph became the king of Hungary. This benevolent monarch endeared himself to the Hungarian people; and though the national spirit had never been quenched, it lay quiescent until his death in 1916. Then the embers of discontent burst into flame and on November 16, 1918, independence was declared and the Hungarian People's Republic came into existence.

Two years later, the old monarchical constitution was restored and the country became, in effect, a kingdom without a king, governed by a regent.

Hungary sided with Germany during World War II. Upon Germany's defeat, Russia occupied Hungary and exacted large reparations from the already impoverished nation. Hungary fell victim to inflation. In 1947, America offered to stabilize the tottering finances with a loan, but withdrew the offer when the Red army of occupation helped the communist minority in Hungary's Parliament stage a coup d'etat. Since that time Hungary has been a Russian satellite.

The Hungarian, tall, high cheek-boned and slightly oblique of eye, loves dueling, horse-racing and games of chance, and can dance for hours, fairly intoxicated by the gipsy music of the country. The Czárdás alternate from rhythms of wild exuberance to those of drooping sadness. The shepherds play a flute, the *tilinko,* and the villagers, the ancient lute. The tziganes—gipsies—believed to have originated long ago in India, have for hundreds of years roved the lowlands of Hungary, though the government has tried to make them settle down. Many of them are horse traders and some are thieves, but nearly all are musicians. The wild rhythms of Franz Liszt's Hungarian Rhapsodies have preserved elements of gipsy music; while the German composer, Johannes Brahms, based his Hungarian songs on their haunting melodies.

The peasant women of Hungary are nothing if not picturesque, with their red stockings, full petticoats—of which they sometimes wear ten or a dozen—their gay aprons and beribboned hair. They never miss an occasion for donning this finery. Easter, Christmas and New Year's Eve are the great events. At Easter, the first young girl to be met must be sprinkled,

CATTLE GRAZING 'NEATH LOMBARDY POPLARS BY LAKE BALATON

The pastures on the shores of Balaton, the largest lake of central Europe, support fine herds of dairy cattle. The region, called Transdanubia, also produces great quantities of grain.

REBUILDING BUDAPEST, IMPORTANT WORK FOR ALL HANDS

Within sight of Franz Josef Bridge, a young woman wields a shovel to clear debris from the fallen blocks of a large building. About 70 per cent of the city's buildings were destroyed in the winter of 1944–45, when the Red Army drove out, block by bitter block, the occupation troops of Germany. Clearing the rubble has been a back-breaking, heart-rending task.

HUNGARIAN CHILDREN IN HOLIDAY FINERY

This serious little boy and his sisters are dressed in elaborately embroidered clothes, copies in miniature of the festival garments their parents wear. The blouses, vests, skirts, aprons—even the tablecloth—are stiff with the famous Hungarian needlework, done in the most vivid colors possible. Hand-made fringe finishes off the edges of the tablecloth and the girls' aprons. All of these pieces represent months of work by the children's mother.

whether she likes it or not, with scent-water, or if she is daring enough to venture out of doors she will promptly be seized and taken to the nearest well, and she will be lucky if she escapes with having only one bucketful of water emptied over her. The men dress as gaily as the women. They wear small, round hats ornamented with feathers and flowers, black sleeveless jackets over loose white undershirts (often with embroidered sleeves) and white trousers that look like petticoats. They also wear bright aprons. The women wear the sleeveless bodice and white blouse and a full, embroidered skirt, with often a handsome shawl, a kerchief for the head, but usually with bare feet. The *suba* and the *szur* are two garments especially beloved by the shepherds and peasant workers. They are the garments in which they live and sleep. The *suba* is a long cloak of sheepskin with the wool worn inside, and the leather elaborately embroidered. The *szur* is also an ornate long cloak, but is made of a felt-like material.

In former years great contrasts of wealth and poverty existed. Most Hungarians are poor today, however, partly as the result of defeat in World War II and partly due to the great political changes that have taken place. Hungary

WATER FOR THE CATTLE ON THE GRASSLANDS NEAR MEZOKOVESD
Much of Hungary is a wide, flat plain with numerous streams. It provides excellent pasturage, for sheep as well as cattle. Elsewhere the land yields bountiful crops.

PHOTOS, EWING GALLOWAY

THATCHED BUILDINGS AROUND AN OLD-TIME FARMYARD
The slabs drying in the foreground are adobe bricks. They are used for the walls of the cottages, which are whitewashed. Thatch is used for the roofs, and floors are tamped earth.

A LINK BETWEEN EAST AND WEST

is behind the iron curtain today. It is very difficult to know for certain how the people live. We do know that the army has been built up to frightening proportions. We also know that the present communist Government stresses the need for building heavy industries.

There are too many people living in the farm regions. Though the Great and Little Alföld are among the most fertile plains of Europe, there is not enough land to go around. There is not enough food harvested to satisfy the hunger of the people. And because Moscow gives the orders, what food there is, is not always eaten in Hungary.

A PLEATED SKIRT BELLS OUT OVER LAYERS OF PETTICOATS
Mother primps daughter in preparation for a village festival. Bright contrasts of color fairly dance in the array of delicate, homemade laces, embroidery and other needlework.

TEXTILE MILL AT SZEGED—WITH MECHANICAL EQUIPMENT IMPORTED FROM THE SOVIET UNION

The Szeged cotton works spins the fibers into thread, yarn and cord for use in the clothing and fabric mills of the country. Mass production and modern machinery—much of it imported from Russia—are keynotes in the Government's program for the build-up of industry. Closely tied in with the industrial planning of the Soviet Union, the Hungarian mills receive the raw cotton from the extensive plantations of Uzbek and the other Soviet republics of central Asia. Yet, in spite of high production, the people find many goods expensive and of poor quality.

TIME TO PLANT POTATOES

Once this field was part of a large manor. After the war the big Hungarian estates were taken away from their owners and parcelled out in small lots. In 1950 the Government instituted a Five Year Plan, with agricultural quotas for peasants. Potatoes are a mainstay in the diet, especially in rural areas, and the Hungarian wife knows many ways of cooking them.

AUTUMN—AND THE CORN IS RIPE

A short length of stalk is left on the ear when corn is gathered in Hungary. The stalks are then braided and the golden garland is hung from the rafters, up under the thatch, to dry. Corn is good family food and excellent feed for livestock as well, during the winter. Most farming in Hungary is now done on the collective pattern. The country is becoming increasingly industrialized.

THE CIRCULAR, DOMED FAÇADE OF A COMMUNIST WORKERS' CLUB

An engineer and several workers from the Hungarian Optical Works in Budapest look over their new culture center. Within recent years a number of similar buildings have been erected at factories and in large farm areas. They contain educational and recreational facilities, such as libraries, rooms for lectures and classes, nurseries, auditoriums and gymnasiums.

FINE CHINA FIGURINES READY FOR A BATH

When the delicate, ornamental figure is first produced it has a porous, dull surface. Then it is dipped into a vat of liquid glaze, a substance similar to glass, that penetrates the figure and clings to the surface. After that the statuette is baked in an oven at extremely high temperatures and emerges at last with a glossy and durable surface.

PHOTOS, EASTFOTO

AN OLD MASTER AT PAINTING PLATES TEACHES APPRENTICES

This experienced artist is one reason why Hungarian porcelain is so well known for its fineness and variety of design. In spite of his years, his hand is steady and sure, his motif original, and his colors delicate. His trainees will learn a deep pride of craftsmanship as well as a fine art from him, and some day they may be skilled masters teaching others.

SZECHENYI BRIDGE AND OLD BUDA BEFORE WORLD WAR II

Szechenyi, spanning the Danube, was one of the greatest suspension bridges in the world until its destruction in the war. Today several pontoon bridges connect the city's two sections.

A MARKET IN PEST—BUCKETS, POTS, PANS AND DISHES APLENTY

People of Budapest browse among the stalls, wagons and random piles of household goods. Pinched between high prices and low wages, they are especially eager to find a bargain.

A SEVERELY MODERN GOTHIC CHURCH IN RAKOSPALOTA
A few miles from the ancient city of Budapest, this recent structure has the pointed arches and the tall, slender pinnacles of the old Gothic without its ornate and elaborate detail.

ALONG THE DANUBE, where even in the driest summer the wells fed by the river cannot fail, the well-wheel is a favorite meeting place for lovers; and a girl who has an affianced sweetheart places two huge pieces of sugarloaf in her window. The costume shown above is that of the countryside near Kalocsa. Hungarian women all do elaborate embroidery.

© CUTLER

WEDDING GARMENTS are worn by the Hungarian peasantry in exact imitation of those of mediaeval times. The bride's flowery head-dress, her embroidered panels and handkerchief the size of a dinner napkin may have taken years to make. The bridegroom's surplice-like robe is heavy with handwork and the flowers in his hat are to be regarded with entire seriousness.

IN A HUNGARIAN FARMYARD, PEASANT WOMEN TEND THEIR GEESE

Hungary is primarily an agricultural country and the majority of its people depend upon their land and livestock for a livelihood. Most of the country's farms are small.

HUNGARY: FACTS AND FIGURES

THE COUNTRY

A republic since 1946. Bounded by Austria on the west, Czechoslovakia and the U.S.S.R. on the north, Rumania on the east, and Yugoslavia on the south. Present territory, as settled by the 1945 armistice, 35,912 square miles; population, 9,800,000.

GOVERNMENT

Hungary entered World War II as an ally of nazi Germany and finally was occupied by German troops. In 1944, Russian troops entered Hungary and succeeded in driving out the Nazis. A provisional government, in 1945, signed an armistice with the Allies, and in 1946 the National Assembly proclaimed the Hungarian Republic. In 1948, pro-Communists gained control of the country, and a new constitution was adopted in 1949, vesting supreme power in Parliament, assisted by a Presidential Council. In 1956 Hungary revolted against Russian control.

COMMERCE AND INDUSTRIES

Chief occupations: agriculture, heavy and light industry, factory building. Wheat, corn, rye, barley, oats, potatoes, sugar-beets and grapes are the principal crops. Livestock raising is important and also fishing. The chief mineral products are coal and lignite, and the bauxite mines are among the largest in the world. Other industries are lumbering, milling, distilling and the manufacture of sugar, hemp, flax and textiles. There are also iron and steel works. The chief exports: poultry, cotton fabrics and, reputedly, industrial manufactures such as railway engines and electrical equipment. Imports consist mainly of cotton. Since 1946, many industries nationalized. Monetary unit, the forint.

COMMUNICATIONS

Mileage: railways, 7,100; highways, 15,900; navigable rivers, 687. There are 122,000 telephones and nearly 1,000,000 radio receivers.

RELIGION AND EDUCATION

Most of the Magyars are Roman Catholic. Elementary education compulsory between ages of 6 to 14 years. In addition to extended facilities for secondary education, there are special adult training schools and also universities.

CHIEF TOWNS

Budapest, capital, 1,780,000; Szeged, 133,000; Debreczen, 120,000; Kecskemet, 88,000; Miskolc, 77,300.

Switzerland and the Swiss

Beautiful Countryside of the Alpine Republic

Switzerland, birthplace of the Red Cross, is the Mecca of the mountaineer and the paradise of the winter sportsman, and the Swiss have made it their chief industry to care for tourists. They are also famed for their watch-making, wood-carving, lace-making and embroidery and for their fine cheeses. The people show varying proportions of German, French and Italian descent, and the newspapers and government reports are printed in four languages.

SWITZERLAND is a tiny country composed of two great mountain ranges with a narrow tableland between. Fir-clad slopes hem in lush valley pastures and blue mirrors of Alpine lakes between glittering snow peaks that reach skyward for two miles and more. This lovely land, with but four million people save as it attracts visitors from America and Europe, becomes one gigantic white setting for the winter sports. The lakes become natural ice-rinks; the meadows, the best of "bob runs," and the steep slopes, the ideal courses for the ski-jumper. It is the Alps that make Switzerland unique.

On the south lies the Swiss portion of the higher Alps, walling off France and Italy from Lake Geneva to Lake Constance; and on the north, the Jura Mountains, united with the main range of the Alps in the west. Between these two high ranges flow two mighty rivers, the Rhone, flowing westward, on the side nearest France, and the Rhine, flowing eastward, toward the Austrian boundary, with the River Aar and that tributary of the Rhine, the Thur, in undulating valleys that dent the plateau between. The rivers are mountain torrents that have to be embanked as a measure of flood prevention; the Rhone has falls of considerable height, and the Rhine, shorter falls of greater volume. In marked contrast to their sonorous turbulence, more than a thousand glaciers creep imperceptibly down the grooves of the ranges, feeding three large lakes and innumerable Alpine tarns. Of these glaciers, there are three in the north which are over ten miles in length—the Great Aletsch, a thousand feet deep, the Fiescher and the Unteraar. Lake Geneva in the southwest is cut by the borderline between Switzerland and France, and Lake Constance, in the extreme northeast is only in part Swiss, but Lake Neuchatel lies wholly within the little mountain republic. Of the snow caps which rise violet-shadowed above all, Mt. Blanc is 15,781 feet high; the Matterhorn, 14,703; and the Aletschhorn, 13,713; while hundreds of less famous peaks are really high mountains. The Alps reach their greatest altitude on the Bernese Oberland. The Great St. Bernard Pass—over which both the armies of Caesar and those of Napoleon passed—is 8,111 feet in altitude and covers a distance of 53 miles.

The mountaineer passes through many climates, beginning with that favorable to vineyards and olive groves; and as he reaches higher slopes or those more exposed to winter storms, through oak and beech woods, pines and firs and the zone of dwarfed Alpine plants, and on—above the clouds to the eternal snows.

An hour before sunrise the challenge of the guide's horn echoes from peak to peak. As one climbs, pale clouds go smoking up the canyons, and the towns beneath become more and more toy-like. At last one looks out over a sea of peaks capped, billow upon billow, with dazzling ice. One of the most memorable sights in all the Alps is the Jungfrau, rising white and solitary, encircled with clouds.

The tableland between the ranges, deep with the silt of centuries, is incredibly rich soil that can be cultivated intensively. Fully half of Switzerland is under grass, however; for every opening in the forest is cleared of stones and made into pastureland. Half of the area is either forested or too rocky to yield anything but scenery.

A WORLD OF SNOW lies above the green valleys and pine woods of Switzerland, a world where everything that the eye can see is dazzling white. Four adventurous amateur climbers, led and followed by trained guides, are approaching the summit of the Allalinhorn, 13,000 feet above the sea, across a treacherous snow-covered glacier, where a slip would be fatal.

THE MATTERHORN, rising solitary and majestic 14,703 feet above the sea, bears on its sheer slopes the blossoms of the edelweiss and the alpenrose, while the meadows at its feet are starred with buttercups. Those who climb must carry pack-baskets or pack-harnesses, that their arms may be free, and a load of more than twenty pounds soon becomes irksome.

SKI RACERS GLIDE skillfully down the steep, snow-covered slopes of the Alps near Klosters. The town is a popular resort in the Grisons canton, in eastern Switzerland.

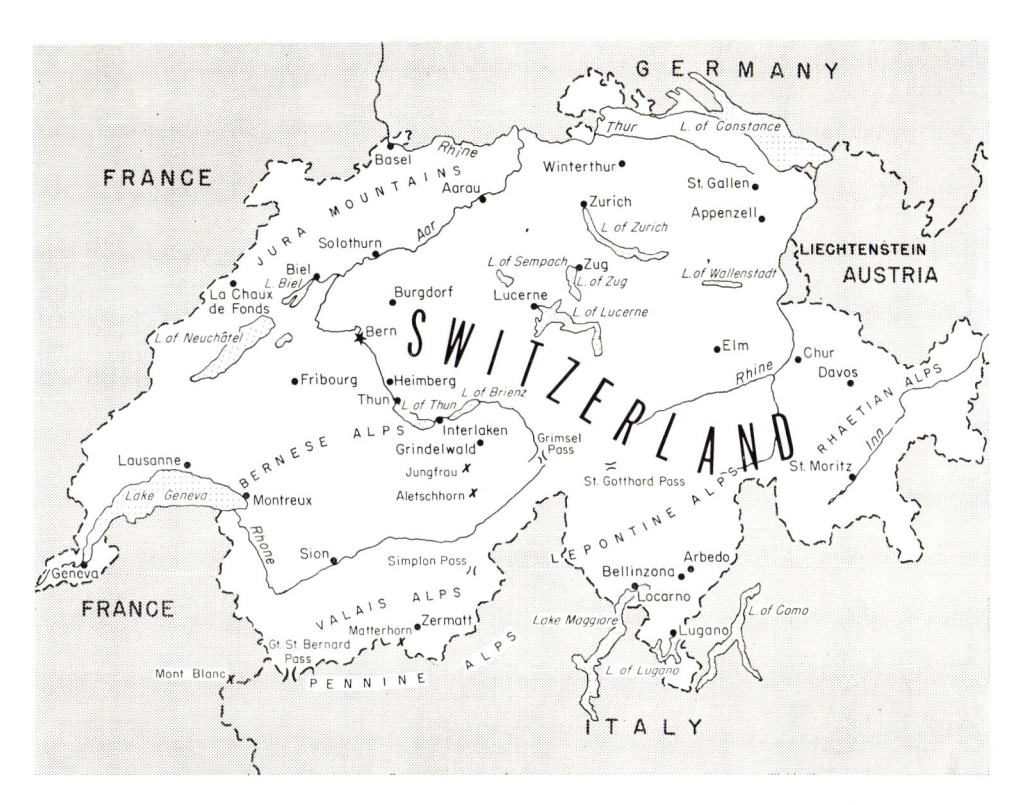

A SUNNY DAY IN BRUGG, a town in northern Switzerland, on the Aar River. Along with modern shops, Brugg has a Romanesque tower and gabled houses of an earlier time.

STANDARD OIL CO. (N. J.)

THESE SWISS GIRLS are wearing the costume typical of Hallau, a diminutive village in Schaffhausen. This small canton, lying a little to the west of Lake Constance, is the most northerly of the Swiss cantons. Indeed, it seems to dip into Baden, Germany. It also possesses the distinction of being the only canton entirely north of the Rhine River.

THESE LITTLE PEOPLE dwell at Unterschächen in Uri, William Tell's native canton, nearly a tenth of which is covered with glaciers. It is autumn and the boys apparently have to wear hoods to keep their close-clipped polls warm, though the girl is barefoot. The wooden carrier on the back of the older boy is a Swiss back-pack, or pack-basket.

SWISS FEDERAL RAILROADS

A STUDY IN BRIEFING

A monk at the Great St. Bernard Hospice receives rapt attention from one of his "pupils." Here, atop a mountain pass in Switzerland 8,111 feet high, the monks train their famous dogs to rescue travelers who lose their way in the snow. In recent years, however, modern methods of transportation have left few opportunities for these animals to practice their skill.

SWISS NATIONAL TRAVEL OFFICE

WHERE SLACKS ARE PART OF AN OLD-TIME COSTUME FOR WOMEN

Long trousers are a very sensible form of dress for the active, hardworking young women of the Val d'Illiez, at the head of which is the small town of Champéry, close to the French-Swiss frontier. Their long trousers are fashioned from locally made cloth, and a headkerchief, usually scarlet, adds a vivid touch to their modern-looking costume.

BY A TINY CHALET which is the stable of their long-horned goats, a peasant of the Bernese Oberland and his wife gaze intently, perhaps at a chamois, the wild antelope of the Alps, leaping from rock to rock on the height above them. The hunter who kills a chamois has a dangerous time tracking his prey among the crags, and a laborious one bringing it back.

THE MOUNTAIN PASTURES are usually communally owned. At twilight the chorus of cow-bells sounds a musical tink-a-tonk that is heard in the villages far below. The cattle are driven higher as the summer comes on, while their owners manure the cropped meadows and grass patches ready for another season. Every farm makes many cheeses for export.

Allied for Mutual Defense

What effect have these mountains had upon the history of the Swiss and how do people wrest a living from this Alpine land? The history of Switzerland is, in effect, that of the drawing together of groups from Germany, Italy and Burgundy for mutual defense against the Hapsburgs. In 1291 three little German forest districts formed a league for self-defense. The league thus formed, in which at first the Teutonic interest was strongest, gradually won its independence during the one hundred and fifty years preceding 1648. Though the French Revolution had its influence on the Swiss mind, it was not until 1803 that the French-speaking subjects were accorded political equality—nor were Italian-speaking people till 1815. In that year the perpetual neutrality of Switzerland was guaranteed by Austria, Great Britain, Russia and other countries.

Originally only an alliance of several small states, gradually the idea of Swiss nationality grew, and in 1848 a proper federal state was formed. The Swiss were ever an independent people, and to-day few are more democratic. Thrifty, inclined to be blond and stocky (with the exception of those nearest Italy, who show evidences of the southern blend), they are finely educated and make the most of their limited resources.

Typical Swiss Châlet

The peasant as a rule has a rough but comfortable châlet built of pine which weathers to a rich light brown. When it is in an exposed position, heavy stones are placed on the roof to prevent its being torn off by the fierce winter gales or by the melting snows of spring. A gallery runs around the house. This is sheltered by the broad eaves, which jut out sometimes ten feet beyond the walls. The stone basement is utilized as a storeroom for the produce of vineyard or dairy. The eaves and galleries are often elaborately decorated with carvings. The living-rooms are large and airy. The furniture is homemade. Large benches and dressers of walnut made by the owner or by the local carpenter are the chief pieces. The dressers are sometimes decorated with painted plates. The house is warmed by a large green tiled stove which stands in a corner of the living-room and is kept burning throughout the winter.

In districts where sheep are reared, the housewife, with the help of her daughters, weaves the wool into cloth; in some places the women make beautiful lace. In winter the menfolk occupy themselves with woodcarving, at which they are most skillful, making anything from furniture down to miniature châlets. These things, like the lace, are sold to tourists.

In addition to the hotel-keepers who offer tourist accommodations of the finest, a large number of the Swiss add to their incomes by acting as guides. Nor can these Swiss guides be excelled the world over; for every school child learns to climb the peaks. Groups go with their teachers for days at a time armed with ice axes, ropes and rucksacks, and in many places the military authorities lend them blankets.

Swiss Alpine Club Huts

The Swiss Alpine Club has erected stone huts where climbers may take refuge when violent thunderstorms and sudden blizzards overtake them among the peaks. It is significant that these huts contain not alone fuel, but first-aid equipment and clogs for the foot-sore.

Those who take their vacations less strenuously may, however, reach high altitudes on the trains, which often tunnel through rock and under glaciers, stopping at intervals to allow passengers to walk to some point from which they may enjoy the view. In Switzerland everything possible is done for the accommodation and pleasure of the visitor, and thousands from every part of the world come every year.

The presence of the mountains has a vast influence on the lives of those who live among them. In winter the postman goes his rounds on a toboggan and the housewife goes to the store with one, dragging it back loaded with her supplies. Farmers wait for the snow that they may transport their firewood by guiding it over

READY FOR A NATIONAL HOLIDAY WITH A BIG ALPENHORN

The alpenhorn may be anywhere from three to twelve feet long and is made of wood. It has a flaring shape and the mouthpiece is cup-shaped. Usually it is used for signaling or calling cattle. The traditional melody played on it—*Ranz des Vaches* (Tune of the Cows)—was used by Beethoven in his *Pastoral Symphony* and by Rossini in his opera *William Tell*.

STANDARD OIL CO. (N. J.)

THE PORT OF BRUNNEN ON LAKE LUCERNE, SWITZERLAND

Summer tourists frequent this place, on Lake Lucerne, in the canton of Schwyz. Lake Lucerne, in the heart of the Alps, is believed by many to be the most magnificent of all the Swiss lakes. It stretches for nearly twenty-four miles through breath-taking mountain scenery. In spite of its high altitude the lake never freezes over in winter.

A CORDIAL GUIDE FOR THE MOUNTAIN HIKER IN SWITZERLAND

Artistic road signs such as this one are made in the city of Brienz, the famous wood-carving capital of the Bernese Oberland. Wood carving is one of the many handicrafts for which Switzerland has long been noted. The city is on the northeast shore of the Lake of Brienz, at the foot of the Bernese Alps, and the spot is very popular with tourists.

PHOTOS, SWISS NATIONAL TOURIST OFFICE

TOYS THAT WILL GLADDEN THE HEARTS OF CHILDREN

This young employee in a Swiss toy factory looks, at this smiling moment, hardly more than a child, as she adds final hand touches to a tray of toy donkeys. Toys come in all sizes and shapes; they imitate all sorts of things; but animals seem to be popular with children everywhere. The toy industry in southern Germany and Switzerland has long been important.

the slippery white crust, and in places they lower it on wires stretched from the high cliffs to the valleys below and operated by windlasses. Everyone skates, but the first skis were brought from Norway in 1883 by the monks for use in life-saving work.

The government has not only subsidized the farmer but aided him by such agricultural engineering works as cableways for the transportation of milk from inaccessible mountainsides.

Danger of Sudden Avalanches

The one ever present danger of the mountains is that of the avalanches, huge masses of snow and boulders that come sliding down upon the valleys, sometimes crushing entire villages. A rockfall crushed the village of Elm in 1881. That was due to quarrying for slate on Mt. Tschingelberg. Mt. Arbino has been left unstable by the retreat of glaciers and for many years has been slowly collapsing. Since the days of Æsop's Fables the idea has prevailed that mountains do not move, yet the Swiss topographical authorities had discovered by annual surveys both the speed and the direction of the movement of Arbino, and so were able to give warning in 1928 to the village of Arbedo and the Ticino Valley through which runs the important St. Gotthard railroad to Italy. Of course the movement has been too slow to be observed by the layman save for the almost constant sound like rolling thunder and the haze of dust over the mountain from the falling of stones and boulders.

Conservation of Forests

The forests are well policed in accordance with a conservation policy which aims at a perpetual timber supply. At the same time, the commune permits everyone a sufficient quantity of wood ripe for cutting to be used in building and for winter fuel. Incidentally, if there were no other reason for preserving the forests, it would be necessary as a means of holding the soil of the mountainsides and so preventing landslides and destructive floods. The government also controls the waters, with their potential electric power —so important in the case of the federally owned railways, which are almost entirely electrified. For irrigation, miniature aqueducts carry glacial waters along the precipices to the vineyards below.

Switzerland employs the initiative and referendum, enforces insurance against illness and old age, as well as industrial, accident and military insurance, and provides work for the unemployed.

Switzerland's Army

The world has long honored Switzerland's peaceful history. But peaceful as they are, the Swiss are ever ready to defend their frontiers. The regular army numbers several army corps, which include fully armed divisions, mountain brigades, light motor brigades and an air force of considerable strength.

All Swiss share the responsibility of military service. From the time he is twenty years old until he is sixty the Swiss man is subject to call. Until he is thirty-six he trains for front-line duty, spending about four months a year for eight years. Older men train over shorter periods of time and are called in times of emergency for lighter, rear-guard action. The disabled are excused from call in the army, but they must pay a special exemption tax.

As Switzerland is almost the least self-sustaining nation of Europe, her people make the most of their skill in manufacturing. In the canton of Appenzell people have been making lace for centuries. On Lake Brienz is a village of wood-carvers and toy-makers; in Zurich, a community specializing in the weaving of silk textiles. The metal workers in the world-famous watch factories can make timepieces the size of a dime, with 170 parts to each one. Where four hundred years ago Swiss watches were made in the homes of the workers, one part by each family, now factory methods are employed. Heimberg manufactures majolica ware and Valais has aluminum works.

Berne, the capital city, named for the bears that are the town emblem, lies in central Switzerland in a crook of the River Aar, where it faces half a dozen peaks

GOATS BROWSE CONTENTEDLY beneath a village cross in a high Appenzell valley. The words mean: "May God protect and safeguard us and our possessions from all misfortunes."

A HAY-GATHERER ON A LANE OF STEPS NEAR LAKE LUGANO

A natural rock garden flourishes by the side of this enchanting byway. The region around the lake, which Switzerland shares with Italy, is one of the loveliest in all the Alps.

TINY ZERMATT IN THE SHADOW OF THE SNOW-CAPPED MATTERHORN
The little Swiss town with its rustic wooden dwellings is a favorite resort with sportsmen. It nestles 5,315 feet high in the Pennine Alps, surrounded by meadows forming a beautiful valley.

over ten thousand feet in height. In the medieval part of town the narrow streets are overhung by tiled roofs, arcaded stores and cross tunnels; while the sight of draft dogs pulling the milk carts, men in aprons and school children in black over-dresses adds to the quaintness. *"Leb' Wohl"* (good health to you) is the greeting heard on every side.

The name Lucerne means lantern. There was a great lantern in the watch-tower of its old fourteenth-century bridge. The high walls and nine watch-towers catch the eye as one comes in by steamer across the lake. The Lion of Lucerne is a splendid piece of sculpture. Cut in the solid rock in 1821, it is dedicated to the memory of the Swiss guards who died defending the Tuileries in Paris at the commencement of the French Revolution. The cathedral is noted for its wonderful organ.

One of the best centres for seeing the beauties of Switzerland is Interlaken, at the head of the valley of Grindelwald overlooked by the Jungfrau. The road near Interlaken is one of the most picturesque in Europe. In some places one drives along the edge of a rushing mountain torrent, in others through pine forests; and sometimes the road winds along with a solid wall of rock on one side and a precipice on the other.

When Mark Twain visited Interlaken in the nineteenth century he predicted that the day would come when every mountain in Switzerland would have a railway up its back like a pair of suspenders. That prophecy is fast coming to pass. Moreover, these and the major portion of all the Swiss railways have been electrified from power provided by the mountain waterfalls. That makes it possible for a tourist to climb mountains by rail. The greater part of the Jungfrau railway tunnels through the rock directly beneath the glaciers, as it worms its way upward through the very substance of the great peak and its neighbor the Mönch.

Grindelwald, a village at the foot of the Wetterhorn is a centre for skiing. Lausanne has a special school for training chefs and hotel-keepers. Zermatt is famous for its guides. From this town the Matterhorn can be seen, its peak outlined against the vivid sky in solitary grandeur. Many lives have been lost on this mountain, but every year fresh enthusiasts set out to conquer its precipitous sides.

SEPTEMBER IS CHEESE-DIVIDING TIME IN THE BERNESE OBERLAND

Although Switzerland is an agricultural country, the only farm products it exports are derived from cattle-raising. Best known are its Emmentaler and Gruyère cheeses which are produced on most Swiss dairy farms. A quaint annual event among dairy farmers in the Justis Valley is dividing the cheese. Here the head dairyman auctions off a freshly made, still soft cheese.

ZURICH CLIMBS THE HILL ABOVE THE LAKE

Zurich, Switzerland's largest city, is pleasantly situated at the northeastern end of Lake Zurich. It was a town in ancient Roman times, and there are buildings still standing that go back hundreds of years. Yet the main part of Zurich is modern and progressive. There is a university, several colleges and numerous schools for special instruction.

PHOTOS, SWISS NATIONAL TOURIST OFFICE

GALA PARADE AT ZURICH'S SPRING FESTIVAL

Beduin horsemen on handsome mounts lead the grand parade of the Sechselauten festival in Zurich. This traditional spring fete has come down from feudal times. It celebrated the pealing of bells at six o'clock in the evening (Sechselauten means six o'clock bells). The bells were silent in the dark winter evenings, so the first ringing in spring was a joyous occasion.

CASTLE OF CHILLON AT MONTREUX ON LAKE GENEVA, SWITZERLAND

The castle, built on a rock close to shore, is the one about which Lord Byron wrote in his *Prisoner of Chillon*. It is near the east end of Lake Geneva where the Swiss Alps rise in sheer beauty all around, and where the mild, pleasant climate and clear air attract travelers and vacationers from far and wide to the hotels of Montreux.

Geneva, famous city where the International Red Cross Society was founded, is located on Lake Geneva where the Rhone River flows from its blue waters. Though the lake is but ten miles at its widest, and forty-five miles long, it lies quite 1,230 feet above the sea. Its assemblage of craft, lateen sails of red or white floating across its surface, appear at a distance like so many gigantic butterflies.

In the old part of Geneva, where close-packed medieval buildings once stood within walled fortifications, stands the tenth-century Protestant Cathedral of St. Peter, and near it, the Arsenal, which contains an historical museum. On two islands may be seen the statue of Rousseau and the Castle of Chillon (where Bonnivard was held prisoner by the Duke of Savoy).

Some idea of the theological controversies that once tore Geneva may be acquired from the fact that it has one monument to Calvin and one to Servetus. For the two men had a controversy in 1553 after which Servetus would have fled to Italy but that he was apprehended at Calvin's instance and burned at the stake for heresy. Calvin published his great work at Basel in 1536 and, banished from Paris, took refuge at Geneva. He founded the Academy of Geneva in 1559.

Geneva has at various times been the sanctuary for religious and political refugees (not all of them welcome), the gathering place of scholars and the focus of humanitarian movements. To this cosmopolitan city came John Knox, Dostoevski and Andrew Melville. The International Red Cross, initiated here after the horrors of the Battle of Solferino by Henry Dunant, appropriately chose for its flag that of Switzerland with the colors reversed. During World War I Switzerland might almost have been

IN THE HEART OF BERNE, SWITZERLAND'S SEAT OF GOVERNMENT

Berne (the name means bears) stands on a high bluff overlooking the Aar. Berne retains its medieval character, with its narrow streets flanked by arcades and its old buildings. The clock tower, once the west gate of the city, marks each hour with a procession of bears and the crowing of a cock. At the left of the picture is a famous old bear statue.

called one great internment camp. In addition, it acted as intermediary for the exchange of seriously wounded prisoners. The country steadfastly maintained its neutrality during World War II, and successfully escaped invasion of its boundaries.

The newcomer, having established himself at one of the excellent hotels that line the banks of Lake Geneva and the Rhone, will approach the Palais des Nations by the quay, a tree-lined promenade behind which the four-story building, designed along unpretentious classical lines, graces the lawns of a beautiful park. When the League disbanded in 1946, its assets were transferred to the United Nations. The Palais des Nations became the headquarters of the European Office of the UN. The International Labor Organization continued to hold meetings in the building. Since the war, Geneva has been the site of several momentous world-trade meetings that have advanced the cause of economic co-operation among many nations.

The tourist ought to see an Aelplifest some Sunday, in spring. This pageant, representative of the moving of the cattle to the Alpine pastures, is one in which people don their local folk costumes and march through the streets with their cattle, sheep and goats and carts laden with their shining copper cheese caldrons, while sometimes floats that look like châlets carry women engaged in cheese-making or men operating the winepress.

Every village has its choral society, and singing competitions are held at Lucerne and elsewhere to which singers come from all over Switzerland.

SWITZERLAND: FACTS AND FIGURES

THE COUNTRY

Land-locked state of Europe, bounded north and east by Germany, southwest and west by France, and on the southeast by Italy. To the south is the central section of the Pennine Alps, comprising some of the greatest heights in Europe. Principal rivers are the Aar, Rhone and Rhine. The lakes include those of Geneva, Constance and Maggiore (these three are not wholly Swiss), Neuchatel, Lucerne, Zurich, Lugano, Thun, Bienne, Zug, Brienz Morat, the Walensee and Sempach. The country's total land and water area is 15,944 square miles, and it has a population of more than 4,978,000.

GOVERNMENT

Legislative power is vested in a parliament, consisting of two chambers—a Council of State with 44 members (2 for each of the 22 cantons) and a National Council of 196 members elected by proportional representation (one deputy for every 22,000 inhabitants). Executive authority is exercised by a Federal Council consisting of 7 members, elected for 4 years by the Federal Assembly. A president and a vice-president, who are the chief magistrates of the Swiss Confederation, are elected by the Federal Assembly for a term of one year. For purposes of local government Switzerland is divided into cantons and demi-cantons.

COMMERCE AND INDUSTRIES

About 22.5% of the soil is unproductive, and of the production area 32% is forest. Arable land covers the greatest acreage, and dairying is the chief agricultural industry. Switzerland is noted for her cheese and chocolate. Wheat, potatoes, sugar-beets, vegetables and tobacco are grown. Apples, pears and grapes for wine are the principal fruits. There is salt-mining and a slight output of iron ore and manganese. Electric-power production is over 10 billion kilowatt-hours per year. Leading manufactures are processed foods, clocks and watches, machinery, metalware, chemicals and dyes, textiles, knitted goods and embroidery. The leading exports are machinery, clocks and watches, textiles and clothing, instruments and parts, dyes, drugs and chemicals. Imports: cereals and other foodstuffs, iron and iron manufactures, motor vehicles, machinery and chemicals. Monetary unit, the Swiss franc.

COMMUNICATIONS

Railways, 3,211 miles, most of which are electrified; roads, 10,500. Basel is the terminus of the Rhine waterway, navigable all the way from the North Sea. The Swiss merchant marine comprises 34 vessels. There is one domestic airline. Telephones, 1,074,216.

RELIGION AND EDUCATION

Protestants are in majority in 12 cantons and Catholics in 10. There is absolute freedom of worship. Elementary education is free and compulsory. There are 7 universities, at Basel, Zurich, Berne, Geneva, Lausanne, Fribourg and Neuchatel, a technological institute and a school of economics and public administration.

CHIEF CITIES

Berne, capital, 146,500; Zurich, 390,050; Basel, 183,600; Geneva, 145,500; Lausanne, 106,800; St. Gallen, 68,050; Winterthur, 67,000; Lucerne, 60,600; Biel, 48,400.

The Toy States of Europe
Tiny Countries and Their Self-reliant People

There are pin-points of color on the map of Europe. You have to look closely to see them. Though almost invisible, the tiny states these dots represent hold up their heads among the free nations of the world. Andorra balances between France and Spain in the Pyrenees. Vatican City, the home of the Pope, is a free state of one hundred acres within Rome. Monaco, a principality, is a famous pleasure resort on the lovely blue coast of the Mediterranean. Luxembourg, a grand duchy, is a busy little triangle enclosed by Belgium, France and Germany. Another principality, Liechtenstein, is in a mountain valley between Switzerland and Austria. And San Marino perches proudly in the Italian Apennines. These states may be Lilliputian in size, but they cherish their independence as much, if not more, than many larger ones.

IN thinking of Europe our thoughts naturally turn to the Great Powers, such as France, Germany and Russia, whose territories practically cover the continent. We forget that among these mighty nations there are the baby states of Europe still existing as semi-independent lands, with curious customs of their own, and in some of which the people live much as they did in medieval days.

Perhaps the most interesting of these is Monaco, which owing to its situation on the Mediterranean, has become the most popular pleasure resort on the French Riviera. Monte Carlo, although not the capital of this tiny state, is the town that attracts most attention, and it is certainly one of the most beautifully situated and fascinating places on the shores of the Mediterranean.

One element that makes Monte Carlo the paradise of the pleasure-seeker is the sunny climate of the Riviera and its location between a background of high Alps, rising in snow-white points above the purple mountain wall. The perfume of orange and lemon blossoms greets one in January, and the whitewashed villas that cling to the green velvet hillsides add rose-colored roofs to the picture. Man has also done his utmost to bait the gold of cosmopolitan tourists, as evidenced by the luxurious wines of the restaurants that line the boulevards, the gaiety of night clubs, theatres and concert halls, to say nothing of the lure of the famed Casino, established in 1863 by a notorious gambler.

Quaint superstitions actuate many of the gamblers, of which there are fully as many women as men. It is, for instance, thought to bring good luck if one stumbles while going upstairs, or if one meets a hunchback and can manage to lay a finger on his hump. Some gamblers also believe that an evil spirit may, when it so elects, preside over the roulette board and cause the ivory ball to behave in a manner contrary to the laws of chance.

Monaco has an area of just about 368 acres and it has an average width of six hundred and fifty yards, so that we might in three strokes send a golf ball right across the state. Its population is approximately twenty-three thousand. Within its limits it manages to compress more excitement and tragedy than probably any other place in the world. The one great source of revenue is the Casino at Monte Carlo, where fortunes are lost and won.

Monaco has its own coinage and postage stamps, its inhabitants are practically free from every form of taxation, and the ruling prince and his council direct the fortunes of the state. It has had a constitution since 1911, and there is a semi-military police force. Monaco suffered during World War II because its prosperity depends on the pleasure-seeking crowds of peacetime.

The late Prince Albert of Monaco, who died in 1922, was not the kind of man we might expect to find as the ruler of such an extraordinary land. He was intensely interested in all that pertains to the sea and the fishes and vegetation in it, and in his yacht he frequently made expeditions in the interests of scientific research and

GRANDE CORNICHE DRIVE FROM NICE TO MENTON IN FRANCE

The motor highway along the French Riviera, part of which was built by Napoleon as a military course, passes through the tiny principality of Monaco. Above it rise the steep Maritime Alps. The Monacan farmers in the foreground are cultivating perfume flowers. In Monaco is the famous resort Monte Carlo, which people visit from all over the world.

oceanography. His museum is the finest of its kind in the world. La Condamine, one of Monaco's three towns, is a bathing resort, set in orange groves on the shore of the bay.

If we travel to Austria through Switzerland we come across another of the independent principalities of Europe—Liechtenstein—set in the midst of high peaks between the Austrian mountains of Vorarlberg and the Rhine. It is larger than Monaco, being about sixty-five square miles in area. It has one claim to distinction in that its inhabitants are exempt from military service, and free to pursue the pastoral life their forefathers led for centuries before them.

Once a Roman camp on the site of Triesen—before that town was wiped out by a landslide—Liechtenstein formed part of the great German Confederation of States; but in the Council of the Diet it maintained its practical independence by holding a separate vote; and when the Confederation was dissolved, Liechtenstein became independent (though economically allied to Switzerland).

In Prince Johann II, whose death in 1929 occurred soon after the fête in honor of his seventy years' reign, Liechtenstein had a benevolent monarch. He not only asked no taxes, but spent of his own fortune for improvements within the boundaries of his toy state, and even kept his palace and garden open to the public. Prince Johann had come of one of the most ancient families in Europe. He had a palace in Vienna with an unexcelled art collection and a telephone line to the capital of his little principality on the Rhine. He also paid out of his own pocket the major portion of the cost of the electric lighting of Vaduz and the hamlets, and the founding of electric sawmills, flax and cotton weaving industries. In 1921 Liechtenstein accepted of him a free constitution with a parliament of fifteen members. Swiss money is used, and the posts, telegraph and customs are managed by Switzerland.

LOOKING ACROSS THE YACHT BASIN AT MONTE CARLO

Monte Carlo is in the principality of Monaco on the southern coast of France, not far from the Italian border. The famous resort has luxurious hotels for wealthy visitors.

TRANS WORLD AIRLINES

SHRUBS AND STATUARY BY THE PRINCE OF MONACO'S PALACE

The sprawling structure, which dates back to the sixteenth and seventeenth centuries, is a mixture of styles. One of the building's most inviting features is the porches open to sea breezes. The palace sits high on a jutting rock cliff that forms a little harbor. Here yachts and small craft sway at anchor in the azure waters glittering in the sun.

THE FAMOUS OCEANOGRAPHICAL MUSEUM ATOP MONACO'S CLIFFS

The museum is perhaps the finest of its kind in the world and contains enthralling exhibits of marine life and other aspects of the sea. It was founded in 1910 by Prince Albert I in the old settlement of Monaco, which is part of the principality. The rocky headland of Monaco was the site of an ancient Phoenician and Greek temple to the mythological hero Hercules.

VADUZ, CAPITAL OF THE TINY PRINCIPALITY OF LIECHTENSTEIN

Overlooking the city from the high promontory is the Castle Liechtenstein, with a back curtain of lofty Alps. Liechtenstein, one of Europe's smallest independent states, has only sixty-five square miles; it is flanked on the west and south by Switzerland and on the east by Austria. Its economy —trade, finance and so on—is closely related to that of Switzerland.

PHOTOS, EWING GALLOWAY

LUXEMBOURG, CAPITAL CITY OF THE GRAND DUCHY

A view of the old prison in the lower part of the city which borders on the Alsette River. The upper part of the city is built on a plateau and was once called the "northern Gibraltar," because it had such a strong military position. The newer parts of Luxembourg, with modern and costly buildings, are laid out along wide, attractive thoroughfares.

A VENDOR'S STAND AT THE NUT FESTIVAL, VIANDEN

The first Sunday in October is nut festival day in Vianden, a village in the Grand Duchy of Luxembourg, near the German border. Children have worked hard gathering the nuts from the hilly countryside; these are carefully washed and sold along with other traditional goodies at the roadside stands. Vianden is an ancient town, dating back to the fourteenth century.

FREDERIC LEWIS
IN THE SHELTER OF THE PYRENEES: LES ESCALDES, ANDORRA
Ancient stone houses, haystacks and Italian cypresses snuggle cosily in the lee of rugged mountains. It is not hard to understand why Andorra has been able to maintain its independence, protected as it has been through the centuries by the ranges that surround it. Besides, there are few resources in the small area of the country to tempt covetous outsiders.

WHEAT FIELDS WITH SAN MARINO ROCK IN THE BACKGROUND

Like many larger countries, San Marino gets a large part of its income from wheat and other agricultural products. San Marino, though, is probably the only nation in the world that depends upon postage stamps for much of its revenue. The Government issues many stamps, knowing that they will be purchased by philatelists, stamp collectors, all over the world.

PHOTOS, EWING GALLOWAY

AERIAL VIEW OF THE INDEPENDENT REPUBLIC OF SAN MARINO

San Marino, the smallest republic in the world, covers an area of less than forty square miles. St. Marinus, a Dalmatian stonecutter fleeing religious persecution, founded the nation in the fourth century. Its capital sits atop Mount Titano, while small villages sprawl along the mountainside. Two regents and a sixty-man council govern the Republic.

Vaduz is an old-world village through which goose-girls drive their flocks. The castle, on a hilltop, has walls twenty feet thick and contains a splendid collection of armor. Though bicycles and even automobiles are seen in this mile-high country, oxen draw the carts and plows.

San Marino is reputed to be the oldest state in Europe. Located on spurs of the Apennines about twelve miles from the Adriatic, it lies between several Italian provinces. Its customs and constitution are survivals of the Middle Ages. The miniature country has had a part in many events of Italian history. It placed itself under the protection of the Italians in 1862.

Founded, according to tradition, in the third century by St. Martin, during the persecutions of Diocletian, the history of San Marino includes the founding of the monastery of St. Marino in 885. The independence of the diminutive republic was confirmed by the Pope in 1631, and it has been the only one of the Italian states to retain its independence. The town stands on Mt. Titano, a rock 2,437 feet high, each summit of which is fortified, and the fortifications of the state consist

BLACK STAR

AN ANDORRAN LAD AND HIS FLOCK IN THE RUGGED PYRENEES

A boy of an Andorran village leads his sheep down a narrow lane that traces its way along a terrace at the base of a massive rock cliff. Sheer escarpments, the severe winters, poor irrigation and indifferent soil make farming and grazing difficult and uncertain occupations. Yet the people, stubborn and resourceful, cling to their isolated spot in the high Pyrenees.

Three Lions

LIBERTY PRESIDES OVER THE SQUARE IN SAN MARINO'S CAPITAL
The majestic statue is in front of the government buildings. San Marino City perches on the western slope of Mount Titano just below the summit, which has three peaks. Each of the peaks is crowned with towers, connected by ramparts, where long ago the San Marinos defended themselves in turn against Hungarians, Saracens and Normans.

of three peaks each crowned with a tower, at the base of which stands Borgo, where oxen are the chief means of transport. The government is democratic.

The Grand Council of sixty is elected by popular vote, and two Regents appointed from their number every six months act as executives.

On the first day of April in San Marino one must be up by sunrise, otherwise there is risk of being hauled out in one's nightdress, placed upon a mule and paraded through the streets to the music of bells and jangling instruments and the jeers of the crowd. San Marino issues its own postage stamps. Tobacco, by international agreement, is not allowed to be grown within the state, but every year a supply is received from Italy, which, in addition, gives a large quantity of white salt.

A COVERED BRIDGE crosses the gently flowing Rhine from the Swiss shore to Bendern in Liechtenstein. The snowcapped Alps lie on the other side of the village church.

The mountainous state of Andorra, the Hidden Valley, lies high in the Pyrenees between the borders of France and Spain. Twelve hundred years ago, when the Moors swept down upon the Visigoths who had for three hundred years ruled Iberia (present-day Spain), a group of Catalan peasants fled from the foothills of Urgel, up the Segre and Valira rivers into a remote valley of the mountains that guard the northern frontier of their mother country. There, amid the deep undertones of mountain torrents, the dark-eyed refugees took up their lives.

Charlemagne came upon Andorra on his way southward to attack the Moslems. The people still treasure a document signed by him enfranchising the state. The present capital was once the scene of a battle in which Charlemagne's son Louis achieved a hard-won victory over the Mohammedans. In those days, of course, Europeans usually called Mohammedans the Saracens.

Louis placed Andorra under the protection of the Spanish Bishops of Urgel. Three hundred years later neighboring French counts disputed it with the Spanish bishop until 1282 when suzerainty was divided between them. Thus it happens that the tiny state finds itself under the joint authority and protection of France and the Spanish Bishop of Urgel. France represents Andorra in foreign affairs and manages public services such as education, post office and telegraph.

Andorra has but five thousand people scattered among half a dozen villages. They speak Catalan, and few of them have ever crossed the rocky frontier. Andorra is a primitive spot; its laws are unwritten and few of its citizens can read.

Government is by a council of twenty-four members who meet in a council chamber resembling the loft of the barn in which they stable their mules while deliberating. No one can serve unless he is married and head of a family. The council elects a First Syndic to be the executive head of the government, with a Second Syndic for deputy.

Andorra is astride the crest that separates the waters flowing toward the Atlantic in the west and the Mediterranean in the east. The passes leading to France are inaccessible for more than six months in the year, as they are then blocked by snow and all transport has to come from

THIS PEASANT GIRL of Vaduz (Vallis Dulcis, Sweet Valley), in Liechtenstein, lives among pastures musical with the bells of cattle on the pine-clad slopes of Vorarlberg.

POLICE HEADQUARTERS IN ANDORRA LA VELLA
The little village of Andorra la Vella is the capital of Andorra, the isolated and romantic little state that perches high in the Pyrenees Mountains on the border between Spain and France. Today a good road crosses Andorra, connecting the Spanish and French frontiers. Andorrans speak Catalan Spanish, and use both Spanish and French currency.

the Spanish side from which there is a good road. Vividly colored shrines carved of native stone are found everywhere.

Until recently the cultivation of tobacco was the leading industry. The plantations in the valleys are watered by a primitive system of irrigation consisting of tiny canals hollowed out of tree trunks. The tobacco grown is smuggled across the frontier. Indeed, smuggling is regarded in Andorra as an honorable profession. The smuggler must have not only the acuteness to avoid the officers of the law, but the physical fitness to carry loads up the mountainside. The natives are pastoral. They drink the acid and slightly sour wine of the country from leathern bottles similar to those their nomadic forbears used centuries ago. There is, however, this difference, that where the latter drank in the ordinary way, the Andorran holds the bottle a few inches from his mouth and lets the liquid pour into it.

The Andorrans have many quaint beliefs. Their fields must each have a sprig of cypress placed in the ground at one side and be blessed by the priest, that evil spirits may be warded off. If an Andorran sets out on a journey and he sees a white cat, he will turn back.

Sheep- and cattle-breeding are important occupations of the Andorrans. The women spin and weave the clothing worn by both sexes, and the home industries include boot-making, pottery and other crafts to supply the simple wants of the community. Andorra's isolation is coming to an end, however.

The Duchy of Luxembourg

The Duchy of Luxembourg is on the heavily wooded Ardennes plateau—a rising shelf of land a few hundred miles back from Europe's northwestern coast. Luxembourg is a land of gently rolling pastures marked here and there with castle-topped hills or steep river valleys. The streams of the north wind through slight highlands and rush into the Sauer, which also wends its way eastward to the Moselle, the river of the Luxembourg-German border. The principal river of the south is the Alzette. It flows northeastward across the southern plains, watering the small farms and providing transportation to the mines and mills of industrial towns.

The minette iron ore of this region is Luxembourg's richest resource. Most of the people of the Duchy work in the iron and steel industry.

Only one man in five now lives off the land. The farmers grow oats, wheat and potatoes and also raise horses, cattle, sheep and hogs. Those along the banks of the Sauer and Moselle tend lovely orchards and vineyards.

The story of Luxembourg begins in the eleventh century when it became a principality in the Holy Roman Empire. Several noblemen of Luxembourg were elected emperor; the son of one of these emperors was the adventurous King John of Bohemia. Made a duchy in 1354, Luxembourg came under the sovereignty of the house of Burgundy in the fifteenth century and later became a possession of the powerful house of Hapsburg.

Freedom Is Won, Bit by Bit

After the French Revolution, Luxembourg was a part of France. In 1815, after Napoleon's defeat, the Duchy passed on to the Netherlands. When Belgium broke with the Dutch King in 1830, she annexed a large part of Luxembourg. The remaining part—what we know today as Luxembourg—became virtually free, though the crown still remained with the royal family of Holland. Upon the death of William III, king of the Netherlands, in 1890, the house of Nassau inherited the Grand Duchy and made a complete break with Holland.

In 1867 the great powers of Europe declared Luxembourg neutral. The following year the people of the Duchy drafted a constitution and wrote this principle of neutrality into the document. Germany defied the declaration in both world wars. Her troops swept through the Alzette and Sauer valleys on their way into France. In World War II, Luxembourg suffered particularly heavy damage.

Luxembourgers themselves abandoned neutrality in 1948 when they amended their constitution and joined the Western

LA ROCCA, the citadel of San Marino, founded in the third century, stands on one of the three peaks of Mt. Titano in the Apennines. Of all the Italian states, San Marino alone has retained its independence. The stronghold is now used as a prison. Like other buildings of the republic, it is made of stone quarried out of the slopes of the mountain.

STREET SCENE in San Julian, a village in mountainous Andorra, a tiny republic that lies between France and Spain. Andorra is the last survivor of the miniature buffer states established by the Emperor Charlemagne along the Pyrenees, and it still treasures a document with his signature upon it. Although the country is very irregular and rugged, there is some excellent pasture land in the valleys on which the inhabitants raise livestock. The people speak Catalan, a Spanish dialect; and they use both Spanish and French currency.

THE TOY STATES OF EUROPE

European Union and the North Atlantic Pact. By these acts of co-operation they stood firmly with their neighbors, contributing troops and products of iron and steel.

Vatican City

In the city of Rome, there is an area that contains less than 110 acres and yet forms an independent and a very important state: the Vatican City. It has its own government, its flag—yellow and white—its diplomatic service and all the requisites of a sovereign country. To 400,000,000 Roman Catholics of the world, it is the residence of their spiritual leader, the pope. To tourists, the Vatican is a treasure house of the arts. The Palace of the Vatican and the Basilica of Saint Peter date from the Italian Renaissance and they are splendid examples of the architecture of that period. They contain paintings, frescoes and sculpture by the most gifted artists of the time: Michaelangelo, Raphael, Titian, Botticelli. There are also magnificent collections of Greek and Roman statuary and Egyptian antiquities. The Vatican has an astronomical observatory; and its library, particularly rich in manuscripts, is one of the most important in the world.

TOY STATES: FACTS AND FIGURES

ANDORRA

Occupies a valley in the Pyrenees between France and Spain and is under the joint suzerainty of the head of the French state and the Spanish Bishop of Urgel. Total area is 175 square miles with a population of 5,700, scattered in 6 villages. The government is in the hands of a council of 24 members elected for 4 years by heads of families. Half the council is elected every two years. Tobacco-growing and sheep-raising are the most important occupations. France represents Andorra in foreign affairs. Both the French franc and the Spanish peseta are accepted units of currency.

LIECHTENSTEIN

A principality on the east bank of the Rhine between Switzerland and Austria. Area, 62 square miles; population, 14,700. The crown passes by inheritance through male line of the house of Liechtenstein. A democratic constitution of 1921 establishes the right of all citizens to elect Diet of 15 members. Capital and largest town, Vaduz (population, 2,772). Roman Catholicism, predominant religion; 14 elementary and 3 advanced schools. Main products are agricultural—corn, wine, fruit and wood. Livestock numbers more than 10,000 head. Small industries produce cotton, pottery and leather goods. Good roads connect the villages. Member of Swiss customs union, uses Swiss currency and telegraphic and postal services; but issues own postage stamps.

LUXEMBOURG

A Grand Duchy ruled by heirs of the house of Nassau, is bounded by Belgium on the north and west, by France on the south, by Germany on the east. The twice revised constitution of 1868 sets up parliamentary government, recognizing social, political and economic rights of the citizens. Principal legislative house, Chamber of Deputies, has 52 members elected by electoral delegates. The sovereign also appoints 15 members to an upper house, the Council of State. Area, 999 square miles; population, 308,000. Primary education compulsory. Farming by about 30% of the people; principal crops: potatoes and grain. Livestock, over 200,000 head. Iron ore, pig iron and steel are the principal products of the very important metals and mining industry. Road mileage, 2,673; 340 miles of railway. Chief towns: Luxembourg (capital), 64,000; Esch-Alzette, 27,000. Monetary unit, Luxembourg franc.

MONACO

A principality on the Mediterranean coast of France near the Italian border, surrounded by the Alpes Maritimes. The Constitution of 1911 provides for National Council of 18 members elected for 4-year terms by universal suffrage. Council assists prince in legislation. Prince and State Ministry have executive control. Area, 368 acres; population, 22,000. Excellent small harbor. Independent postage system; in French customs union. Monetary unit, the French franc.

SAN MARINO

Is a republic located in the Apennine Mountains of Italy near the Adriatic Sea. The area is 38 square miles and the population, 14,500. The republic is governed by the Grand Council of 60 members elected by popular vote. Two of the members are appointed to serve as Regents for a term of 6 months. The chief exports are wine, cattle and building stone. About 35 elementary schools, a technical and a high school. Monetary unit, the lira.

VATICAN CITY

Independent papal state on west bank of Tiber within city of Rome. Executive, legislative, judicial authority rests with pope, the spiritual head of the Roman Catholic Church. Temporal powers are delegated by the pope to church dignitaries and to the college of Cardinals, which acts as a senate and meets at the death of a pope to elect his successor. The Vatican maintains a railroad station, postal and monetary systems, radio station and official papal journals. Area, 108.7 acres; population, about 940. Monetary unit, the Vatican lira.

THE LURE OF ITALY
Its Vital People and Their Land

Of all the striking things that can be said about Italy, none suggests more than this: that, century after century, it has attracted more visitors than any other country in the Old World. Whether to conquer or to admire, to learn, to worship—or merely to relax for a season in the sun where the food is superb and the people are a joy—sooner or later, the traveler has found his way to the Italian Peninsula. It was so before the dawn of history; it is even more so today. Italy is a great crossroads for major air and shipping lines. (Rome, Venice and the island of Sicily are discussed in separate chapters.)

WHAT is Italy's attraction? In ancient times it was the land and the climate. The successive swarms of invaders who came down from the north, even before the days of pagan Rome, were doubtless drawn by the fertility of the soil, the mild, semitropical climate and the general charm of the landscape. To these—the attractions of nature—were later added the attractions of the mind and the heart. Italy soon excelled in the fields of art and literature, science and religion. At the time of the Empire, under Augustus, when Rome had inherited and absorbed the civilization of ancient Greece, the Italian Peninsula became the center of learning in the Western world. With the reign of Constantine, who in the fourth century made the Empire Christian, Rome and Italy became the seat of Christendom. At the height of the Middle Ages, two great Italian minds dominated the world of learning: St. Thomas Aquinas, who surveyed and interpreted all Christian knowledge; and Dante Alighieri, the Florentine poet who wrote *The Divine Comedy* and became both the interpreter and the prophet of his age. After these came the giants of the Renaissance: Leonardo, Michelangelo, Machiavelli and the rest; and after them, a continuous line of distinguished minds down to the present day: Ignazio Silone, Enrico Fermi, Carlo Levi.

For centuries, scholars and artists and men of religion have been going to Italy in increasing numbers for professional purposes—and, incidentally, to enjoy the sun and the landscape and the food and the people. And what of the ordinary travelers—the men and women who go to Italy primarily because it is a lovely country in the Mediterranean? Are they not also pleasantly aware that they are going to a country rich in the achievements of the human spirit? In the thirteenth century, Dante called Italy *"il giardin dell' Impero,"* the garden of the Empire. The Empire has long since disappeared; but those who have seen Italy, even since the ravages of World War II, will affirm that the garden remains—as lovely as ever.

The Italian Peninsula is small and densely populated. It projects south and east from the mass of central Europe, extending 700 miles into the Mediterranean. It is shaped like an enormous boot, bound on the north by the Alps, on the south by the Mediterranean, on the east by the Adriatic and on the west by the Tyrrhenian Sea. The breadth of the peninsula nowhere exceeds 150 miles. There are 389 inhabitants for every square mile—double the ratio in France. In addition to the long, irregular coast line, Italy's main topographical features are the range of the Apennines and the basins of the Po, the Tiber and the Arno rivers. The Apennines stretch from the Gulf of Genoa east toward the Adriatic to a point near Ravenna, whence they turn south and extend as a backbone down the full length of the peninsula.

The country may be divided into three main geographical areas: northern, central and southern Italy. Each of these areas has distinct regions. There is, of course, a certain amount of overlapping

GRANDEUR in the midst of Lake Maggiore. The slim cypresses and classic statuary are on a terrace of Isola Bella. The islet, once barren, was transformed into a fabulous garden in the seventeenth century.

SYMPHONY IN BROWNS on a farm in Umbria, in central Italy. Beside the huge haystacks—winter fodder—plods a team of the white, long-horned oxen that have been bred in Umbria from ancient times.

PHOTOS, AMERICAN HOME FOODS, DIVISION OF AMERICAN HOME PRODUCTS, INC.

TIVOLI lies astride a ridge, seventeen miles northeast of Rome. The town was a favorite resort of the ancient Romans and is still famous for its breath-taking waterfalls.

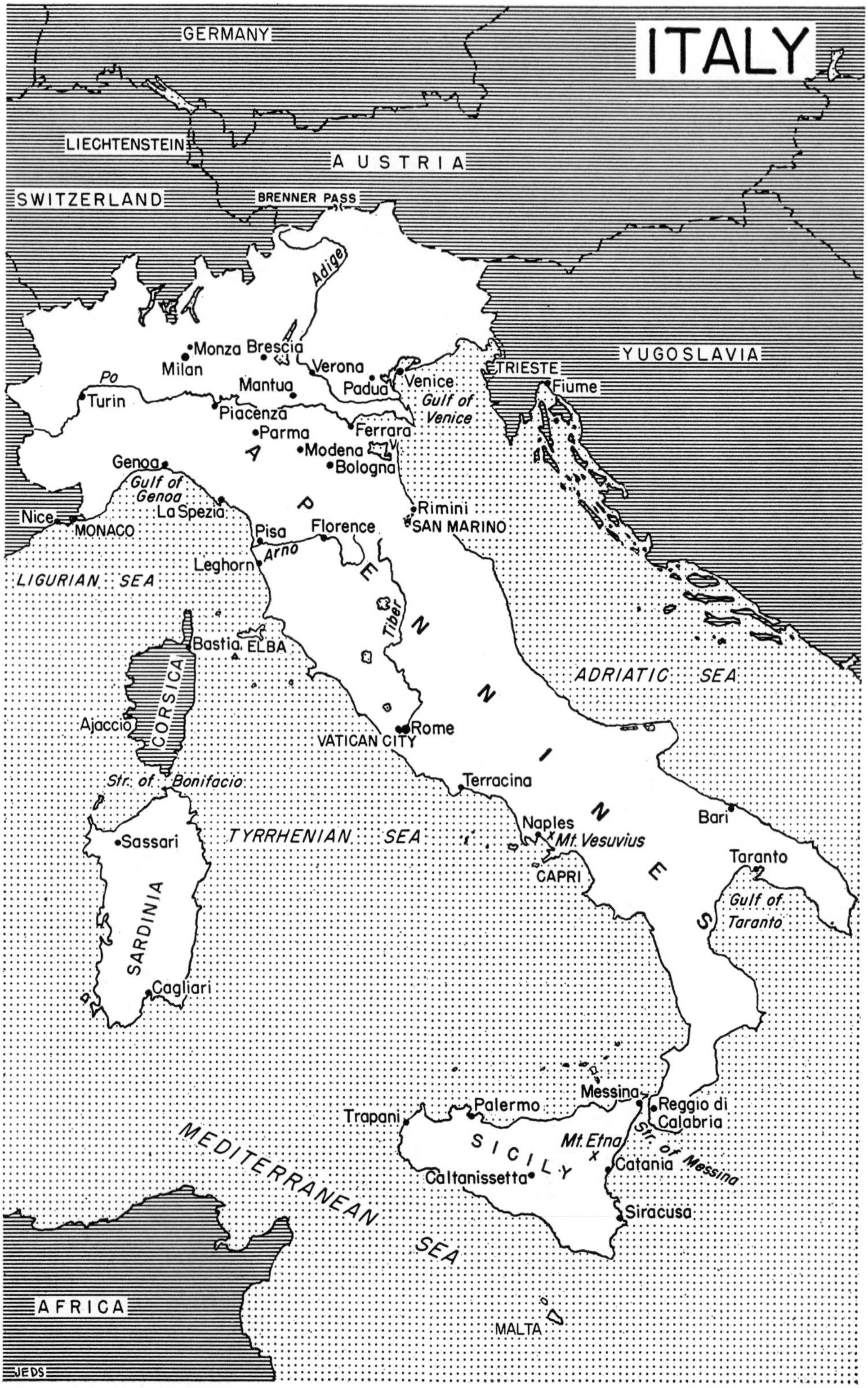
ITALY
GERMANY
LIECHTENSTEIN
AUSTRIA
SWITZERLAND
BRENNER PASS
Adige
Monza
Brescia
Milan
Verona
Po
Mantua
Padua
Venice
Turin
Gulf of Venice
Piacenza
Parma
Ferrara
Modena
Bologna
Genoa
Gulf of Genoa
La Spezia
Nice
MONACO
Pisa
Florence
Arno
Leghorn
Rimini
SAN MARINO
TRIESTE
Fiume
YUGOSLAVIA
LIGURIAN SEA
Tiber
Bastia
ELBA
CORSICA
Ajaccio
ADRIATIC SEA
Rome
VATICAN CITY
A P E N N I N E S
Str. of Bonifacio
Terracina
Naples
Mt. Vesuvius
Bari
Sassari
TYRRHENIAN SEA
CAPRI
Taranto
Gulf of Taranto
SARDINIA
Cagliari
Messina
Reggio di Calabria
Trapani
Palermo
SICILY
Mt. Etna
Str. of Messina
Catania
Caltanissetta
Siracusa
MEDITERRANEAN SEA
AFRICA
MALTA
JEDS

THE LURE OF ITALY

in any such division of a country, but on the whole, each area has its own identity.

Northern Italy lies north of the east-west range of the Apennines and is composed of the regions Piedmont, Lombardy and Venetia. Central Italy extends from the southern slopes of the Apennines to Rome and is composed of the regions Emilia, Liguria, Tuscany, Umbria, Latium and the Marches. Southern Italy is made up of Campania, Abruzzi and Molise, Basilicata, Apulia and Calabria. Except for Naples, all the important cities are north of Rome. Siena, Florence, Pisa, Bologna, Ravenna are in central Italy. Genoa, Turin, Milan, Venice are in northern Italy.

Italy is one of the hottest countries in Europe. Yet the effect of its southerly position is tempered by the seas which bound it on the east and west, by the range of the Apennines and by the Alps to the north. The result is a great variety in climate. The Po Basin in the north is chilled by the cold winds from the Alps, so that the winters there are generally cold and the summers hot. Thus in the whole region north of the Apennines, no plant will grow that cannot stand severe winter frosts. On the other hand, the strip of coast between the Apennines and the sea, which extends from Genoa south, has a semitropical climate in which olives, grapes and citrus fruits flourish.

In central Italy the climate is generally mild and favorable to the cultivation of the olive, the mulberry and the vine. But when we reach the central range of the Apennines, we find the coldest districts in Italy. In the upland valleys of Abruzzi,

A VILLAGE CHURCH, tile-roofed and whitewashed, beside Lake Como. At the tip of the promontory beyond, which divides the lake into two arms, is the little port of Bellagio.

ITALIAN STATE TOURIST OFFICE

SAN GIULIO (St. Julius) lies like an enchanted island in the turquoise waters of Lake Orta (or Cusio), seven miles west of Lake Maggiore. The buildings on the rocky islet are those of a seminary and the ancient basilica of San Giulio. This church was founded in the fourth century by St. Julius, who came to the district to convert the residents of the town of Orta.

WASHDAY AT OMEGNA, a small town at the north end of Lake Orta. At this spot a stream emerges that flows toward Lake Maggiore so that the waters of the small lake are always being poured into the large one. Both Lake Orta and the stream furnish water to Omegna's various industries—iron and steel works, an aluminum factory, tanneries and cotton and paper mills.

on the eastern flank of the mountains, snow begins to fall early in November and heavy snowstorms occur as late as May. In the district around Lake Fucino, directly east of Rome, there are heavy snowstorms even in June. About forty miles away, on the shore of the Adriatic, from Ortona to Vasto, the fig tree, the olive and the orange thrive luxuriantly. Likewise, in and around Naples, the thermometer seldom falls to the freezing point; but twenty miles to the east, in the Avellino Valley, encircled by high mountains, frosts are not uncommon as late as June. Farther south and east, in the heart of Basilicata, Potenza has the coldest summer temperature in Italy.

However, the effect of the mountains and the sea upon the climate is nowhere more strikingly revealed than in Calabria, the foot of the boot which reaches out into the southern end of the Tyrrhenian Sea and nudges the island of Sicily. Its entire shore line is a continuous grove of olive, orange and lemon trees which grow to a size and luxuriance equaled nowhere else in Italy. Here also thrive sugar cane, cotton plants, date palms, pomegranates and the Indian fig. Yet if we go inland for a few miles we are in the foothills of the southern Apennines, on whose lower levels are groves of oak and chestnut trees. On the higher reaches, where snow begins to fall in late September, grow conifers.

Italy is not and never has been an industrial nation. While she has the skilled labor and great natural water resources for the development of electric power, she lacks both solid and liquid fuels and most of the basic raw materials necessary for an industrial economy. Nevertheless, her industrial achievements, mainly in the northern cities, have been noteworthy for quality. Where raw materials are lacking, there cannot be quantity production; but a people whose inventive and artistic talents are second to none cannot be restrained from producing an automobile, a sewing machine, a typewriter equal to any

PIAZZA FRATELLI CAIROLI in Milan. Over it looms the clock tower of Sforzesco Castle, which today is a museum. In the foreground, traffic circles around a statue of Garibaldi.

WITH MILAN CATHEDRAL, Italian Gothic architecture reached its height. In places the lacy marble carving is so delicate that it must be held together and braced with iron rods.

FOUNTAINS AND GARDENS of the Villa Lante, a superb Renaissance mansion at Bagnaia, central Italy. In such landscaping, the Italians' gift for gardening left a record, kept exquisitely precise, of the luxurious Renaissance taste.

PHOTOS, J. BARNELL

DANCING in a courtyard at Scanno, a village mid the rugged mountains of the Abruzzi district. The lovely costumes of the girls date from the 1600's.

produced in the chief industrial centers of the world. For the same reason, Italy has excelled for centuries in the various artisan industries—in any craft that requires imagination, patience and dexterity. The furniture of Lombardy, the marble and alabaster work of Carrara, the pottery of Faenza, the leatherwork of Florence, the jewelry of Venice, the glass and beads of Murano—these and a dozen other artisan products are well known to people of taste everywhere.

Indeed, Italy is modestly at work in all industrial pursuits, from shipbuilding to the making of mouth organs. Nevertheless, the core of her economy is agriculture. One half of the people are on the land. More than a third of the national income comes from agriculture. A little less than half of the land is tilled; and except for a serious lack in wheat, Italian farm production meets home needs. Various reforms begun in the 1950's hold promise for the future. When these reforms, which include land reclamation and new methods of farming, become a reality, the country will yield even more richly than has been possible before.

Cereals, Olives, Grapes

The variety in climate, as we have noted, makes possible a remarkable variety in crops. However, the main products of the soil are cereals, olives, grapes, fruits, nuts and vegetables. There are also some important industrial crops. Hemp and flax are grown in great quantities. Enough tobacco is produced to supply the home market. Cotton, oil seeds and sugar beets are also grown, though on a limited scale.

Of the cereals, wheat, maize and rice are the most important. From the first two come the basic items in the Italian's diet—bread, *pasta* and polenta. Rice is grown primarily in the Po Valley, though there is some produced in the low, moist valleys of central Italy. Wheat and corn are grown anywhere that appropriate soil is available, though normally about half the wheat crop is harvested north of the Apennines.

The olive and the vine grow profusely throughout the peninsula. The grape varieties that produce the finest wines are grown mainly in Piedmont and Tuscany. The best olive oil is pressed from the olives grown in Tuscany near Lucca. Citrus fruit thrives along the Ligurian coast southeast of Genoa; but the main and best crop is harvested along the Tyrrhenian coast of Calabria. This region forms the "toe" of the Italian peninsula.

The Rich Basin of the Po

In looking over the total economy of Italy, industrial and agricultural, one cannot escape being impressed by the leading role of the north. The basin of the Po River, which is the key to the geography and economy of northern Italy, is one of the largest and most fertile in Europe. More than half the population of peninsular Italy is in the north. About half the agricultural and industrial workers of the country are in the north. The north produces the bulk of the vital cereal crops. The major industries—textiles, woolens, motor vehicles—are in northern Italy. Thus it is not unfair to say, by way of summary, that Italy is basically an agricultural land, rich in the north, fairly prosperous at the center and poor in the south. There are no large rivers in the south, the peninsula is narrow, and, save for the small, fertile basins along the coasts, the grim realities of the landscape are the barren, rocky Apennines.

Before going on to a glimpse of the people and their achievements, there is another matter of importance to be noted—the importance of the tourist trade. What the Italians call *turismo,* tourism, is a major industry, or, as they say, "an invisible export."

Italy *must* import fuel, raw materials and certain foodstuffs. She cannot survive without these materials. To pay for them she exports other foodstuffs and certain manufactured and semimanufactured goods. But since she must buy more than she can sell, she is always plagued by what the economist calls an unfavorable balance of trade. To make up this trade deficit, she has depended upon receipts from shipping, remittances sent back by

ON THE GULF OF SALERNO. Above the houses of the fishing hamlet winds the Amalfi Drive. This highway twists along the cliffs of the Sorrento Peninsula, which divides the gulf from the Bay of Naples. Now the road dips close to azure waters and then climbs high through orange groves, planted in narrow terraces on the cliff face.

SERENE SIMPLICITY—the remains of an exquisite Greek temple at Paestum (south of Naples). A tiny village today, Paestum was a Greek colony as early as 600 B.C.

GLITTERING in the light, stalactites and stalagmites form a natural altar in a grotto near Bari. Dripping water and the sea have created many caves in Italy.

ITALIAN STATE TOURIST OFFICE

THE JAGGED PEAKS of the Italian Dolomites, an extension of the Alps, have a wild, strange beauty. At certain hours, the rocks reflect the light in a dazzling display of color.

CALTEX

OIL PIPELINE at Savona, on the Gulf of Genoa. Through it, crude oil delivered at the port is carried for ninety-seven miles to refineries near Milan, in the industrial heart of Italy.

MARITIME STATION at Genoa, where passenger vessels dock. For centuries Genoa has been a great port and trading center, and it still welcomes ships from every quarter of the globe.

her emigrants and, mainly, upon money spent in Italy by tourists. Consider the following facts:

In the decade 1931–40, the credit balance of the tourist trade was in the neighborhood of 1,374,000,000 lire a year. For the same period the average annual deficit in the balance of trade was around 2,606,000,000 lire. Thus the tourist earnings for that decade covered about half of Italy's trade deficit with the rest of the world. In the best of those years, 1937, over 5,000,000 foreigners visited Italy. Since 1949, the number of visitors has been steadily increasing. In a recent year over 7,000,000 tourists brought to Italy a grand total of 154,000,000,000 lire. So may we not say that Italy's major export is sunshine and flowers and historic and artistic treasures—and her gracious self? And that thus her beauty and her grace are a main prop in her economy?

When we turn from the land and its products to the people who inhabit it, what do we find? A distinguished English traveler is said to have remarked that the visitor cannot enjoy Italy until he gets her monuments off his conscience. Did he mean that you cannot enjoy to the utmost, as you certainly should, the Roman landscape or *fettuccine* at Alfredo's if you are haunted by the feeling that you must prowl through the Colosseum and gaze in awe at Michelangelo's Moses and take pictures of antiquities? If so, there was excellent advice in the observation. If you are not interested in monuments and art treasures, forget that they exist and go with a clear conscience among the people. You will find there more than you could possibly absorb in a lifetime of summers. In the end you will have missed nothing, for the people will see to it that you become acquainted with the monuments.

First, a word of warning. You will be frequently baffled by contradictions, by an apparent lack of order in the midst of a people noted for their keen minds, their art, their civility. Suspend your judgment and, at your journey's end, reflect upon what you have seen in the perspec-

SPRING BLOSSOMS brighten a "trullo" farmhouse. "Trullo" refers to the early rough-stone buildings found in southern Italy.

HARPOON ready for a swordfish off Scilla. The town perches on Scylla rock, in legend one of the perils of the Strait of Messina.

A SKIER CONTEMPLATES a mass of the Dolomites, a jagged eastern arm of the Alps. The fluted formation seems to rise straight up like the walls of some enormous medieval fortress.

THE HILLTOP CITY of Traui, between Florence and Rome. Almost everywhere in Italy, towns cling to heights rather than nestle in valleys. In time of strife, lofty location made defense easier.

PHOTOS, J. BARNELL

BASILICA OF ST. ANTHONY in Padua. The thirteenth-century church contains the tomb of the saint. It was to Padua that Petruchio came to woo Katharine in *The Taming of the Shrew*.

tive of the history of the Italian people.

The discerning visitor will soon discover that he is among a people who have a gift for the enjoyment of life. If it may be said that the Americans have a talent for the accumulation of wealth, the English for government, the French for orderliness, then it may surely be said that the Italians have a gift for life. Perhaps a more accurate way of putting it is that they are a people who live intensely, without reservation. Whether old or young, at work or at play, they extract everything from every moment. That, surely, is their genius. They have a gift for tears as well as for laughter; for hate as well as for love. They mourn without restraint; they love without restraint; they hate and they quarrel without restraint. They never compromise with life; to live is to live fully.

For every important event—birth, baptism, communion, marriage—there is the appropriate celebration in the grand manner. Friends and neighbors unite; choice bread and wine are shared. There are song and dance and tears and laughter. And when one of them dies, the survivors mourn long and generously and record their sorrow in eloquent epitaphs:

> Here lies the mortal remains of
> Cavaliere Professore Alfredo Mori,
> Remembered for his exemplary virtues,
> His devotion to learning and to the arts,
> Whose zeal in the service of man was surpassed
> Only by his devotion to the Eternal Father,
> To whose memory his inconsolable consort
> Raises this monument in love everlasting.

A people in whom there is so much sympathy, such an abundance of passionate interest, cannot let a single moment of life go unobserved and uncelebrated. Everything that is human is their business. They may therefore appear excessively curious or even meddlesome. The fact is that they are simply interested. Even a minor traffic accident summons them to the spot—not as spectators, but as participants in a moment of life. They bring no order to the scene, only life. They ask questions; they dispense advice; they quarrel; they take sides.

It has been frequently said that the Italians are a very artistic people. It is true; perhaps the word "creative" more accurately defines them as a people. Quite apart from their continuous achievement in all the arts, their instinct for creating—that is, for bringing into being—is evident in their total conduct of life. Note the artisans at work; the passionate interest they bring to their labor. Watch the peasants in the fields, pruning, plowing, planting, harvesting. See how they have terraced the mountain slopes. Each little plot is protected by a retaining wall of stone, and the soil in which the vine is growing was carried up the mountainside in baskets. Observe the housewife in the kitchen; with a few herbs, a few weeds, a sliver of meat—from practically nothing she creates a savory meal. There is order in their labor; there is meticulous husbandry; but, above all, there is passionate

A STREET VENDOR of Arezzo displays her Lenten candles. All during the season of Lent, Italian churches, great and small, are ablaze with candles, some of them highly ornate.

STANDARD OIL CO. (N. J.)

THE "SIREN CITY," Naples, located in front of the ankle of the Italian boot, lies upon the shore of a lovely bay, north of Mount Vesuvius' lofty cone. It is a beautiful city in a beautiful position, but it is noisy and, in many parts, squalid. In the great harbor lie all kinds of vessels— warships, liners, cargo steamers, pleasure and fishing boats. It is the last that we see here, graceful craft with huge lateen sails that overtop the buildings, craft manned by sailors whose fishing ground is the blue Mediterranean. Boats and sails are of many colors.

THE CASTLE OF ARCO, from its lofty crag 930 feet above the River Sarca, once protected from all enemies the town that lies in a half moon at its base. Destroyed by the French in 1703 during the War of the Spanish Succession, its ruins remain to crown the jutting peak. The town of Arco, among olive groves at the base of the mountain, is today a winter resort, largely because of its sheltered situation. The Sarca flows into the north end of Lake Garda and emerges on the south as the Mincio River. The waterway is the boundary between Lombardy and Venetia.

care. Whether you call it the artistic or the creative instinct at work matters little.

Or you may say that they have a gift for survival. So many people in a country not richly endowed by nature in raw materials, and where there has been such uneven distribution! Yet they manage to live. In inland Calabria, in Lucania, in metropolitan Naples—to name only the better known dens of misery—it requires talent to survive, to be sure; but before the talent is the passionate care, the love of life.

An ancient story, well known among Italians—really a popular classic—dramatizes not only their gift for survival but also the humor with which they confront their misery. It is the story of *Bertoldo*, written in the late sixteenth century by Giulio Cesare dalla Croce. The hero is the fool of the Longobard King Alboin. For some misdeed he is condemned to die. He asks and receives one grace; he may choose the tree from which he is to hang. For twenty years he travels far and wide at the King's expense, searching diligently for the tree fit to be his gallows. Of course, he does not find it.

Yet a people who so love to live and who know *how* to live, have so little talent for living together. They know a great deal about the techniques of surviving as individuals, but they have much to learn about the practical politics of surviving as a group. There have been as many as twenty political parties competing for power. Even today in the beginning years of the Republic and after the sobering effects of fascism and war, there are nearly a dozen parties vying with each other.

The Gift of Eloquence

Italians love rhetoric—speechmaking—in the same way they love opera. They delight in applause. Every eloquent man is the possible leader of a party. If he cannot win leadership in the party to which he belongs, he may resign—with eloquence—go across the street, hire a hall and declare himself the leader of a new party. Italians are capable of the most exalted ideals of liberty, and no one can state them more effectively than they. But they generally take a rigid stand—without give-and-take. So they fail to advance, as the British, for example, have advanced, in the art of government.

Walking along the Corso in Rome one Sunday morning when the streets were deserted, I was approached and engaged in conversation by an amiable Italian who was apparently in search of an audience. Before I knew exactly how it had happened, he was delivering to me a terrible denunciation of the Government. It was a fiery, full-dress performance, complete with gestures and facial expressions dominated by sparkling eyes and such expressive lip movements as would have been eloquence to the deaf. He stood at the curb and I leaned against the wall of a building listening intently and observing closely. When he had finished he came near me and asked, "Wouldn't you say that I speak rather well?" I assured him he had spoken very well indeed. With that he bade me good day and departed, and I continued my walk.

Key to the Italian Character

The political clumsiness is perhaps, in some measure, the result of the Italian's excessive individualism. He is jealous of his personal identity. He wants to be a wheel rather than a cog. No man who loves life so dearly as he does is happy in the shade. Observe a group of Italians in conversation. They are flushed with excitement. They gesticulate violently; their voices rise and explode. They seem ready to leap at each other's throats. Yet they are not actually mad, nor really excitable; they are individuals in earnest, desperate competition for survival.

They are a people to whom the family tie and the obligations that stem from it take first place over all earthly considerations. This does not mean that their family life is always happy, nor that one may find in the Italian home an unusually high degree of friendliness and easy relationships. Whatever the feeling between members, however, the Italian family is bound together by the conviction that an injury to one is an injury to all.

In a novel by Ignazio Silone, a mother

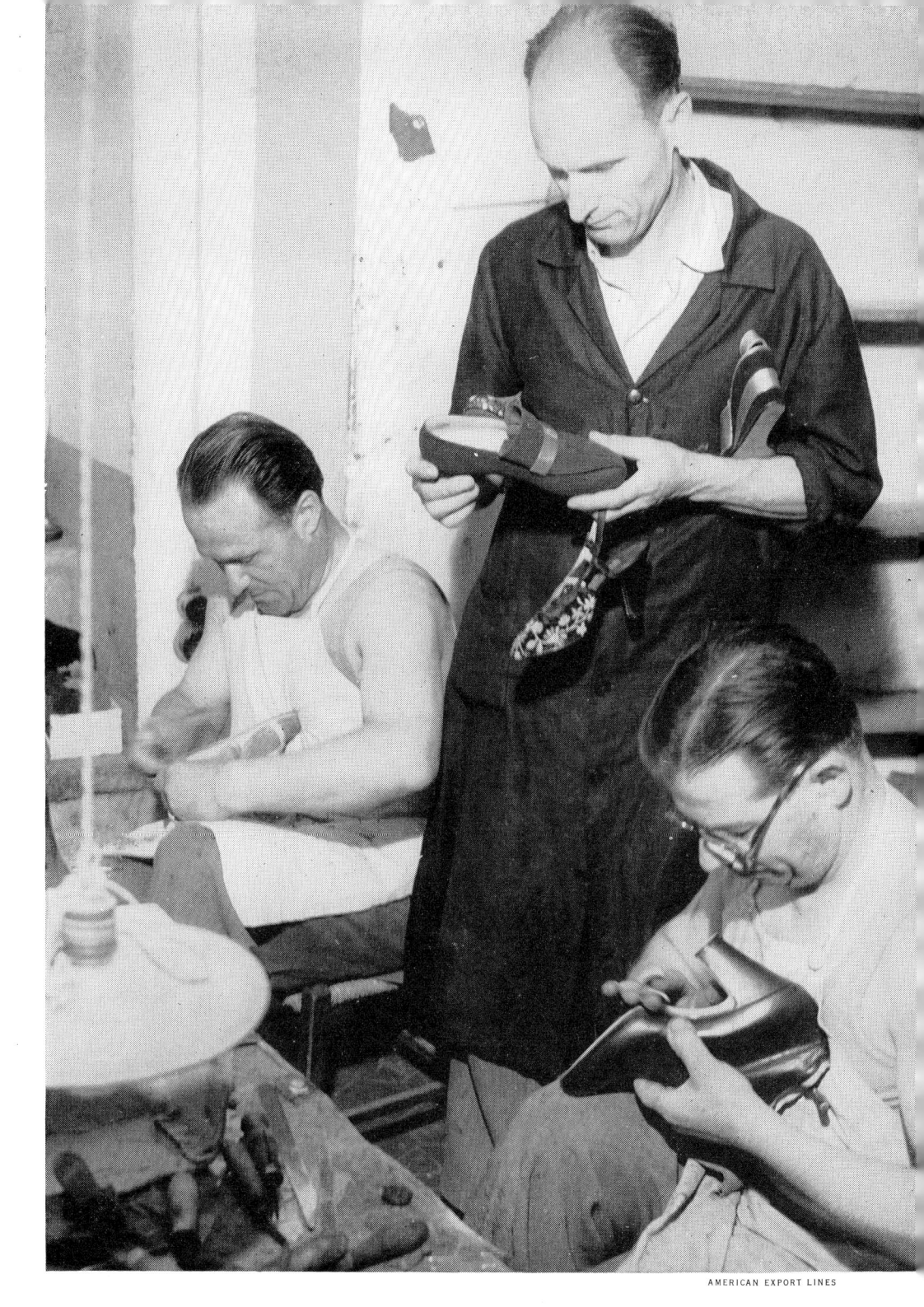

HAND-MADE SHOES for the world's fashionable women. Italian designers and craftsmen turn out footwear, in the finest leathers and fabrics, that cannot be excelled for quality.

PIAZZA VECCHIA of Bergamo, Lombardy city near Milan. The square is the center of the ancient walled section, which crowns a high summit. Standing in the midst of massive Romanesque buildings, the visitor is wafted back to the early Middle Ages.

LEATHER SHOP in Florence. The city is not only a world center of fine arts but is also famous for its production of leather goods made by master craftsmen.

D. FORBERT

THE PONTE VECCHIO in Florence. Above the old shops and dwellings that clutter the bridge runs a roofed passageway—the Vasari "corridor"—which leads from the Uffizi Gallery on the north side of the Arno River to the Pitti Palace on the south.

AMERICAN HOME FOODS. DIVISION OF AMERICAN HOME PRODUCTS, INC.

defines perfectly the meaning of the function of the family in Italian culture. A grandson is in trouble, and she is urging one of her sons, the grandson's uncle, to help her protect the young man: "You are right in saying that he has committed wrongs; but you, my son, must admit that I am right when I say that, notwithstanding all your allegations against him, he is none the less one of ours. No man-made law can change his blood. That which binds us together is in our bones, in our blood, in our viscera. We may refuse, certainly, to share his wrongs and his sins; but we cannot refuse to share his pain. Families exist to sustain each other in misery and in sorrow. If life should become permanently and absolutely happy, places of amusement would thrive; but the family would disappear. For the first time in my long life, my son, I have known shame; not because one of ours has created a scandal, but because we have not lifted a finger in his defense. It is true that the Spinas have always been known for their stubbornness, their tough hides, their hard bones; but they have also been known for their heart. Whoever has laid hands on one of them has had to reckon with the entire family. You, my son, have lost all but their stubbornness. Who has changed your blood?"

Yet in a land where the heart matters so much, where there is so much civility, kindness, humanity, the intelligent and sympathetic traveler will find much that is difficult to understand. Like so many countries whose history goes back for long, long centuries, Italy is two worlds: the world of privilege and the world of poverty. Now, since the end of World War II, there are signs of such reforms as may bring the two worlds closer together.

Meanwhile, the stranger who visits Italy must expect to be accosted by beggars and other parasites, as he must expect it wherever poverty and hunger prevail. They are not violent. They will implore; they will beseech; they will importune you with pathetic tales of suffering; and they

PONTE VECCHIO, the famous "old bridge" that spans the Arno in Florence. There are shops above the arches. Before World War II there were six bridges across the Arno here.

A GODSPEED FOR FISHERMEN. In beautiful Portofino, a small town on the Italian Riviera, a blessing is invoked on the fishing fleet. Under the canopy a priest carries the monstrance.

THE LURE OF ITALY

CHRISTOPHER COLUMBUS is supposed to have been born in this house in Genoa.

may cheat you. They bring to their parasitic occupations the finesse and ingenuity acquired through centuries of struggle for survival. No, they will not slug you; but be prudent and hold fast to your possessions. Remember, too, that where one of them wounds you, another may come to soothe your pain. A friend of mine with whom I was exploring Florence was cheated of $300 by a street money changer. On the following day he stopped at a newsstand and bought a paper. When he had walked about a block the news boy came running up to him. "You paid me too much, sir," he said. And he handed him thirty-five lire. There you have it: saints and sinners, the whole of life.

The differences in climate, topography and in the growth of the soil are balanced by an interesting variety in culture. North, south and central may be said to correspond to three main cultural as well as geographical divisions of Italy. Dozens of dialects are spoken in the peninsula; yet it is much easier, for example, for a Calabrian and an Abruzzese (two southerners) to communicate with each other than for either of them to communicate with a Genoese. It is also interesting to note that the north's main contribution to the peninsula's culture has been in statemanship and affairs: Garibaldi and Count Cavour; central Italy's has been mainly in the arts: Dante and Michelangelo; the south's main contribution has been in philosophy: Giordano Bruno and Giambattista Vico. There have been exceptions, of course, but this historical pattern is quite noticeable.

The different dialects enrich the language and literature of the whole peninsula. They are not, moreover, a barrier to communication. There is a national language—literary Italian—spoken everywhere and taught in the schools. It began as the common speech of Tuscany and was cultivated in the early thirteenth century at the court of Frederick II, king of southern Italy, then called Sicily. Later, Dante and the various Renaissance writers perfected it.

As one travels south from the Po Basin

A CLASSIC POSE along the ancient Appian Way, which runs between Rome and Naples.

A CERAMIC MENAGERIE awaits removal from an open kiln at a pottery works in Florence. The animal figures, ornate vases and plates and cups are destined for shipment overseas.

FLAG-WAVING DAY is an old festival in Siena. The merrymakers wear Renaissance costumes —reminders of the Tuscan city's days of glory. Siena was a center of early Renaissance art.

to Calabria, among all the other differences none is more fascinating than the variation in food.

A word, first, about Italian cuisine—food and cooking. It ranks with the finest in Europe. Many travelers say it is the best. It is a balanced cuisine: many vegetables, many fruits and nuts, much cheese, always good soup, excellent bread, good wine. With the exception of a few extreme dishes found in this or that province, it is a cuisine to which the traveler takes immediately—as if he had been raised on it from the day he first drew breath.

To begin with northern Italy, one must remember that it is the land of rice, dairy products, truffles and fine wines. (Like mushrooms, truffles are fungi.) Butter, for example, rather than olive oil, is basic in cooking. *Risotto alla Milanese,* rice cooked in butter, broth, onions, flavored with saffron and served with grated cheese, is one of the characteristic dishes of the north. So is *fonduta,* which is a mouth-watering blend of melted Fontina

SHOPPING BAGS, beach hats and other articles woven of straw turn up almost everywhere. Gay and inexpensive, they are among the most popular souvenirs of a visit to Italy.

A BLOCK OF MARBLE—raw material for a work of art. The marble quarries, especially those of Carrara, have been famous for more than two thousand years, and are still yielding.

cheese, butter, milk, egg yolks and a layer of white truffles from Alba. So is *bagna cauda,* a sauce made of butter, anchovies, garlic and truffles, into which are dipped hearts of celery and cardoon (a relative of artichoke). *Osso buco,* veal shank and marrow (the vegetable) cooked with rice, is a specialty in Lombardy, as is also *busecca,* a soup made of selected tripe and various vegetables, seasoned with herbs and served with grated cheese.

In the north are produced three of Italy's famous cheeses—Bel Paese, Gorgonzola and Stracchino—and most of the peninsula's great wines. Northern Italians are fair and tall, hard workers, ambitious and hearty eaters; they take their cuisine seriously. They will insist that the white truffles of Alba are better than the dark truffles of France. Have you ever heard of *grissini,* the long, crunchy bread sticks? It was a northern Italian, Antonio Brunero, who created them, in 1679.

Central Italy, properly explored, is a paradise for the lover of fine food. Along the Ligurian coast, from Genoa to Livorno (Leghorn), one will find a wide variety of Mediterranean sea food. Anywhere along the coast, but especially at Spezia, one may have *boiabesa,* a fish soup made by combining choice sea food, flavored with herbs, and white wine. (On the Adriatic coast, at Ancona, the same soup will be called *brodetto.*) *Buridda,* fish cooked in oil with a variety of vegetables, and *scabeccio,* a subtly pickled fish, are two other specialties of the Ligurian coast.

The Art of Making Pasta

Emilia is famous for its pork products: *prosciutto, salcicce, mortadella;* for its home-made *pasta,* for *ravioli* and *tortellini;* and for Parmigiano, one of the most widely known among Italian cheeses. Nowhere else in Italy is the art of making *pasta* so perfected as in Emilia. An ordinary housewife, in half an hour, can make enough *taglierini,* a kind of *pasta,* for a dozen people. With eggs and flour and just a drop of water she makes the dough and kneads it until it is firm enough to roll. Then with a rolling pin a yard or

GRAPE HARVEST near Monti Chianti, Tuscany. A wine is named for the mountain range.

MARINA PICCOLA BEACH on Capri. The rocky island is one of the loveliest spots on earth. Covered with luxuriant vegetation, it is like a giant emerald in the sapphire Bay of Naples.

PHOTOS, TRANS WORLD AIRLINES

THE BLUE GROTTO of Capri, the most famous of the caves that have been pounded out by waves. When the sun shines outside, the grotto waters seem almost alive with an electric-blue light.

FIAT DIESEL TRACTORS, which are helping to modernize Italian farming. The country is a leader in European automobile production. Among its best-known cars are Fiats and Lancias.

more long she presses it out into circular sheets, paper thin. She then cuts it into ribbons a quarter of an inch in width. In Rome this *pasta* will be called *fettuccine,* and will be boiled and drained like spaghetti, and served swimming in butter and grated cheese. In Emilia they prefer it served with a sauce of meat, tomato, herbs and mushrooms. In Genoa, the same *pasta,* made in exactly the same way, is served *al pesto*—with an uncooked sauce of garlic, fresh basil and olive oil. No matter where you have it, it will be a memorable experience; and it is the quality of the *pasta* itself that matters, the making of which is really a folk art.

In Tuscany the traveler will find the very best cuisine Italy has to offer. It is light, simple, savory, balanced. The olive oil here is the finest in Italy. It is light and nutty, with the full flavor of the ripe olive. The sauces are lean rather than overly rich. There is an emphasis on soups and green vegetables. Carrots, beans, peas, lettuce, artichokes, fennel—all the vegetables are picked young and may be served with a light dressing of olive oil deliciously seasoned. *Bistecca alla Fiorentina,* beef steak as prepared in Florence, is grilled and seasoned only with salt, pepper and a few drops of olive oil. Another example of the taste and simplicity of Tuscan cookery is *fritto misto alla Fiorentina.* This is a mixed fry—brains, sweetbreads, artichokes, zucchini and very small lamb chops are dipped in a thin batter and fried in a small quantity of olive oil, then served with a light spray of lemon juice.

The cuisine of southern Italy is noted for an excessive use of tomatoes, hot peppers and macaroni products. In fact, *maccheroni* and spaghetti are the principal items in the diet of the Neapolitans. South of Rome there is an abundance of eggplant, peppers of various kinds, tomatoes, asparagus, artichokes, olives and chicory. The southerners cook them very well, although the visitor may find them somewhat too hot and spicy. On either coast there is a great variety of fish, especially tuna, eels, trout, and oysters along the Gulf of Taranto. Game is plentiful, such as boar, mountain goat, snipe and other small birds. All of these are available in the restaurants of southern Italy. And, of course, oranges and lemons, nuts, figs and luscious table grapes are at home in the region south of Naples.

In food and wine and many other matters, there is much good-humored rivalry between the various regions. The Italian is proud of his region, his province, his campanile. Few towns are without a campanile, or bell tower. The visitor need not take sides. A wise rule to follow is that wherever he goes he should ask for the special food of the province. He

THE AMPHITHEATER at Pola, a port of Istria, is a relic of the ancient Romans, and could seat 25,000 people. The Venetians, who took the town in 1148, used its stone seats as building material. Taken by Austria in 1850 and by Italy after World War I, Pola was ceded to Yugoslavia in 1947. Italians form a large part of its foreign population.

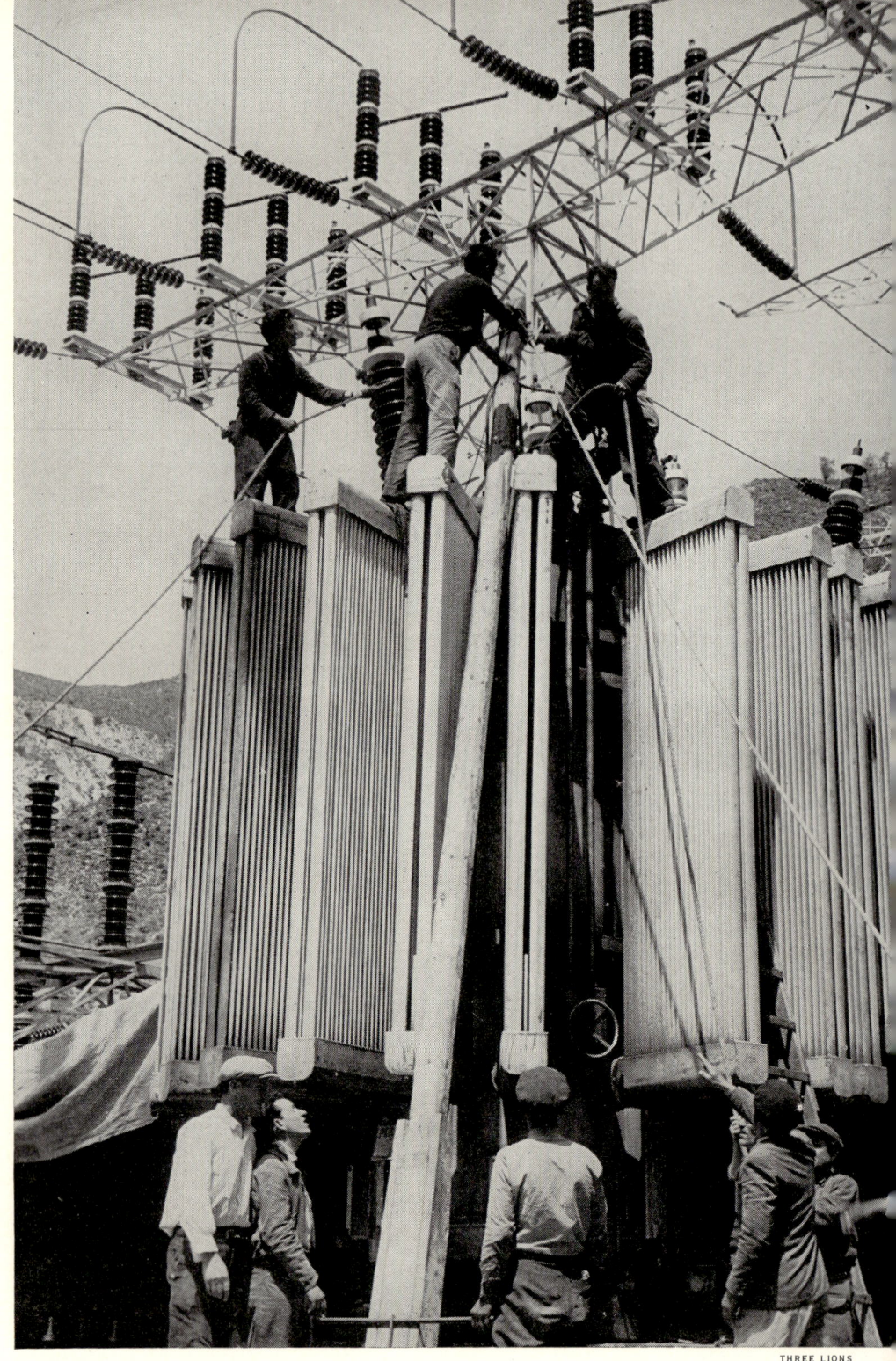

AN ELECTRIC-POWER PLANT is installed in Calabria, the "toe" of Italy. Such projects are beginning to transform the south, which has been neglected over a long period.

will seldom be disappointed. Moreover, the request will bring him closer to the people.

As he reflects upon his Italian journey, the thoughtful traveler is likely to be puzzled by a people who know how to live so well and yet govern themselves so ill. It is a paradox; but the reason is not far to seek. What we know as Italian culture has been in the process of development since the time of the Etruscans, at least five hundred years before Christ. Yet, as a nation, Italy is less than a century old. Before 1870 she was a cluster of cities and towns, in conflict among themselves and the special prey of various continental rulers. It is one of the major ironies of the Western world that Italians should have begun to make distinguished contributions to political theory, the idea of liberty and the art of government a full six hundred years before they could unite themselves into a nation. Finally, inspired by Mazzini the writer, directed by Count Cavour the statesman and led by Garibaldi the soldier, they expelled the foreigner and formed a united Italy in 1870—though as a monarchy.

LIFE SPILLS OUT into the streets in the old, crowded and poor section of Naples.

MODERN NAPLES is to be seen partly along the water front. Wide avenues follow the curve of the bay, and facing the water are a number of up-to-date hotels and office buildings.

THE LEANING TOWER of Pisa, the cathedral's bell tower, is famous, neither for its beauty nor for the tone of its bells, but because it is about fourteen feet out of perpendicular.

THE DUOMO, the handsome cathedral of St. Maria del Fiore in Florence, is the fourth largest church in Europe. The square campanile is considered to be the finest of its kind.

After World War II, they took another step toward the achievement of democracy: they voted against the continuation of the monarchy and established a republic. The first Parliament under the new constitution was elected in 1948. In 1953 was held the second general election. There has been much to do in a country that was deeply scarred by twenty years of fascism and nearly ten years of war. The deputies elected by the people have been hard at work. There have been bitter rivalries. The problems have been extremely difficult. Some progress has been made; and there is every reason to believe that, given time, the Italians will learn how to govern themselves. With a people so wise and so sane, it cannot be otherwise.

ANGELO M. PELLEGRINI

THE CONVERSATION may be on art or food. Whatever the subject, talk is eloquent.

ITALY: FACTS AND FIGURES

THE COUNTRY

Central peninsula of southern Europe. On the east is the Adriatic Sea; on the south, the Ionian Sea; on the west, the Tyrrhenian and Ligurian seas; on the north, forming a natural boundary, the Alps. Area, 116,305 sq. mi., which includes 81 sq. mi. from zone A of Trieste; population, about 50,000,000. There are 19 regions (divided into 91 provinces) as follows: Piedmont, Valle d'Aosta, Lombardy, Trentino-Alto Adige, Venetia, Friuli-Venezia Giulia, Liguria, Emilia-Romagna, Tuscany, Umbria, Marches, Latium, Abruzzi and Molise, Campania, Apulia, Basilicata, Calabria, Sicily, Sardinia.

GOVERNMENT

Italy became a republic by a vote of the people in 1946. A new constitution was approved by the assembly in 1947 and took effect January 1, 1948. It provides for a strong central government, a Parliament of two houses, a president to hold office for 7 years and equal voting rights for all over 21. The Vatican City of 109 acres became an independent state in 1929.

COMMERCE AND INDUSTRIES

About 43% of the total area is under crops, 22% under meadows and pastures, 10% devoted to horticulture, 19% to forest, and 8% is unproductive land. Fruit, wheat, corn, potatoes, olives and sugar beets are grown. The textile industry (silk, rayon, wool and cotton) is the largest and most important. Dairy farming and cheesemaking are also important industries. Manufactures include lace, machinery, foodstuffs, lumber and woodwork, art goods, wine and automobiles. Minerals found are sulfur, building and decorative stone (granite and marble), zinc, iron, mercury and lead. Petroleum has been discovered though production waits on development.

The chief exports are vegetables and fruits, rayon, cheese, felt hats, rice, olive oil, gloves, marble and alabaster. Imports are meat, wheat, coffee, fish, wool, raw cotton, coal and coke, machinery, mineral oils and crude rubber.

COMMUNICATIONS

Railway lines, about 13,000 miles, of which about 10,000 are state-owned. Telegraph lines, about 37,000 miles. There are 10,150 telegraph offices. Total length of national highways, 105,938 miles. In a recent year, 2 airlines were in operation with regular flights to Tunis, Tripoli, Athens, Cairo, Beirut, Istanbul, New York and Buenos Aires.

RELIGION AND EDUCATION

Roman Catholicism is the established religion, but freedom of worship is allowed. Education is regulated by the state, which maintains public schools of every grade, but only the lower grade instruction is compulsory. There are 27 state and free universities, technical schools, higher institutes, and a national institute for the instruction of illiterate adults.

CHIEF CITIES

Populations: Rome, capital, 1,735,354; Milan, 1,288,301; Naples, 1,044,586; Turin, 712,596; Genoa, 680,563; Palermo, 483,777; Florence, 376,383; Bologna, 339,195; Venice, 316,228.

The City that Ruled the World
Rome and the Ruins of Its Ancient Splendor

In the days of its grandeur as the heart of the far-flung Roman Empire, Rome was already being called the Eternal City. Some Latin writers, Vergil among them, prophesied that the city and the empire would endure forever. Alas for their dreams, the empire eventually shriveled away. The city, however, has remained in existence, for almost three thousand years. For some centuries its greatest influence has been spiritual for within it is the headquarters of the Roman Catholic Church. Present-day Rome also has another kind of importance, political, as the capital of the Italian Republic.

AS we approach Rome we enter what is known as the Roman Campagna. It is a low plain, marshy but very dry in some seasons, that extends like a sea to the walls of Rome. In the days of the Caesars the Campagna seems to have flourished. Then it was abandoned, partly for lack of water and also because malaria was rife. In this century, the marshes have been drained and the land has been restored to some extent.

The founding of Rome is veiled in myth. No doubt there was a village on the site, chosen perhaps because the hills were free of malaria, in very early times. The ancient Romans believed that their proud city was founded by Romulus in 753 B.C.

Rome is usually said to be built on seven hills. Actually it spreads out over ten hills, one of which, the Janiculum, lies west of the Tiber.

South of the Janiculum is the colorful Trastevere (across the Tiber) quarter. The people who live there—clerks, artisans, small tradesmen—speak a dialect all their own. They also boast that they are the only true Romans. Ever since the quarter came into existence in the Middle Ages, the fiercely independent people of the Trastevere have held aloof from the rest of the city, even though they may work in other sections.

Nevertheless—except for Vatican City, also west of the Tiber—what most of us think of as Rome is east of the winding river. Ancient Rome centered around the Palatine hill, with the Forum at its foot. Just northwest is the Capitoline hill, surmounted by an enormous monument to King Victor Emmanuel II. The structure faces the Piazza Venezia, the heart of the modern city. On one side is the Palazzo Venezia, whose little balcony was the scene of many of the dictator Mussolini's public speeches.

Perhaps the most familiar street to today's visitors is the Via Veneto. It begins at one of Rome's loveliest squares, the Piazza Barberini, where a fountain spouts from a triton on a sea shell. Along the wide avenue are hotels, shops, sidewalk cafés. Late in the afternoon it is where everyone goes who wants to see and be seen. The Via Veneto leads toward the stately Borghese Gardens, the walks shaded by great ilexes.

Crowning another hill, the Quirinal, is a magnificent palace of the same name. It was begun by Pope Gregory XIII in 1574. Later it was the king's residence, and today the president of Italy lives there. Nearby is Rome's largest and most spectacular fountain, the Trevi. The water cascades down over rocks into a pool, presided over by Neptune and other deities. If you toss a coin into the pool you will be certain to return to Rome.

Another popular meeting place is the Spanish Steps, where in warm weather you can buy flowers by the armful. The long graceful flight is the stairway to the church of Trinità dei Monti. At the foot of the steps is the Piazza di Spagna (Spanish Square), around which the artists' quarter clusters.

If the day of our arrival at Rome is clear, presently the eye is caught by what looks

COLOSSEUM. Though worn by time and weather, it is still an awe-inspiring symbol of the Roman Empire's days of glory.

FOUNTAIN OF THE NAIADS (water nymphs) in the Piazza Esedra. Modern Rome is a city of fountains, the water splashing against figures out of myth.

CASTLE OF SANT' ANGELO (right) and Sant' Angelo Bridge across the Tiber. St. Peter's dome is in the background.

MONUMENT to Victor Emmanuel II, united Italy's first king. The monument surmounts the Capitoline Hill.

ALL ROADS—and air routes, too—lead to Rome. Most of the world's major airlines operate to the Italian capital from European cities, the Americas, Africa and the Orient.

ST. PETER'S BASILICA, CROWN OF ITALIAN RENAISSANCE ART

St. Peter's Basilica dominates the right bank of the Tiber. A small chapel and a basilica built by Constantine preceded St. Peter's on the present site. The façade is resplendent with baroque decoration. Floating over all is the great dome, begun by Michelangelo and his architectural masterpiece, all the more magnificent for the beauty and purity of its simple design.

THE PIAZZA OF ST. PETER'S AND THE AVENUE TO THE TIBER

Statues of Christ, St. John the Baptist and the Apostles look down on the Piazza, the masterpiece of Bernini. In the center is an obelisk; gigantic fountains are off to the sides. Doric columns, 370 in all, form the graceful half-ovals of the enclosing colonnades. Leading toward the Tiber and the rounded tomb of Hadrian is the wide Via della Conciliazione.

FROM THE PINCIO GARDENS we look across a modern quarter of Rome to the glittering white mass of St. Peter's on the farther bank of the Tiber. The Pincio, which is a favorite resort of the Romans in the cool evening, was turned from a vineyard to pleasure grounds at the beginning of the nineteenth century; but it was not the first time that it had been laid out in such a fashion. It was the "hill of gardens" of the ancient Romans, famous for the luxurious villas there of notable men such as Lucullus, a Roman general who gave fabulous banquets.

THE TEMPLE OF SATURN, now reduced to eight meaningless pillars, looms above the triumphal arch of the Emperor Severus on the Capitoline Hill. In early times the public treasure was stored in the Temple of Saturn, which, from the remains still existing, must have been a magnificent building. It was approached by a lofty flight of steps. The splendid church of Santa Martina e Luca, which was first built in the seventh century on the ruins of the hall in which the Senate of ancient Rome held its secret meetings, faces the temple.

VATICAN CITY ART GALLERY—STOREHOUSE OF PRICELESS TREASURES

The Vatican Pinacotheca—its gallery of rare paintings—houses a collection of the works of Raphael, Leonardo da Vinci, Fra Angelico, Murillo and many other Italian and Spanish masters. The gallery is a favorite visiting place for art lovers. By copying the paintings, students hope to recapture something of the mood and technique of the originals.

THE CITY THAT RULED THE WORLD

like a cloud on the horizon. This is our first glimpse of Rome. It is the dome of St. Peter's, and in those marks against the sky, like pencil scribblings on a slate, is the eternal city of the empire of the Caesars, of the dominion of the Popes and now of the Republic of Italy.

The city by the Tiber is a strange admixture of old and new. The drive from the station reveals a street which might well be found in any modern city. Street cars rumble, newsboys shout—and there are more newspapers than can be counted in New York City. Sturdily built flower girls give color to the scene. Gowned priests push through bustling crowds—for all Rome hurries in these busy days, and tourists with red guide-books add to the bustle.

Every now and then we come upon a piazza or public square, with obelisks, columns, fountains and perhaps a few trees. We are impressed by the many squares, the balconies of the palaces, and the colonnades, the fine churches, the obelisks, the ruins, no less than by the colorful gardens, the cafés, the bookstores and the smart shops. Above all looms St. Peter's gigantic dome, while the columns of the Caesars brood over all.

COURTESY, ITALIAN TOURIST INFORMATION OFFICE

MAGNIFICENT GARDEN OF THE HISTORIC PALAZZO COLONNA

The Palazzo Colonna, an impressive reminder of the greatness of the Colonna family, stands on the broad Corso Umberto, near the center of Rome. The construction of the Palazzo was begun in the 15th century by Pope Martin V, one of the Colonna. The Palazzo has a fine gallery. It also boasts of beautiful gardens, of which the above photograph gives us some idea.

SWISS PONTIFICAL GUARDS are always on duty at the Vatican, and form part of the Pope's train in processions. Their uniform had altered considerably through the centuries, and had become really ugly. In 1914-15, the above distinguished garb was provided for them. It is an exact reproduction of the uniform worn more than three hundred years ago.

STONE RELIEF RECENTLY FOUND AMONG THE RUINS OF THE TRAJAN FORUM

The vanished splendor of Imperial Rome appears again in the stone sculptured in high relief recently found among the ruins of the Trajan Forum. Last and most magnificent of all the fora of ancient Rome, it was built early in the second century A.D. The griffin represented above was supposed to watch over hidden treasure. It was consecrated to the sun.

The Palatine Hill (Palatium) overhangs the Forum. This is the hill on which Romulus built the first Rome. Today the place is a mass of débris, but we may trace the Servian Wall (which was probably built by Servius Tullius), as it has been disclosed by excavations reaching from the Tiber straight to the Capitoline Hill, thence to the Quirinal, and see how it was made of two-foot blocks of tufa quarried on the spot. We may even see the cave—known as the Lupercal—in which the twin founders of the city were supposedly suckled by the wolf.

The Forum Romanum, which begins in a hollow of the eastern slope of the Capitoline Hill, was the heart of ancient Rome and the meeting-place of the first citizens. It became in time the centre of the civic and political life of the city. On this spot were raised memorials to Roman heroes, temples to their gods and tribunals of justice.

Barbarian conquerors burned and pillaged it; the makers of Christian Rome took its stone to build their churches; ruin and neglect fell upon it, so that the greater part lay buried for centuries beneath forty feet of rubbish, and its surface was used as a cattle market and as a place for washer-women to hang out their clothes to dry.

Now, thanks to the excavators, a great deal of the ancient Forum has been revealed, and we shall stand before the relics of temples, prisons, tombs and basilicas. We shall see what remains of the Old Senate House, and the depression known as the Lake of Curtius. According to legend, in 362 B.C. a chasm had suddenly opened in the Forum and an oracle declared that it would close only if Rome's greatest possession were thrown into its depths. Marcus Curtius, believing that a good citizen was the city's greatest possession, mounted on his horse and in full armor leaped into the chasm, which instantly closed again.

The tourist season begins with Christmas. During the two weeks from Christ-

QUIRINAL PALACE ATOP ONE OF ROME'S HIGHEST HILLS

Once the summer residence of the popes, the palace on the Quirinal was the home of the Italian royal family from 1870 to 1946. Facing it are two superb marble groups of horse tamers.

PHOTOS, BLACK STAR

CORAZZIERI, COLORFUL REMINDER OF THE ITALIAN MONARCHY

The brightly clad Corazzieri are today at the service of Italy's president. This group of a hundred specially chosen men was originally organized as a royal guard of honor.

THREE GRACEFUL COLUMNS ALONE REMAIN OF A BYGONE SPLENDOR

In the heart of Rome, amid ruins of the ancient Forum, stands a remnant of the temple built to honor Castor and Pollux, the warrior twins who figure in Greek and Roman mythology.

MODERN APARTMENT DWELLINGS HAVE INVADED AN OLD, OLD CITY
New buildings going up in Rome still have balconies, though streamlined, to please romantic tastes. Since bygone times Latin peoples have liked these artistic, projecting galleries.

TRAJAN'S COLUMN COMMEMORATES A TIME OF ROMAN TRIUMPH
Bas-relief figures on the column chronicle the exploits of the Roman army that conquered the Dacians. The lopped pillars and tumbled marble are all that remain of the ancient Forum.

mas to the Epiphany, the Romans give themselves over to feasting and merry-making. On New Year's Day everyone from the postman to the man who mends your typewriter must receive a gratuity, and in return, one receives gifts from the trades-people. The custom is traced to Janus, for whom the hill known as the Janiculum was named, and to whom after his death a temple was erected. The first month was also named in his honor. He it was who is supposed to have introduced the custom of giving gifts. In the old days bouquets, especially of verbena, were the usual gifts, but as Rome grew in splendor the practice of gift-giving grew to such proportions that in the time of Augustus families were beggared by the necessity of distributing gifts beyond their means. Today at both the Vatican and the Quirinal New Year's Day is spent in receiving calls of state.

The modern city promenades in the fashionable Corso. From the Piazza del Popolo one may retreat to the coolness of the Pincio Gardens, famous even in antiquity, on Monte Pincio. Around five o'clock the band plays and all Rome walks.

Along the Corso, one of Rome's principal streets, friend meets friend for a cup of coffee at a nearby restaurant, say, the Colonna or the Fagiano in the busy Piazza Colonna about halfway down the street.

Centuries now have passed since the

AMERICAN EXPORT LINES

OXEN AND AQUEDUCT RECALL THE FLAVOR OF ANCIENT ROME
The aqueduct at which these oxen are drinking dates back to the fourth century B.C. So well did the Romans build their water systems that some of the ancient aqueducts are still in use.

Forum swarmed with the busy life of ancient Rome and the Colosseum echoed to the cries of the gladiators and the roaring of hungry lions. Despite the ruin, they are still imposing and typify the city which once gave its laws as an example to every nation. The broken columns of the Forum and the ruined buildings are reminders of the days when ancient Rome was the mistress of a mighty empire and the center of civilization.

One thing we shall notice in our wanderings through Rome is the great number of churches, most of them handsome and impressive and many of them full of pictures and statuary. Rome is one great museum. One could spend years without exhausting its possibilities.

St. Peter's, with its great colonnaded piazza, its dazzling fountains and its yellowish-white stone glistening in the sunshine, is perhaps the most magnificent church in the world. The vast interior is a wilderness of gold and marble, presided over by colossal statues of the saints, past prelates of the church and great Christian kings. The dome, over 404 feet high, was built as a canopy above the tomb of St. Peter. The dome's four supporting piers are the work of Bernini who also designed the colonnade in the piazza, the pulpit and the baldachin, or marble canopy, over the papal altar.

The Vatican Palace

Near the Basilica is the Vatican Palace, which became the residence of the popes in 1377. Its galleries contain the largest collection in the world of Greco-Roman and Roman sculpture. The magnitude of the palace is staggering. There are twenty courts, two hundred staircases and more than one thousand rooms, including picture galleries, museums, chapels, libraries and the apartments of the pope.

Many of the world's great artists have assisted in decorating the Vatican. The Sistine Chapel with its ceiling and altar-wall frescoes by Michelangelo is a wonder of Renaissance beauty. Though Michelangelo dominates the chapel, there are also notable works by Botticelli, Domenico Ghirlandaio and other masters of a great age. The Loggia and Stanze are rich with tapestries and paintings designed or executed by Raphael; his Transfiguration is in the Pinacoteca, or Vatican Picture Gallery; and there are other paintings by him throughout the palace. Tapestries by Fra Angelico are in the Chapel of Nicholas V. In the Vatican Museum we find the original of the celebrated Laocoön group, supposed to have been sculptured in the first century B.C. There are also fine copies of other Greek statues, such as the Venus of Cnidus, the Apollo Belvedere and a Belvedere torso.

The Temporal Realm of the Pope

The Vatican, the Lateran Palace (the papal residence before 1377), other buildings in Rome, and the Castel Gandolpho, a summer palace ten miles from Rome, have been outside the jurisdiction of the Italian Government since 1929, when the Pope gained temporal authority of the little state. More on Vatican City will be found on page 294 of this volume.

Across the Tiber from the Vatican toward the Colosseum are many famous monuments, churches and other buildings clustered about the Capitoline Mount, religious center of ancient Rome, and the Piazza Venezia, center of the modern city. Within the massive Palazzo Venezia is a museum containing works by Titian and Fra Filippo Lippi. Near by is a twentieth-century statue in memory of King Emmanuel II and the tomb of the Italian Unknown Soldier.

The Piazza del Campidoglio, in the vicinity of the Capitoline Mount, is largely the work of Michelangelo. In its center the equestrian statue of Marcus Aurelius, a fine example of second-century Roman sculpture, stands on a graceful base made from plans by Michelangelo. Michelangelo's artistry is further represented in the design of the near-by Senatorial Palace, modern Rome's city hall.

After just a short tour of the most famous parts of Rome we can easily see that it is, indeed, one great museum. Yet for all its antiquity and its superb treasure of art from the past, it is as alive today as it was two thousand years ago.

THE FAMOUS APPIAN WAY HAS BORNE THE TRAFFIC OF CENTURIES
Extending from the center of Rome southward to Capua and then southwest to Brindisi in the heel of the Italian boot, Via Appia takes a motorist past crumbling ruins of ancient glory.

STURDY MEMORIAL TO A POWERFUL OFFICIAL OF ANCIENT ROME

The Pyramid of Caius Cestius, people's tribune in the days of the mighty Caesars, has lasted through the centuries. The tomb's heavy walls are of brick encased in blocks of marble.

AS THE HOUR STRIKES ABOVE ST. MARK'S SQUARE

This is one of the two gigantic bronze figures of Moors that regularly sound the hours at the top of the Clock Tower. It is over an arch on the north side of the square. Below the Moors, in the façade of the tower, is a great gilt and enamel clock face. In the background, rising still higher, is the Campanile, bell tower of St. Mark's Cathedral.

BEAUTIFUL VENICE

Born of the Marriage of Land and Sea

Like a city in a haunting dream, Venice has the most improbable site. For it spreads out over 118 islets that are only a few feet above sea level. Among the islets run 160 canals, crossed by some 400 bridges. The whole cluster lies within the Lagoon of Venice, in the northwest corner of the Gulf of Venice. Only a chain of sand dunes shelters the Lagoon from the open Adriatic Sea. The Lido, the noted beach resort, is on the largest of the sand bars. The city's buildings have no ordinary foundation. They stand on piles driven deep into the mud and are anchored with heavy blocks of stone.

VENICE—Venezia to the Italians—at first impresses the visitor with its quiet. No roar of street traffic assaults the ears. Instead one hears the faint lisp of the salt tides lapping the walls of the canals, the cries of gondoliers, the chug of motorboats, the slosh of the little steamers against the piles. It is a city of beauty and mystery, and its history is romantic.

Once a great sea power, Venice remains important for shipping and shipbuilding. After World War I, modern docks and loading equipment were installed, and an improved channel was dug to the Adriatic. Venetian artisans have long been noted for jewelry, mirrors, mosaics, silks and laces. Above all, today, Venice is geared to the tourist trade.

To account for the beginnings of the city, the Venetians usually claim that Attila the Hun was responsible. The story goes that refugees, fleeing before the fifth-century Asiatic conqueror on the mainland, found safety on the islets in the Lagoon. It is likely, however, that some fishing hamlets were already there. Also, there was not one but a number of barbaric invasions into Italy, by Huns and then Lombards, during the fifth and sixth centuries. With each invasion the Lagoon population grew. By the end of the sixth century the community was established permanently. It consisted of twelve townships, and the people had come to believe that they were born free.

With the final breakup of the Roman Empire, the community came under the Eastern, or Byzantine, Empire—though more in theory than in fact. As early as 697 the Venetians elected their first doge (chief magistrate). From then until 1797 Venice was really a republic.

It was attacked repeatedly by Dalmatian pirates during the early Middle Ages. Strong castles were built, and the canals were guarded against enemy craft by chains stretched across their mouths. Houses clustered around the churches, and the canals between these villagelike groups were deepened. In places trees were planted on the banks. Land was reclaimed from the sea and vineyards and orchards were set out.

While most of the canals were spanned by simple wooden bridges, the first bridge across the Grand Canal was a pontoon one—supported by boats. The earliest of the stone bridges to be built, some time before 1170, was San Zaccaria. The original Rialto bridge—a pontoon structure—was designed in 1178. It was twice rebuilt in wood during the thirteenth century. Today's Rialto bridge, designed by the same architect who built the Bridge of Sighs, was not completed until 1591. The early bridges had no steps but were for the most part inclined planes which could be crossed by the horses then in universal use. By a law of 1392 all horses and mules had to wear bells, as a warning to pedestrians, and no horses could be ridden in the crowded Merceria. As early as the thirteenth century, brick pavements began to appear and ferries to run to the mainland and to some of the outlying islands.

Gradually the city grew to be a power-

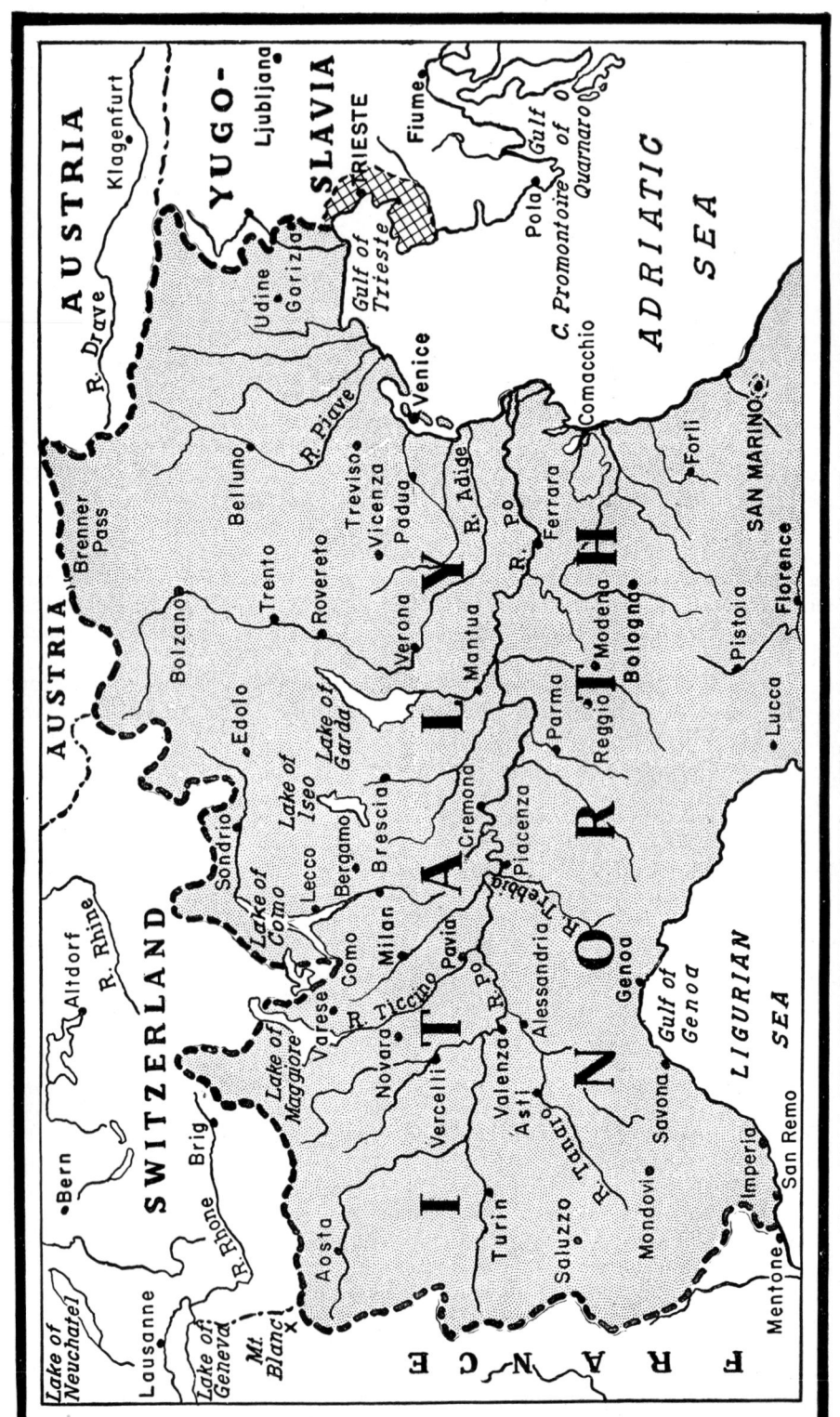

TWO SEAS AND THE LAKE-STUDDED ALPS GUARDING THE PLAIN OF NORTHERN ITALY

CAUSEWAY LINKING VENICE, THE CITY IN THE SEA, TO MAINLAND
The city of Venice consists of about 120 small islands in a shallow lagoon in the Adriatic. It is connected with the mainland by a motor bridge (above) and a 2½-mile-long railroad bridge.

ful republic, with a fleet that enriched itself on the commerce of the world. Great oaks were felled in the forests of the mainland for the building of ships. These vessels went to England for wool and to India and China for merchandise for Italy. They penetrated through the Black Sea for furs. By taking part in the Crusades, Venice even secured trading stations in the Holy Land.

As the Eastern Empire weakened, Venice obtained colonies in Cyprus, Crete and the Ægean Islands. When Genoa, aided by Greece, began disputing the trade routes, Venice established a Latin empire in Constantinople (1204-61). In 1379 the Genoese blockaded Venice: the island city in turn blockaded the Genoese fleet and compelled its surrender. The fall of Constantinople came in 1453, and thereafter Venice had to fight the Turks in defense of her eastern colonies. (This warfare did not, in fact, cease for over 250 years.) A body blow was struck at her commercial supremacy in 1486 by the discovery of a sea route to India.

Venice now acquired Padua, from which some of her people had fled so many centuries before, together with Cremona (home of the famous violins), Verona and certain other towns and provinces, and ruled them wisely. Because of her growing power she was attacked by the League of Cambrai (aided by the rulers of France and Spain), and in 1509 lost most of her mainland territory. After about 1797 the government had become an oligarchy of wealthy families ruling through the Grand Council and the smaller Council of Ten. The latter body made the Doge a mere figurehead. Napoleon destroyed the republic in 1797, but by the Treaty of Campo Formio Venice fell to the lot of the Austrians. A revolt in 1848-49 freed her for a time, although, becoming weakened by the cholera brought about by poor sanitation, she again fell under Austrian domination, from which this time she struggled free in 1866. Her history from that date is united with that of the Italian people.

Picture the world in the days of the greatness of Venice. When Nicolo Polo and his brother Maffeo, jewelers, returned from their first wanderings in China, the empire of Kublai Khan reached from the Steppes of Siberia to the Punjab of India. Marco was but a stripling of seventeen at the time (1271) he elected to accompany his father and his uncle on their return journey. Little did he dream of the wonders he was to witness during the next twenty-three years. For not until he was

VENICE FROM THE STILL BLUE WATERS OF THE LAGOON
Venice, on her 120 islands, looks out upon a peaceful lagoon, or arm, of the blue, blue Adriatic. Most of the streets are canals and most of the buildings are erected on piles.

a bearded man of forty was he again to set eyes on the dome of St. Mark's, and not for several hundred years thereafter were the tales he told of the unknown lands of farthest Asia really credited.

Kublai Khan had requested oil from the lamp of the Holy Sepulchre at Jerusalem, and the trio made their way bearing a vessel of this oil through what is now eastern Turkey, Georgia and the Desert of Gobi. It is interesting today to reflect that they passed Mount Ararat but pronounced its ascent impracticable, that they noted in Georgia where petroleum has lately become important that "there is a fountain from which oil springs in great abundance," and that the oil was good to burn, though not to flavor a salad. They witnessed the recruiting methods of Moslem chieftains who administered hashish to their victims. Entering the region now known as Persia, they fingered the softness of the Kerman "shals" on which the shawls of Kashmir were later modeled. They were astounded by the fat-tailed Armenian sheep, the caudal appendages of which sometimes weighed thirty pounds. They plunged desperately into the unknown fastnesses of Badakhshan, where salt was mined and rubies dug from the mountainsides. They crossed the Desert of Gobi, with its mirages of sight and sound and the peril of its sand-storms. The Great Sea of Sand, as the Chinese termed it, was vividly described by Marco Polo in a way that has been verified by subsequent explorers.

At Kanchow they found themselves in the homeland of the Mongol tribesmen who were riding into Russia, capturing Budapest, and even harrying the English. Not until four years of weary journeying did the travelers reach Chandu, the Xanadu of Coleridge's poem. The "stately pleasure dome" of the Khan's palace at Peking gleamed violet, green and vermilion above walls plated with gold and carved with the figures of dragons and Buddhas; and in the great hall the monarch of all Asia and Eastern Europe could entertain six thousand at dinner. It was said he had a million retainers. Within the walls of his summer residence he kept ten thousand milk-white horses. His New Year's parade included five thousand elephants, each of which carried two coffers of treasure.

Kublai Khan was pleased with Marco and the tales he could tell and made possible his further travels, and for seventeen years Marco roamed Cathay. In the end he returned with a small fleet, the seams of his garments filled with jewels of incredible value. Marco Millions was the nickname given him, and for years the Venetian carnivals contained the figure of a Munchausen who related tales on a par with Marco's. Since for the time the Mongols had beaten back the Moslems, it was possible for Venetian silk merchants to profit by the route Marco had blazed across Asia. The tale of his travels, which added greatly to Europe's knowledge of the strange lands he visited, came in this wise to be preserved. During a battle between Venice and her rival Genoa, in 1298, Marco was taken prisoner and passed the

PIGEONS THAT HAVE ACQUIRED WORLD FAME

From their roosting places among the pillars and arches of buildings that line St. Mark's Square, Venice, pigeons flutter down in their thousands to the piazza to be fed by tourists. Hawkers sell grain to those who wish to feed the birds, which fraternize fearlessly with visitors from all over the world. No traffic is permitted in the square.

time dictating his reminiscences to a fellow prisoner who was gifted with the pen. The story was translated into many languages, but not till 1447 could it be printed.

Gondolas Are Painted Black

To-day Venice is beloved of tourists. Leaving the mainland, the jog-trot Italian train seems to run straight into the sea. Presently we espy a vision of domes and towers rising sheer out of the water, with never a trace of land so far as eye can see. At the station there are no cabs, only black gondolas and motor boats. A law was passed in the fifteenth century requiring gondolas to be painted black. On a star-lit summer night the lights gleam across the waters and even a whisper carries.

One might spend a month in Venice and scarce set foot on land, for 150 canals lead to almost every doorway. But behind the waterways lies a maze of narrow streets and paved squares connected with one another by curved bridges like those of which Marco Polo told on his return from China. It is puzzling, though, to find one's way about afoot, when so many areaways come to a sudden end, perhaps against the blackened walls of some old palace with iron-barred windows. In few places would it be so easy to disappear without a trace. One's thoughts turn to abductions and assignations, secret societies, conspiracies and deeds of darkness.

Banishment for Outsize Bread

The old republic of the Doges was cruel in a way that would now be regarded as absurd. For instance, between St. Mark's, the great cathedral, and the Rialto bridge over the Grand Canal, is a sort of tombstone on which is an inscription that threatens everything from penal servitude and torture to banishment and fines of many ducats, for anyone who baked round loaves exceeding a certain weight and offered them for sale to the public in any square, street, alley, thoroughfare, or on any barge, gondola, or boat of any kind!

Most of the streets retain names handed down from ancient times. Just behind St. Mark's Square is the Street of the Assassins, a narrow lane between high houses, with a suitable bend in the middle where the assassins could lurk for their prey. Nowadays it is usually deserted. Several streets recall a sort of bull fight which used to be popular at carnival time. It arose out of a revolt by Ulrich, patriarch of Aquileia, against Venice in the thirteenth century. The Doge, the ruler of the Venetian republic, sent a fleet and took him prisoner with twelve of his canons. They were, however, forgiven and released on condition that their town should send a fine bull and twelve pigs as tribute every year on Carnival Thursday.

A Carnival Custom

The animals were received in great state in one of the salons of the Doge's palace, which was decorated with a number of wooden models of Ulrich's fortresses, the Doge appeared in his robes and solemnly sentenced the bull and pigs to death, and presently martial music heralded a procession of the smiths' and carpenters' guilds with flags and swords. Seizing their victims, they led them into St. Mark's Square where a mob received them with applause. As soon as quiet could be restored, a signal was given for the sacrifice. The bull was more or less released—that is to say, he was tied by a long rope which prevented his charging further than a certain distance. Thereupon amateur bull-fighters danced about with huge, two-handed swords, endeavoring to strike his head off at one blow. Now came the turn of the pigs, which were chased about with swords by the populace. At last the Doge led the way back to the palace, and trumpets were sounded while he destroyed the wooden fortresses with his stick. It was a childish game, but appealed to the humor of the people.

In the old days the carnival of Venice was celebrated throughout the world, visitors flocking to it from all over Europe. Masked balls in theatres and public places, fun and frolic were incessant day and night for a week. Little of all this now remains beyond a few masquerades. Various quarters of the city still keep up many of their old-time local festivals, but modern Venetians dislike the idea.

FLAG WAVERS from Siena add the richness of medieval costumes to St. Mark's Piazzetta—the little square from which the main square, piazza, opens out.

THE GONDOLIERS have a day of their own on the Grand Canal during the regatta held in April. The gay striped poles serve as moorings for the gondolas.

PHOTOS, CHARLES J. BELDEN

In the sixteenth century there were no fewer than ten thousand gondolas. Their high prows, called dolphins (resembling sea horses), were gilded; the little hut in the center was of velvet; the cushions were of bright silk and satin. But all this display was finally repressed, and the simplicity of the republic revealed in the black wooden fittings and steel prow which characterize the modern gondola. In summer the shelter is replaced by a light awning. There are special arrangements when a gondola is used as a hearse or a prison van; otherwise the boat is standardized.

Nowhere are funerals so impressive as in Venice. In the dazzling sunlight, when the reflections of the rose-colored palaces are dancing in the water, there comes a long file of black gondolas. The first attracts attention by the number of wreaths attached to the prow and a huge silver cross on a black cloth over the cabin, where priests in surplices are murmuring prayers. Immediately behind, propelled by

SYMBOL OF SPLENDOR AND A GLORIOUS PAST, THE DOGES' PALACE
The palace is a fanciful blend of architectural effects. Between the upper story of white and pink marble and the colonnade with pointed arches is a gallery of delicate arches and foils.

AT THE ENTRANCE TO THE GRAND CANAL, ORNATE BAROQUE

Restless ornament—swirled carvings, statues—crowds all free space on the eight-sided Santa Maria della Salute. Inside are paintings by Titian and Tintoretto.

CUTLER J. COULSON FROM SHOSTAL

THE BASILICA of St. Mark's, splendor of Byzantine architecture. The west (main) front is shown above. Below, the gallery over the main door, where the famous bronze horses forever prance. Above them, in the center of the pointed arch, is a winged lion, ancient symbol of Venice.

CAMERA CLIX

364

RIALTO BRIDGE across the Grand Canal. The single-arch span, constructed of marble in 1590, is lined with shops. Below it one may sit or saunter on a wide sidewalk.

CHARM AND QUIET on a watery byway. It is on the "little" canals, rather than on the bustling, noisy Grand Canal, that one is likely to capture the city's most enchanting flavor.

SHALLOW LAGOONS and narrow canals make it necessary for the gondolier to stand at the boat's stern, to see his direction. A weight at the prow balances the weight of his body.

four gondoliers in black livery, glides a gondola bearing the coffin beneath an awning laden with flowers. A black cross stands out at the helm, and an angel spreads his silver wings at the prow.

To-day gondoliers rely for employment chiefly on their ferries, which have been fixed at certain points from time immemorial and form a kind of trade-union with schools and strict laws and benefits attached. Every gondolier must join a brotherhood, paying certain fees and drawing his share of the profits.

When one wishes to cross the Grand Canal, one can do so by bridge or steamer, but those who prefer old-fashioned ways will find a ferry and step aboard a waiting gondola. Or one shouts "Poppe!" (which literally means "poop") and a boat comes across from the other side. The custom is to deposit fares on the ledge of the boat. The Doge used to be transported through the Grand Canal enthroned on his ivory chair.

Decorated by Great Artists

Weeks could be spent looking at the Doge's palace where lived the rulers of the old republic in the days when it was incredibly wealthy. The outer walls are upheld by arcades of rose marble, the inner walls are gorgeous with paintings by the great Venetian artists. The pillars that support the arcades are rich with carvings. The sculpturing at the top of one pillar exhibits the whole life of man in exquisite miniature—first the baby in a cradle, then a Romeo and Juliet scene at a balcony, a wedding, the appearance of an heir and, finally, a death-bed. Other carvings represent seasons, industries, birds, beasts and fishes, sins and virtues and biblical scenes.

In St. Mark's Square, where street-peddlers importune the tourist to buy their wares, let us go into one of the old coffee-houses. In winter-time we enter a succession of small, over-heated rooms whose walls are lined with divans of red plush. Here we may see what a coffee-house was like in the seventeenth century. But when spring comes, we may take one of the hundreds of chairs and tables then set far out into the square.

The Cathedral of Gold

The Cathedral of St. Mark's is likely unparalleled in the richness of its decoration. Originally the private chapel of the Doge, it began its career in 828 as a small wooden building erected to contain the relics of St. Mark which had been brought from Alexandria. This church was burned in 976 in an insurrection, but was rebuilt and later altered, on which occasions Byzantine workmen and artists as well as Lombard were employed. The resulting blend represents a unique type of architecture.

As the cathedral became the religious centre of the growing state, it was adorned with spoils brought back from the East and from the mainland of Italy by merchant traders. The general plan of the building is that of a Greek cross, with a dome over the centre and one over each of the arms. The pavement is in part of red and green porphyry mixed with marbles, while walls and ceilings are covered with delicate mosaics set in a background of gold. These mosaics, millions of tiny bits of marble, gold leaf and enamel, colorfully picture the stories of the Bible—the Creation, the Fall of Man, the Flood, Noah's Ark, the Tower of Babel, the story of Moses, the life of Christ, the life of St. John and countless other subjects. Over the doorway at the northwest angle the mosaics show the translation of the body of St. Mark—which now rests within the high altar.

Adventurous Bronze Horses

The Pala d'oro, the retable of this high altar, is one of the finest specimens of goldsmiths' and jewelers' work known. Representing the figures of Christ, the saints, the angels and the prophets, it is set with no less than thirteen hundred pearls, four hundred garnets, three hundred emeralds and an equal number of sapphires. The work was ordered in 976 and was several times enlarged and enriched between that date and 1345.

The four bronze horses over the doors of St. Mark's are said to have come from an arch of Nero, or perhaps to have been

THE CENTRAL ARCHED PORTAL OF ST. MARK'S BASILICA

On the terrace above are four bronze horses brought from Constantinople. Decorating the arches are carvings and reliefs. In the lunette beneath the outer arch is an exquisite mosaic.

looted from Constantinople. Napoleon carried them off to Paris, but they were brought back after his fall. At the outbreak of World War I they were taken to a place of safety, but were later restored to their old position.

The tall campanile, or bell tower, too, has had its adventures. The foundations had long caused anxiety, on account of their subsidence. Suddenly in July, 1902, the tower collapsed with a mighty roar in a storm of dust and rubble. Reconstruction was immediately started and was finished in 1910.

On certain high days at the hour of noon the venerable clock over the arch at the entrance to the Merceria, one of the main thoroughfares, gives a unique entertainment to the curious. Scarcely have the bronze Moors beaten the hour on a gong than a little trap-door opens and figures of the three wise men emerge,

ROBERT LEAHEY FROM SHOSTAL

VENETIAN GLASS, delicate and exquisitely colored, has been prized for centuries. With improved methods, today the industry has acquired new vigor.

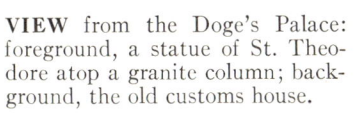

VIEW from the Doge's Palace: foreground, a statue of St. Theodore atop a granite column; background, the old customs house.

HEART of Venice: the church of Santa Maria della Salute, left; Grand Canal; Library of St. Mark, behind the piazzetta's columns.

369

solemnly raising their hats as they pass in procession before the images of the Virgin and Child seated upon a throne.

Venice, with her shining-marble buildings and mirror-like stretches of water, never seems to look the same. Her colors are always changing. Sometimes the whole city seems in mourning, with dark canals, gray palaces and sad lagoons beneath clouded skies. Again canals, lagoons, roofs and windows are red with reflected fire and the pavements are molten gold.

During World War I, there were aerial bombardments during which over six hundred bombs were dropped on Venice, destroying the Church of Santa Maria Formosa, though it has since been restored. (The bronze horses of St. Mark's were temporarily removed to Rome for safety.) In 1917 a Venetian patriarch vowed that if the city were saved he would build a votive temple in honor of the Virgin. The church, located on the Lido, has in its foundations a brick from St. Peter's and a rock from the Grotto at Lourdes where so many miracles of healing have been performed. During the second World War Venice was spared serious damage, though many of her sister cities lost priceless treasures.

EWING GALLOWAY

ACROSS FROM SAN GIORGIO, GONDOLAS CROWD THE SHORE LINE

Above the calm waters of San Marco Canal rise the bell tower, dome and noble façade of San Giorgio Maggiore. It was built on the island of San Giorgio in the sixteenth century by the great Venetian architect Andrea Palladio. His designs were adapted in England by Inigo Jones; and other architects, long afterward, continued to build in the Palladian manner.

The Jewel of the Mediterranean

Sicily's Beauty, Its People and Historic Places

When we look at a map of Italy, which quaintly resembles a booted foot with a high heel, we see, close to the toe, a triangular object which the foot seems about to kick. This is the island of Sicily, for centuries a scene of conflict between East and West. Many races have struggled for possession of the land. Phœnicians, Carthaginians, Greeks, Romans, Vandals, Saracens, Normans, Germans, French, Italians and Spaniards either have had settlements here, or have in turn ruled the island. The ancient ruins with which it is strewn tell its stirring history. The island has a place in modern history, as well. In World War II the Allies made it a stepping-stone for their invasion of Italy from Tunisia. Now peace has settled once more upon this land of olive orchards and orange groves. The chief cities are Palermo, Catania and Messina, all of them on the coast.

AS our steamer plows its way through the blue waters of the Mediterranean, the gray haze seen from a distance out at sea becomes Sicily. Violet shadows fill the valleys, and the vivid green of grass, with the darker shades of the olive groves, complete the brilliant setting. Barely separated from the mainland by the Strait of Messina, two miles wide at one point, Sicily rises on the north in steep cliffs, between which lie Palermo and other good harbors. Here the lower slopes of the limestone mountains blossom into oranges and olives, grapes, lemons and mulberries. The mean temperature ranges between 51½ degrees of rainy January and 77 degrees of sun-drenched July. The one drawback is the parching wind storms of the sirocco, red with dust, which blow from Africa, especially in April and September. The coast to the west and south lies low and malarial between the rising hills and the sea; but the east coast is steep and rocky, save for the plain of Catania and Mt. Etna, whose hardened lava streams radiate for twenty miles in bold promontories. The central plateau is a region of waving wheat fields. Through the northern half there runs a chain of mountains which is regarded as a continuation of the Apennines of Italy. The slopes of the lower hills are everywhere extremely fertile.

The mountains are of volcanic origin. Etna rises over 10,750 feet from the vast plain of Catania, with its lowest slopes, especially toward the southeast, densely populated and clothed with olive groves and vineyards, and is believed to be more ancient than Vesuvius. Higher up, its sides are densely wooded. In winter the peak is covered with snow. An observatory has been built a thousand feet or so below the summit, the ascent to which is usually made from Catania. History records more than eighty serious eruptions of Etna. That of 1928 sent a wave of molten lava three hundred yards in width creeping down the mountainside to meet the sea. This wave piled up, in places, two hundred feet in height and buried the houses in its pathway, while people fled with their livestock through days torrid with the mountain's furnace glow and nights sulphurous with the red stream of destruction. The towns of Mascali and Santalfio were completely buried and parts of Nunziata and Carrabba destroyed.

Not since 1669 had Etna's lava reached the sea. That time it entered Catania. That city has also been laid low many times by violent earthquakes. Messina was destroyed by a big quake in 1908, and 150,000 people killed by an accompanying tidal wave.

In the north of the island there are fairly good harbors. Not one of the Sicilian waterways is navigable for more than a short distance. The people of Sicily have suffered from winter floods and summer droughts. In many cases the rivers dry up altogether so that the plains become parched and arid. Added to these natural causes of misfortune are the people's

HEAVY WITH JUICE, ripe oranges are plucked in a grove on Mt. Etna's fertile slopes.

RICH EMBROIDERY adorns the old costume worn by a girl of Piana dei Greci (near Palermo). Many Albanians are settled there.

GAUDY HUES make the traditional high-wheeled cart one of the gayest sights in Sicily.

VANCE HENRY

J. BARNELL

DREAMING in the sun—a byway in ancient Taormina. Its beach is a popular resort.

SLENDER COLUMNS and graceful arches—the lovely cloister of the Benedictine monastery, founded in 1174, at Monreale, near Palermo.

CHARLES J. BELDEN

SICILIAN LANDSCAPE—A TERRACED VILLAGE AND ROCKY CLIFFS
Precipitous bluffs tower above a village on the Mediterranean coast. The entire island is a continuation of the Apennine range, the rugged spine of the long Italian peninsula.

SICILIAN FISHERMEN BEACH THEIR BOATS AT THE END OF THE DAY
Sicilians often sing folk songs to the rhythm of hauling in their nets and bringing in their day's catch. Though the fishermen lead a hard life, they are a cheerful folk, full of zest.

ANCIENT GREEK TEMPLES of golden stone dating from before the Carthaginian conquests are found at Girgenti. This fragment is called the Temple of Castor and Pollux.

ignorance and indolence. Little reforestation is ever attempted so that Sicily has lost much of the woods for which it was once famous. Surprisingly, in winter many of the mountain towns are swept by bitter winds. Yet the tourist remembers Sicily as a land of roses.

The soil is fertile even in the drier regions, and the vegetation luxuriant. In the southwest there are dwarf palms, and further inland, date palms, Indian figs and prickly pears. Even here diligent irrigation makes it possible to raise groves of lemons and oranges, mulberries and pomegranates, and vineyards of the finest wine grapes. Spring in Sicily is a riot of color, and as the season progresses, quantities of fruit are exported to Italy. Another item of export is copper from the vast mining region at Caltanissetta in Central Sicily.

Glimpses of the Past

At Palermo, on the northern coast, some of the most charming old buildings raise their turrets almost directly out of unspeakably dingy streets. Here and there a fine arched gateway remains standing in good repair, or an old doorway or a colored window demands inspection. The secret of Sicily's appeal lies in these glimpses of bygone days, carrying with them all the charm of ancient legends. Formerly unwashed beggars, descended from countless generations of their calling whined their pleas for alms before every tourist.

As far as it is possible for historians to discover, the first inhabitants of Sicily were a race of people called the Sicani, doubtless Iberians, the Siculi, who dwelt along the eastern shore, and a more cultured race, the Elymi, that came to the northeastern part of the island. By 1000 B.C. the Phœnicians had established trading posts along the coast, but were driven out by wandering parties of Greek settlers known as Sikeliots, who during the next hundred and fifty years formed extensive colonies on the east and south coasts and founded the real civilization of Sicily. The Greek colonies included Syracuse, Naxos, Catania, Messina (at first called Zancle), Girgenti (then known as Agrigentum), Gela and Himera. At first they remained separated from the Siculi, carrying on their own occupations and building after their own style. Many relics of their temples still stand. After some years they gradually intermarried with their Siculi predecessors.

A Succession of Conquerors

In those early times Sicily was over-run by the Phœnicians and the Carthaginians, and later still became the cause of wars between Rome and Carthage. The Romans expelled the Carthaginians in the First Punic War (264-241 B.C.), and in 210 Sicily—then largely a Greek-speaking country—submitted to Rome. For over six hundred years it now remained a part of the Roman Empire. At first a granary for Rome, it came in time to give up the effort of raising corn and allowed the land to revert to pasturage. Palermo (the ancient Panormus), became the leading city, as it is to-day. In the fifth century A.D. the Vandals conquered Sicily but later lost it. For over three hundred years it was a part of the Eastern Empire at Constantinople; and in 878 it was taken by the Saracens. For nearly a hundred years Mohammedan rule was in force. In 1061, came the Normans, at first as plunderers, but afterward as conquerors. Under Robert Guiscard and his brother Roger they over-ran the island for the next thirty years. Robert Guiscard conquered southern Italy and made his brother Count of Sicily. Under Roger's son the by no means unified racial elements of dukedom and county became united as the Kingdom of the Two Sicilies.

Some time later, Sicily passed by marriage to the Hohenstaufen Emperor Henry VI, whose son introduced a high degree of culture to Sicily. But Pope Urban IV, a Frenchman, in 1264 gave the ruling of Sicily to the French Count of Anjou.

The Sicilian Vespers

This period was one of the darkest in Sicily's turbulent history. The Count of Anjou imposed every form of tyranny and taxation upon the people until, in 1282, they massacred almost every man, woman

A SCENE IN THE MARSHY SALT FLATS OF TRAPANI, SICILY

Sicily, part of the Italian Republic, is the largest of the Mediterranean islands. It lies just off the toe of the Italian boot. Salt-manufacture for export is a vital occupation of both the city and province of Trapani; and because the city is the safest port on the western coast of the island it makes an excellent shipping point for the product.

and child of the French population. The massacre took place at Palermo on the evening of March 30, the signal for its commencement being the first peal of the vesper bell. Thus we have the term Sicilian Vespers.

The result of the overthrow of the Angevin power was that Sicily passed into the hands of the House of Aragon, starved, revolted, and eventually became a separate kingdom. Subsequently the island belonged in turn to Spain, Savoy and Austria. Then it was united with Naples in a separate kingdom until the coming of Garibaldi to the island in 1860. He defeated the king, Francis II, and treated the people with great discretion and justice, so that in a short time they and the Neapolitans, with whom they had been linked for centuries, voted to attach themselves to Italy.

Although Sicily once produced a large percentage of the world's sulfur, its output has fallen off in recent years as a result of competition from other countries. The mineral isn't sufficiently valuable to have created great industries. The making and exporting of salt is another industrial activity, particularly on the coasts where sea water can be used. But the island is chiefly agricultural, and many of the people pursue the industries related to farming: canning and preserving of fruits, tomatoes and other foodstuffs, and the making of olive oil. Of late years, Sicilians have started small businesses such as tanning, furniture making, the manufacture of gloves and matches. The fine wines of Marsala have been renowned for hundreds of years. Many Sicilians find employment in deep-sea fish-

A VIEW OF CEFALU, ON THE NORTH COAST OF SICILY

Facing on the Tyrrhenian Sea, a twelve-hundred-foot cliff rising abruptly behind it, Cefalu has limited harbor facilities, but many of its residents earn their living as fishermen. Others work in the marble quarry. The mild climate and the fertile soil of the countryside on the coast near the town are highly suitable for growing grapes and oranges.

PHOTOS, TRANS WORLD AIRLINES

ORANGE RINDS FOR ENGLISH MARMALADE

Milazzo, on the northeastern coast of Sicily, is a small port city that exports the citrus fruits and wines of the vicinity. Many Sicilian towns, this one included, were once Greek colonies. Milazzo's ancient name was Mylae. The island of Sicily had its own government until the middle of the nineteenth century, when it became part of the kingdom of Italy.

CLASSIC TRADITION ADDS CHARM TO A MODERN SYRACUSE GARDEN

Almost hidden in a lush growth of shrubbery is a little replica of a pagan temple. The slender columns are Greek Ionic, but the garlands around the top remind us of ancient Rome.

MOUNT ETNA, ETERNALLY HISSING A THREAT OF DESTRUCTION

A few miles north of Catania, near the eastern coast, the volcano soars to a height of almost eleven thousand feet. Still active, it periodically brings disaster to villages and fields.

A RELIC OF THE DAYS WHEN SYRACUSE WAS A GREEK COLONY

Syracuse was an important outpost of Greek civilization, in the days when this amphitheater was built. The oldest part of the town is on the island of Ortygia in Porto Grande Bay.

THE CATHEDRAL OF PALERMO IS THE WORK OF MANY GENERATIONS
Palermo Cathedral, begun in the twelfth century, is a curious mixture of many styles. Perhaps the finest parts are the delicate arcade and modest doorway of the south side (center).

ing, selling their catches in home ports and in the markets of North Africa.

A glance at the map will remind you of the nearness of Sicily to Greece. As a matter of fact, the ancient Sicilian city of Syracuse was a center of the highest Greek culture. Many leaders in the arts and in government lived here for a period; famous plays were written around her, and some dramas were first produced in the Syracuse theater before being shown in Greece. Syracuse is one of the lesser cities now; and it is an Italian city. The Sicilian of today in appearance has olive-tinted skin and dark hair, and his features, influenced by the ancient infusion of Grecian blood, are delicately molded.

The agricultural products of the island are varied. There are the lush orange and lemon groves of the coast. The rich nectar of the citrus fruits is extracted at factories in most of the cities. Vineyards, though often ruined in the past by killing diseases, produce great quantities of wine. Within reach of all the cities are productive vegetable gardens and olive groves. Almonds, figs, hazelnuts, peaches, pistachio, manna ash, the sumach shrub and the prickly pear all grow in the fields of Sicily. The leading dairy product is cheese.

Today the prosperous, few in number, prefer living in the big towns. Everywhere the farms are small, except in the plains where are large fields of wheat. Owing to the droughts of summer, it is possible to grow good crops only by using alternate patches of the land, allowing each piece to lie idle, except for grazing, for one or two years, so that it may regain its strength. For so poor does the land become after the summer heat that a single animal requires several acres for a pasture. The farmers live in the nearest villages and their laborers walk several miles each day to and from their work. In the villages and towns a family often lives in a single room, sharing the space with pigs and poultry. The smoke from the fire passes out through a hole in the roof, and rain and wind enter through this crude chimney, making the conditions doubly wretched. Dust, dirt and soot discolor every article in the place. Strips of matting cover the bed, and the only dressing-room these laborers have is the road or a parched plot in front of their dwellings.

For food the Sicilian depends more upon vegetables than meat. Oxen and cows are bred only for plowing and carting, and go to the butcher when they become too old for work. Butter is used only by the rich. The chief items of the peasant's diet are black bread—the staple food of the country—macaroni, beans, herbs and onions, a light wine and a hard cheese which the farmers make from goats' milk. The fruit crops, except prickly pears, are rarely eaten; they are closely guarded for export.

Among the Sicilians there is a great love of poetry, and their language is not unlike the soft Neapolitan, which increases the charm of their folk songs.

Over the distant peaks of the mountains the rose hue of day is fading; the purple is gradually darkening the valleys. We can still see bright color, the yellow from the lemon groves, the greens of the olive groves and mulberry trees. Perhaps, as we gaze over the nodding ears of wheat, we catch a glimpse of the blue waters of the Mediterranean. Sicily, unprogressive as it may be, is yet truly the jewel of the Mediterranean, and no tourist who has ever visited there but longs to return.

ROUND ROMAN ARCHES AND LANCELIKE CYPRESSES AT TAORMINA
Crumbling stones and masonry are all that remain of the theater that stood here in ancient days. Along the curving shore below are hotels for winter visitors who come to bask in the sun.

ARCTIC OCEAN
Ellesmere I.
GREENLAN
Baffin Bay
Bank I.
Victoria I.
Baffin I.
ASIA
Bering Strait
Yukon River
Mackenzie River
Great Bear Lake
Great Slave Lake
Bering Sea
Davis Strait
Hudson Bay
ROCKY
R. Nelson
L. Winnipeg
Aleutian Islands
Vancouver Island
NORTH AMERICA
Great Lakes
St. Lawrence R.
Newfoundlar
Columbia R.
Missouri R.
MTS.
APPALACHIAN MTS.
Azore
Colo. R.
Rio Grande
Miss.
ATLANTIC
Bermuda I.
Gulf of Mexico
Bahama Is.
West Indies
Cuba
Hawaii Islands
CENTRAL AMERICA
Caribbean Sea
OCEAN
PACIFIC
Panama Canal
Orinoco R.
Gilbert Is.
EQUATOR
Amazon River
Phoenix Is.
Solomon Is.
Marquesas Is.
ANDES
Madeira R.
SOUTH AMERICA
São Francisco R.
Society Is.
New Hebrides
OCEAN
New Caledonia
Fiji Is.
Tuamotu Archipelago
Paraná R.
MTS.
NEW ZEALAND
Falkland Islands
Strait of Magellan
Cape Horn
Drake Strait
ANTARCTIC CIRCLE
Weddell Sea